Work, Sleep, Repeat

LONDON SCHOOL OF ECONOMICS MONOGRAPHS ON SOCIAL ANTHROPOLOGY

Managing Editor: Laura Bear

The Monographs on Social Anthropology were established in 1940 and aim to publish results of modern anthropological research of primary interest to specialists. The continuation of the series was made possible by a grant in aid from the Wenner-Gren Foundation for Anthropological Research, and more recently by a further grant from the Governors of the London School of Economics and Political Science. Income from sales is returned to a revolving fund to assist further publications. The Monographs are under the direction of an Editorial Board associated with the Department of Anthropology of the London School of Economics and Political Science.

Work, Sleep, Repeat

The Abstract Labour of German Management Consultants

FELIX STEIN

**LONDON SCHOOL OF ECONOMICS MONOGRAPHS
ON SOCIAL ANTHROPOLOGY**

VOLUME 83

Routledge
Taylor & Francis Group

LONDON AND NEW YORK

First published 2017 by Bloomsbury Academic

Published 2020 by Routledge
2 Park Square, Milton Park, Abingdon, Oxon OX14 4RN
605 Third Avenue, New York, NY 10017

Routledge is an imprint of the Taylor & Francis Group, an informa business

British Library Cataloguing-in-Publication Data
A catalogue record for this book is available from the British Library.

Library of Congress Cataloging-in-Publication Data
A catalog record for this book is available from the Library of Congress.

Series: LSE Monographs on Social Anthropology

Cover design: Adriana Brioso
Cover image: *The Son of Man*, 1964 (oil on canvas), Magritte, Rene (1898-1967).
Private Collection. (© Christie's Images / Bridgeman Images / ADAGP, Paris and
DACS, London 2017)

ISBN13: 978-1-3500-2779-4 (hbk)
ISBN13: 978-1-3501-0868-4 (pbk)

Typeset by Deanta Global Publishing Services, Chennai, India

Dedicated to my nieces Sara and Louisa,
in the hope that the work they find
some day will be fulfilling.

CONTENTS

List of figures viii
Acknowledgements ix
Note on the use of German terms xi

Introduction 1

1 Background: A Brief History of Management Consulting 25

2 Selling Speed: Capitalist Acceleration and Temporal Angst 41

3 Economies of Legitimacy 63

4 Abstract Labour and the Absurd 93

5 Selves and Commodities 119

6 Uncertainty at Work 147

Conclusion: In the Business of Critique 177

Notes 193
Bibliography 199
Index 227

LIST OF FIGURES

Figure 1 The final Change Matrix 100

Figure 2 A slide on planned staff increases 109

Figure 3 Gaps in a slide 151

Figure 4 Career descriptions 160

Figure 5 A slide depicting intimate relationships 184

ACKNOWLEDGEMENTS

I would like to acknowledge a great debt to my colleagues, friends and interviewees in the German consulting sector. They often had to squeeze interviews into very short weekends and all of them trusted that I would anonymize their identities.

I am equally grateful for the unceasing support from my PhD supervisor Sian Lazar. With relentless encouragement she has guided me through many difficult situations and continuously provided important challenges to my ideas.

Laura Bear, Chris Hann, Elizabeth Hull, Deborah James, Giulia Liberatore and Maryon McDonald have also generously dedicated much of their time to previous drafts of this book. Their lucid insights have improved it substantially.

The arguments presented here have also benefited from the Cambridge 'Writing-Up Seminars', organized in a most supportive spirit by James Laidlaw. Thanks go to him and to Lys Alcayna-Stevens, Oliver Balch, Ben Belek, Ryan Davey, Clara Devlieger, Marilena Frisone, Sazana Jayadeva, Chau Minh Lam, Matthew McGuire, Patrick McKearney, Patrick O'Hare, Alexander Orona, Falk Parra-Witte, Joseph Philp, Yu Qiu, Marlene Schäfers, Steve Schiffer, Sertaç Sehlikoglu, Jonas Tinius, Max Watson, Tom White and Rachel Wyatt. I also would like to thank Matei Candea and Susan Bayly for their ongoing backing during my time at Cambridge.

The accidental nature of the research that led to this book meant that it was a highly unlikely project from the start. I therefore greatly relied on the encouragement and support of friends to see it through. I would like to thank Blandine Bénézit, Nick Courtman, Igor Dolgalev, Emmanuel Freudenthal, Sarah Ganter, Christian Hampel, Paolo Heywood, Nick Levine, Steven Lowe, Ana Isabel López, Emily Parker, Tobias Pforr, Laura Sauls, Alexa Steinberg, Alice Thorpe, Janice Winter and Jonathan Woolf for being incredibly supportive.

Much of the research funding underpinning this book has generously been provided by the Heinrich Böll Foundation and the Wenner-Gren Foundation. Salary support during copy-editing has been provided by the Wellcome Trust, grant number 106635/Z/14/Z.

My warmest thanks go to my family. My parents Bernhard and Ruth Stein, my uncle Joseph M. Wiesbacher, my sister Andrea and my brother Sebastian have always shown great faith in my decisions. They remain a tremendous source of love and inspiration.

NOTE ON THE USE OF GERMAN TERMS

Translating many of the expressions of my mostly German colleagues and informants into English was surprisingly difficult. On the one hand, consultants used a lot of fairly specific terms that slightly change meaning when rendered into English. I have decided to translate most of these, so as not to interrupt the flow of the writing too often. However, on the few occasions when these terms seemed particularly semantically rich or insightful, I have added the German original as a footnote.

On the other hand, German consultants used Anglicisms (both English terms and German-English neologisms such as 'versliden') with astonishing frequency. I have put them in italics in the body of the text, and sometimes added them as footnotes. While Anglicisms are readily used in Germany, the public awareness of the distinction between German and foreign expressions remains strikingly high (Hilgendorf 2007: 143), which made their ubiquity in consultancy speech and thought all the more remarkable. Anthropologists and linguists have long pointed out how linguistic ideologies and practices are involved in establishing and reproducing notions of modernity, globalization and internationalization (Bauman and Briggs 2003; Clyne 1995: 201). I hope that leaving the Anglicisms in the text fosters the argument that consultants try to personify market values associated with modernity and internationality.

Moreover, I take the frequency of Anglicisms to have two additional effects. First, these terms created considerable semantic opacity for German listeners. This has often been deplored and joked about by the media and by my colleagues, as few of the latter were sure what was really meant by having 'strong *people skills*' or by 'going the *extra mile*'. One of my colleagues even went so far as to publish a blog post on a subsection of the company intranet, arguing that we should stop using them altogether as he considered them inherently vacuous, confusing and unnecessary. I contend that the frequent use of Anglicisms in an environment that is often described as one of knowledge production points to the high degree in which consultants valued the social effects of language, rather than just its representational accuracy.

Finally, it is also worth mentioning that English management expressions often replaced existing, clear and useful German terms that continued to bear negative connotations by being associated with the Third Reich. In a country that is still very much attempting to come to terms with its own past (von Bieberstein 2016), the frequent use of business lingo regarding *leadership, team work* or *management skills* allows German consultants to make reference to notions of order, discipline and hierarchy, without using the heavily – and now often humorously – charged fascist terminology of being a Gruppenführer or Gruppenleiter (cf. Clyne 1996: 200–1; Parkes 1997: 167).

All three of these aspects of language use – their reference to modernity and global connectedness, their opacity and their allusion to notions of order, discipline and hierarchy – will be relevant to the argument presented in this book, which holds that German management consultants primarily work to alter the social relationships of corporate life.

Introduction

The year 2011 marked a peak in Europe's greatest economic and fiscal crisis in recent history. Greece's potential exit from the continent's currency union seemed to threaten the future of the Euro, and government representatives struggled to make policy reforms on the fly. At the same time, people around Europe protested for greater socio-economic equality (e.g. *The Washington Post* 2011). As a result of the global financial meltdown three years earlier, several European governments had become so indebted that they were now unable to borrow money on bond markets. Without the option of devaluing their currencies, they were forced to request loans from the European Union and the International Monetary Fund (IMF), who in turn required them to implement so-called 'austerity measures', meant to allay the concerns of financial analysts and corporate investors (Lane 2012). The resulting mixture of reduced government spending, dried-up banks, stagnant economic growth and severe worker disenfranchisement led European unemployment levels to new record highs. In Spain, about a fifth of the entire labour force was without a job that year, while in Ireland and Greece, relative unemployment had doubled since 2008.[1] People fortunate enough to keep their jobs often faced great losses in real income and increasingly precarious working conditions. Pensioners and the unemployed, particularly around the Mediterranean, were similarly forced to shoulder much of the burden of failed national and regional economic policies of the past decades.

While social hardship was on the rise throughout Europe, I joined an economic elite that remained largely unaffected by these developments. I had dropped out of my PhD programme in social anthropology and – with a five-digit student debt weighing on my shoulders – decided to join Strategy Partners,[2] a firm that provided consulting services and operated in Berlin. During my time as a consultant, from September 2011 until June 2013, and during several months of interviewing consultants and clients afterwards, I gained an insight into a life that existed very much in parallel to that of most Europeans. My colleagues and I moved mostly in luxurious environments, took taxis and planes like other people take the bus, and most of us received salaries of around three times the German national average (Destatis 2015). In the light of the politico-economic circumstances under which our work took place, this book thus asks how economic privilege was created and sustained, even when the societies in which consultants operated were confronted with growing economic misery (Carrier and Kalb 2015; Shore and Nugent 2002: 9).

This book holds that one of the drivers of increasing socio-economic inequality is rooted in the nature of the work regime in question. Surprisingly, this work regime combined a strong belief in its own importance with a considerable degree of cluelessness on the side of consultants as to what it actually consisted of. Let me briefly outline what I am referring to here: Only a few months after going through the job interview with Strategy Partners, I found myself together with other men and women in their late twenties from all around the globe in a consulting training camp. During one of our initial training sessions, in which we were taught the basic functionalities of Microsoft Excel, Rahul, a charismatic middle-aged consultant turned software coach, welcomed us with a curious joke. He told our group of initiates with relish that he knew how we felt at this moment. Most of us, he said, did not have a clue what consulting actually was. As well-educated but largely ignorant college graduates, we probably feared that we had been employed by mistake and that sooner or later we would get 'found out'. His remarks were met with considerable laughter, as well as blushing and occasional nodding. He continued in his self-assertive manner, now reassuring us that we were in fact not 'staffing mistakes' and that teaching us how to use spreadsheet software would equip us with the basic tools that we needed to 'hit the ground running'.

While Rahul did teach us some very helpful Excel tricks and formulas that day, our uncertainty as to what management consultants did exactly persisted for my colleagues and me. It was linked to the fact that we did not produce much in terms of tangible output, as we mostly just created Excel analyses and Microsoft PowerPoint slides. As Rahul put it: 'All that remains after a client has paid millions of dollars for a [consulting] project is a *deck* [of printed PowerPoint slides], about this big.' He held up his hand, indicating a space of just a few centimetres between thumb and index finger. 'This is the only thing left when you will have moved on to the next company.' His observation held true over the following months of my active consulting life. As consultants we usually worked on short-term projects in temporary offices that our clients had reserved for us within their company buildings. At the end of each such project, we packed up our laptops, shipped off the rest of our equipment (mostly printers, scanners, modems, shredders and some stationery) and made sure that nothing was left at the client site. The only material remainders of our work were thick single booklets, handed to company board members and sometimes to other senior staff involved in project activity. Printed in colour and neatly bound, they contained the innumerable PowerPoint slides that we had presented to clients in weekly or biweekly meetings and workshops.

Equally bewildering was the fact that even these printed *decks*, as they were called, did not constitute our actual work output. I was told that once a project was over, clients might not look at past *decks* anymore. Instead, they would often just remember a few key recommendations, slides or numbers, on the basis of which the success of our project would be judged. The material remainder of our work thus mattered little, and references to the elusiveness of our activity often led to humorous exchanges among colleagues about how nobody could explain with certainty what exactly we did, or sold, or how much it was really worth. Rahul's joke that no one truly knew what consulting was resonated with my colleagues and me for a long time.

Three aspects rendered the elusive nature of our work all the more surprising. First, management consultants prided themselves on quickly understanding and summarizing issues of great complexity, especially when they pertained to capitalist production. Thus, during our first training camp we sat through a series of lectures, role plays and case studies to learn how to define the productive essence of other people's work routines. Once this had been established, we could 'cut out' non-productive activity, also known as 'waste'.[3] Yet, while the definition and redefinition of other people's work turned out to be our bread and butter, investigating the nature of our own jobs was nowhere near as easy. My colleagues constantly insisted on, and were frequently astounded by, the radical diversity of consulting projects. Only in this profession, they argued, could one project be about devising a new marketing strategy for a chewing gum producer in Germany, while the next might be about reducing production costs in a South African gold mine.

The tenuous nature or our work was equally startling in the light of the extraordinary salaries and bonuses that consultants received. These ranged from around EUR 60k per year for the most junior consultants in their early twenties to over EUR 1mio for some of the profit-sharing senior consultants known as partners (*The Financial Times* 2013). This meant that management consultants earned roughly between twice and over forty times as much as the average German, whose annual gross salary lay at around EUR 30,960 in 2013 (Destatis 2015). One would expect people who earn this much money to have a very clear idea of how they make it.

Finally, the obscurity of management consulting stood in stark contrast to the importance that my colleagues and I gave to it. We mostly worked for over 14 hours a day, struggling with spreadsheet formulas until late at night or frantically aligning text boxes on PowerPoint slides until the morning hours. Our work was also marked by a constant urgency, often visceral in nature, that became evident whenever we rushed to check-in to our flights at the last possible moment, or when colleagues of mine jumped in panic at realizing that they were late for a conference call, or needed to finish a slide within the next few minutes. Consultants also systematically prided themselves on how important their past projects had been, insisting that most if not all of their assignments had had incredible *impact* for their clients. Thus, almost every project was celebrated post hoc as somehow transformational or otherwise extraordinary.

These and many other paradoxes of this work regime sparked my ethnographic interest in it. It took over half a year for the idea of writing an ethnography about my work to solidify. I had originally planned to write a PhD in anthropology about resource extraction in the Bolivian highlands, and the thought of studying German businessmen instead took some getting used to. However, after the first year of working as a consultant I asked my employer and my university to write an ethnography about this work regime and after getting clearance from both sides I began taking notes on it for another six months. During this time, I mentioned my research to my colleagues and bosses whenever possible. Once I had stopped working at the office, I spent an additional three months in Berlin, interviewing over 80 management consultants from different companies, so as not to write a mere first-person account of my job experience but instead an ethnographically grounded analysis of an industry. I returned to my provisional home in Berlin for another three months, during the summers of 2014 and 2015, acting at one point as a not-for-profit consultant for a small café in Berlin, Neukölln and catching up with former colleagues, friends and interviewees from the consulting business. I also attended recruiting workshops for aspiring consultants in Munich and Cambridge and complemented my own data with publicly available online material of major management consultancies as well as secondary literature.

The result of this research can be summarized as follows. This book contends that the work regime of management consultants is best described as 'abstract labour'. In my field site, this was true in four senses of the term. On an epistemic level, consultants were knowledge workers who bought and sold abstractions, that is, representations that constantly referred to entities and activities that lay far beyond the concrete, observable environment. Similar to nations and nation states, large corporations were 'imagined communities' (Anderson 1991) in which tens of thousands of employees, at times even millions, were put in relation with one another. Consultants managed to conceive of these corporate entities and of their own employer as limited, purposeful and fertile in nature. Limited, not only because corporations were never co-terminus with mankind (ibid.: 7) but also because they were institutions through which labour was organized, an activity that by definition did not encompass the entirety of human striving. Purposeful, because the discourses through which corporate activity was justified tended to focus on pragmatic efficacy, rather than, for example, sovereignty (ibid.), shared substance (Carsten 1995) or mutuality of being (Sahlins 2011a,b). Fertile, because corporate activity was tightly bound up with the miracle of production and of creating money from nothing (James 2015; von Braun 2012). The abstractions that consultants provided, fostered and co-created this guiding vision of corporate relations, enabling both managerial rule and shareholder value.[4]

Secondly, their work was abstract in the sense that it was premised on and conducive to creating relations with vast amounts of people that were marked by an emotional and affective disengagement from them (cf. Herzfeld 1993). The analyses, plans and presentations of consultants were meant to alter the labour of corporate employees, yet consultants were not supposed to become intimately connected to them in any way. Instead, their emotional and affective engagement was supposed to lie with work as such, with wider industries (e.g. they were supposed to have a *passion* for working in the automotive sector or the chemicals industry) and with particular managers who were not part of their analyses but who commissioned their work. Rather than being wholly disembedded, consultants were thus meant to rigorously channel their emotional and affective ties to the substratum of management that was most directly involved in paying their salaries.

Thereby, consultants themselves constituted a technology for the establishment of detached relations (Candea et al. 2015) by the managers who hired them. They provided management with descriptions of staff that enabled high-level decision-making without too much personal engagement with the employees in question. Physical reclusion was an important way in which detached relations were achieved, as management consultants did not usually spend the majority of their time with low-level corporate employees. In fact, it was often possible to successfully complete a consulting project without spending hardly any time with low-level employees at all.

Thirdly, consulting tended to be abstract in that it was often several steps removed from those parts of corporate activity that were considered directly responsible for economic value creation. Consultants neither made nor sold the goods and services around which the work of client companies was supposed to be organized. Of course economic value creation is always highly contested, and understandings of it are as much observations about the essence of economic life as they are political claims as to who should reap its fruits (Harvie 2005; Graeber 2001). However, the consultants, clients and corporate employees that I met in my field site tended to agree that consultants were only indirectly involved in productive activity and that corporate production and reproduction were in theory conceivable without their presence. For example, one of my very senior colleagues held the conviction that the frequent use of our services indicated that a client's own strategic or managerial capabilities were simply not up to the job.

Finally, consulting was abstract in that it ultimately remained opaque, both for client companies in general and for the people directly involved in a project (Christensen, Wang and Van Bever 2013). This kind of work was by no means 'immaterial', even if it did not drive at immediate material output (Hardt 1998; Hardt and Negri 2000; Lazzarato 1996). It was carried out on a series of concrete referents, usually by working on computers in *team rooms* and hotels or by presenting analyses in boardroom meetings, and it had profound impacts on the bodies of the people involved in it. However, the delayed and diffuse nature of its product (viz. improved corporate performance), as well as the use of frequently opaque technologies and concepts meant that it created a myriad of moments of ambiguity, opacity and uncertainty.

Abstract labour thereby crosscuts Arendt's (1998) distinction between 'action' and 'work'. In her terms, consulting could be considered action, since it fell within the realm of speech and sociality. Neither driven by necessity nor mere utility, much of it was simply an act of reconfiguring social relations. In its busyness, its performative elements and its strong preoccupation for client concerns, consulting was an expression of people's desire to please and to interact with one another. At the same time, however, consultants subsumed these aspects to those of 'work' in Arendt's sense. Their abstractions were at least in part meant to provide managers with short to medium-term stability and their frequent reference to pragmatism made abstract labour ultimately the work of *homo faber*, to whom all that is done must at least in theory immediately be useful (ibid.: 22).

Before I go on to outline how the argument presented here fits wider anthropological scholarship, I would like to briefly explain my use of the terms 'work' and 'labour'. Essentially, the German word 'Arbeit' can be translated into either, which is why I have here used them largely interchangeably. While 'the work of abstraction' would have made for an equally apposite title of this book, I have decided to use the phrase 'abstract labour' because it comes with two useful connotations. On the one hand, previous translations of Marx's foundational writings on 'Arbeit' under capitalism have established the term 'labour' in English. The term thereby highlights its ties to the production of socio-economic inequality (Marx 2005). On the other hand, the English term labour refers to fertility, which I hold a lot of corporate activity to be preoccupied with in one form or another (Pande 2014; von Braun 2012). All that said, the distinction of the two terms over the following pages is not hard and fast.

Abstract labour, bureaucracy and corporate forms

Anthropologists confronted with abstract labour regimes have a wide variety of relevant bodies of literature to draw from. While I will not review these in great depth in this introduction, I would like to emphasize that anthropology, as both an explicitly comparative and historically informed discipline, puts us into a unique position to use the study of non-capitalist work regimes, so as to elucidate the contemporary condition of corporate life (e.g. Gudeman and Rivera 1990; Gudeman 2016). The writings by Spittler (2016), for example, helpfully compare the work of peasants in Niger and Hungary to Tuareg pastoralism and work at McDonald's. This allows him to define work as a goal-oriented activity marked by some degree of routine and longevity that constantly exceeds its own functionalist nature (ibid.: 22). Harris (2007), in her study of Andean peasants, has made similar observations. While the work practices of the Laymi, whom she had studied since the 1970s, were usually geared towards a practical outcome, their work was also always a site of meaning-making that involved the ritual construction of personhood as well as of wider community. The fact that work is goal oriented does of course not mean that it necessarily aims at a maximization of production (Sahlins 1972). This peculiarity of capitalism is instead an outcome of culturally and historically specific developments grounded in metaphysical beliefs (Weber 1920) as much as sociotechnological change (Marx 2005). Neither is the desired goal of work ever unitary or clearly defined in corporate work settings. As the following chapters of this book will show, professional consultants are one of the institutional mechanisms which ensure that the consequentialist nature of work – be it bureaucratic efficiency, managerial standing, profit maximization or the increase of shareholder value – triumphs over its tendency to unfold into a multiplicity of sociocultural interactions. Moreover, consultants are meant to discipline and focus the myriad of goals that people work towards according the objectives of the managers who hire them.

The explicitly comparative study of work also permits a heuristically useful division of forms of workplace domination. Thus, Spittler (2016: 126ff) divides workplace rule into that of the lord ('Herr'), the master ('Meister') and the manager. While 'lords' do not directly take part in work processes but define their nature and reap their benefits, masters do interfere to a much higher degree and dispose of the necessary skills to teach newcomers on how to conduct their work properly. Managers are hybrids of the two in that their decisions tend to exert a great deal of influence over the work processes of subordinates, even if they themselves often lack the knowledge and skills necessary to carry out the labour themselves. This classification is of course not set in stone, and many hybrids exist that complicate it in praxis, yet, it usefully points to a managerial legitimation deficit, in which consultants intervene as agents of management support (see Chapter 3).

In addition to studying labour regimes in different times and sociocultural settings, anthropologists have been avid analysts of public and private corporate entities of all sorts. They have recently subsumed this field as the study of 'corporate forms', a term that emphasizes the similarities of private and public sector institutions (Welker, Partridge and Hardin 2011) and that foregrounds the complexity, heterogeneity and often-confused nature of white-collar work (Jordan and Caulkins 2013; Lupton and Wilson 1959; Wright 1994). While this term may not put enough emphasis on the profit motive and shareholder value as the guiding concepts in private sector activity, it does allow us to undermine the distinction between 'private sector efficiency' and 'public bureaucracy' that has long obscured scholarly investigation and legitimized private sector sway (Graeber 2015).

Within the study of corporate forms, ethnographies frequently draw on Weber (2002), who emphasized the role of bureaucracy in the exercise of state domination, describing it as rationalistic, in the sense of being rule-bound, impersonal and focused on means–ends relationships (*zweckrational*) (ibid.: 677). Building on this description, anthropologists have pointed out that relations of power often define apparently rational work regimes (Shore and Wright 1999). Thus, bureaucratic standardization has been shown to lay the conceptual groundwork for authoritarian rule over and above practical knowledge (Scott 1998), while discourses of state and development institutions can frequently perpetuate rather than overcome the difference between reformers and those in need of reform (Escobar 1991, 1995; also Englund 2006: 145–96; Graeber 2012). Corporate activity is thus both ideological and political, not least because it can seem to 'depoliticise' itself, while at the same time consolidating and expanding bureaucratic sway (Ferguson 1994; Foster 2014). Resulting power relations can be incredibly pervasive, re-encoding the sexuality of female employees to turn them into docile bodies (Ong 1987), heightening racial stigma (Benson 2008) and altering the bodily rhythms of those involved in them (Wolf-Meyer 2011). In service sector jobs, workforce discipline has shown to be structured around the notion of being 'flexible' and self-motivated (Massey, Quintas and Wield 1992; Sennett 2006) and changes in temporality that shifts from the rhythms of production to those of contractually set project deadlines, which all too often result in longer working hours (ibid.; Amrute 2014). Large parts of this book can be considered to stand in this tradition. For example, in spite of German consultants' frequent assertions of being mere *problem solvers* in the service of corporate efficiency, Chapters 2 and 3 of this book show that they actively work on the reconfiguration of intra-corporate power relations, so as to favour the dominance of management.

However, just like labour cannot be reduced to power relations, nor can corporate activity. Instead, a close look at work in different parts of what is now frequently called the 'service sector' shows that it is also marked by ritualistic efforts (Harper 2000; cf. Herzfeld 1993), moments of improvisation and imagination (Quattrone 2015: 24; Shore 2000: 26–9), and a considerable amount of culturally inflected drama and spectacle (Tsing 2005: 55–77). Recently, anthropologists inspired by Latour and Woolgar's (1986) study of scientific activity have paid particular attention to the vast array of material carriers that enter into and co-structure corporate life (cf. Riles 2006: 13; also Latour 1993). They have shown that the sociotechnical arrangements of trading offices have a decisive influence on the knowledge that is created in them (Knorr Cetina and Bruegger 2002a, 2002b; Zaloom 2006a, 2006b). The architectural make-up of trading floors and offices can uphold corporate hierarchies (Zaloom 2006b; Ho 2006; Silver 2010), while frequently slow and tedious documentary practices may alter corporate temporalities (Mathur 2014), thereby exceeding their defined purposes in various ways (Gupta 2014; Hull 2012; Jacob 2007). The dense format of documents often means they can be seen to 'expand' into a panoply of potential meanings, guiding political activity and fostering bureaucratic claims of expertise (Riles 2001, 2010, 2011; Reed in Riles 2006). This book attempts to build on these insights, by pointing at the great relevance of ritual activity and information technology through which consulting is enabled. It argues that the abstract nature of consulting heightens the ritualistic and performative aspects of labour and that its strong reliance on technology frequently blurs the line between referent and representation (cf. Keane 1997).

The work that management consultants carry out is linked to the increase of social inequality in a variety of ways. First, as Chong (2012) drawing on Mol (1999) has argued for IT consultants in China, they are engaged in a project of 'ontological politics', which consists of 'transforming the productive economy into financial assets' (ibid.: 40). Consultants turn out to act as agents of financialization, a trend which is itself closely tied to the increase of social inequality, both in the spheres of high finance and increasingly in people's personal lives (James 2015; Weiss 2015). While Chong has provided us with a first detailed analysis of consultancy work that focuses mostly on its effects, this book deals more closely with the concepts, emotions and social practices that this particular form of labour elicits.

Investigating the day-to-day work practices of consultants allows us to see two further ways in which consulting and social inequality may be linked. First, consultants enable and foster intra-corporate hierarchies through which vast differences in pay are made possible. As Chapter 3 will show, consultants work on social relations so as to enable and legitimate the dominant position of top managers who hire them. Secondly, since consultants are removed from many of the epistemic, social and value-creating referents that they speak about, and create little in terms of immediate material output, a panoply of legitimation techniques opens up to justify their work's importance. Opportunities for the 'ritual construction of political reality' (Kertzer 1988: 77) are thus amplified, the more abstract work regimes become, and aesthetics (Riles 1998, 2001, 2010), habitus (Ho 2009a, 2009b) and communicative techniques (Holmes 2009, 2014) become increasingly relevant.

A side effect of the increasingly hierarchical and abstract nature of this form of labour is that it generates a constant pressure on management consultants to prove that they are worth the money that is spent on them, rendering accusations that their work is ultimately worthless more and more popular (Graeber 2013).

Non-places as field sites

Apart from the sociocultural insights outlined so far, this ethnography also raises a couple of issues regarding research methods, in particular the delineation of field-site boundaries. Defining a somehow geographically bounded field for this study was not easy, mostly because consultants travelled a lot. While I did rent an apartment in Berlin during my research, it actually stood empty most of the time, as I spent almost all of the weeks of my working life in other cities, living in hotels in Dresden, Dublin, Düsseldorf, Essen, Frankfurt, Munich, New York, Paris and Rome, as well as towns in Austria and Poland. I only returned to my own apartment in the German capital for the fairly regular 'office Fridays', often spending my weekends with colleagues and friends. On several other occasions, however, I visited my partner in London or my family in Munich and worked from the consultancy offices in these cities on a Friday. Thereby I spent several weeks at a time outside of Berlin, sometimes with colleagues from other cities, whom I had met during special work events.

Tying this patchwork of locations up into a single 'field' was self-defeating due to the striking diversity of municipal histories, local self-understandings and territorialized forms of cultural expression. The cities and towns my colleagues and I lived and worked in differed vastly, both because they were located in different continental, national and linguistic areas and because Germany itself is a strongly federal country in which municipal and regional identities as well as normatively charged East–West divisions continue to dominate people's self-perceptions (Borneman 1992, 2000: 305; Boyer 2000; Herf 1997; Parkes 1997: 180–83). Thus, they did not have any shared cultural characteristics that distinguished them over and above many other conceivable groups of European municipalities. The most that can be said about them is that the middle and upper management bodies of several client companies were located there.

The larger cities of the list above thereby roughly corresponded to the command centres of the global economies that are marked by a locational concentration of producer services (Sassen 2001, 2011; Smith in Fisher and Downey 2006). Consulting work in smaller and often more 'remote' towns reflected the parallel dispersion of production, away from major urban centres.

Moreover, my colleagues and interviewees did not systematically try to understand the local idiosyncrasies of the cities they worked in. Either they did not familiarize themselves with them beyond the level of weekend tourism or they did not even have time for a stroll around town. For example, I spent four days working in Rome, without ever getting to explore the city for more than 30 minutes at a time. Confined to airports, taxis, hotel rooms and offices I was so occupied with work that upon my return to Berlin I felt as if I had never really been there. Most of my colleagues shared this feeling of being physically present yet socially and culturally removed from the places they worked in. They lamented not being able to 'see', 'spend time in' or know anyone in the places they worked, bewildered by the fact that geographical space and social relations did not map onto one another (cf. Cook, Laidlaw and Mair 2009). Consulting was thus carried out in the 'non-places' of super-modernity. Here human relations were predominantly contractual, personal identity mattered most in terms of the socio-institutional position that it conferred at borders, on airplanes and in offices, and the local histories and cultural particularities of place predominantly stood in the service of spectacle (Augé 1995: 77–8). The latter was evident every time consultants posted and re-posted on Facebook and in emails which faraway city or countries they were currently working in.

It was hard to establish links to the social and cultural worlds of these spaces, as most of our colleagues were not from the municipality, region or country in which we worked either. Our graphics support staff, that is, the people who would either draw up or embellish the PowerPoint slides we created, were located in South Asia, Eastern Europe and other parts of Germany, while fellow consultants, researchers and industry experts with whom we worked via phone and email sat in India, China, Italy, Japan, Spain, the United States and the United Kingdom. This is how Serdar, the taxi driver with whom I consistently travelled in Berlin, became the person I had the most sustained face-to-face interaction with during my consulting days. For more than a year we met whenever I was in Berlin, as he drove me early on a Monday morning either to Tegel airport or to one of Berlin's train stations and picked me up late on Thursday evenings to drive me home.

If this field could not easily be circumscribed on a two-dimensional map, it did nevertheless have a series of substantive attributes. The three most important of these were institutional affiliation, a shared aesthetics of people and space, and the monetization of social interaction. Unsurprisingly, institutional affiliation to our employer turned out to be the most significant of these. Upon beginning our jobs my colleagues and I would receive new computers and telephones that included business-wide address directories. With this kind of equipment, any corporate employee could find and contact any of their colleagues via email, chat or telephone within just a couple of seconds. Institutional affiliation also meant access to the company-wide intranet, where each consultant could scan their colleagues' 'profiles', complete with a picture, a personal CV, a history of past projects and a self-written description of topics of economically relevant 'expertise'. Such institutional technology was explicitly designed to render geographical distance irrelevant, while fostering group cohesion. Moreover, my colleagues and I had access to company offices around the globe, and we could use any of the company's landline telephones by means of a personal code, so as to be available via our landline numbers irrespective of where we were. With just a few mouse-clicks we were even able to connect our company printers, as long as we specified which continent, country, city, building, floor and room we were currently working from.

Beyond the affordances and constraints of technological connection, institutional affiliation was also a social structure that defined with whom, how and why we would interact. Roughly speaking, our division of labour as consultants worked through clear-cut social hierarchies. Partners tried to meet regularly with the upper management of major German corporations so as to 'sell a project' to them. They presented their project ideas either in private conversations or in formally organized *pitches*, in which they competed directly with other consulting companies. Once a project had been sold, the partner in charge assembled a team to work on it. As an unwritten rule, partners started by contacting their former teammates, with whom they had made positive experiences in the past, asking them if they were presently available and keen to collaborate. If they needed to expand their team further, they would also get in touch with human resources (HR) staff, who provided them with names of currently 'unassigned' consultants. The latter were then either placed on a project, or – depending on their seniority and the general policy of the management consultancy in question – asked whether they agreed to work on it.

Consultants whose project work had been confirmed would soon after hear from the designated *team leaders*, who ran the project's daily business either together with or in the name of the partners in charge. *Team leaders* would let them know what exactly the project was about, where and when to meet, and how to prepare for the work ahead. They would also provide consultants with project-specific 'budget codes', enabling them to book flights and hotels through the company's travel office or to get their taxi and restaurant bills reimbursed. Abusing the budget code was sanctioned, since the partner in charge would sign off all code-specific expenses at regular intervals.

Lastly, institutional affiliation also defined how consultants interacted with the staff of client companies. On the client side, the corporate managers in charge of a commissioned project would announce our arrival to their subordinates, asking them to cooperate with us. They had their secretaries provide us with a *team room*, keys and access badges for the duration of the project. Subsequently they would meet with us on a regular basis in so-called *Steering Committee Meetings* or *steercos*, during which we would brief them on project progress.

All of these instances of establishing and transforming consultant–client relations relied on an almost militaristic awareness of corporate hierarchy. Within the consultancy firm, hierarchy determined one's function in a project-specific division of labour. Roughly speaking, junior consultants would do most of the data gathering and spreadsheet analyses, *team leaders* were held accountable for their accuracy and relevance, partners were in charge of the overall narrative of the project and would liaise with the most important clients. Consultant–client relationships equally began through a series of contracts and top-down orders, since top management would need to permit our access to their companies. Hierarchy was not an explicitly expressed value of management consultants, who frequently emphasized the egalitarian spirit in which junior company members were encouraged to *challenge* the opinions of partners or take charge of their own sets of tasks, known as *workflows*. While these ideals were important in that they guided consultants' explicit understandings of their work, they could not gloss over the fact that institutional hierarchy was one of the enabling structures of this field site, where corporate hierarchies were a constant preoccupation.

In creating and reaffirming institutional membership, the roles of technology and hierarchy frequently intersected. For example, members of the graphics, IT or research departments did not have the same expensive smartphones or company cars as consultants. Thus they lacked important symbolic markers of belonging to the consultancy company's 'core' as well as the same kind of immediate and around-the-clock access to all other company members. *Team leaders* had different kinds of laptops that allowed them to use an electronic pen on the screen, with which to edit and comment on PowerPoint documents of lower-level colleagues. Once edits had been noted and emailed back, consultants would need to incorporate them into their slide shows. Finally, *team leaders* and partners had often accumulated so many air miles that they would not remain in the business lounge at the airport but disappear into even more exclusive Senator or First Class lounges, to which access was granted only if the automated doors or the lounge receptionists confirmed one's eligibility.

A second defining aspect of this 'field' was a shared aesthetic. As described above, management consultants mostly travelled in a closed-off international corridor, consisting of airports, taxis, hotel rooms, restaurants and office spaces. This corridor was incredibly homogeneous, even across municipal, national and regional boundaries. One of its most immediately notable features lay in its imposing, yet abstract, minimalism. While some of the hotels that my colleagues and I lived in celebrated baroque opulence, most of them stressed glass, steel and concrete as well an ostentatious plainness in their architectural make-up. The entrances of spacious hotel lobbies, expansive client headquarters and all glass-and-concrete consulting offices were often decorated with abstract sculptures, while their generally commanding architectural modernism echoed the impersonal feel of airports. These spaces were meant to invoke both luxury and the functionalist virtues of neutrality, efficiency and precision (Sassen 2011: 480–6). They dealt in abstraction and replicability to such an extent that my colleagues and I regularly joked about how we could not find our hotel rooms because we misremembered which room, city or country we were currently staying in. The aesthetic spanned from the material environment that surrounded us to the clothing we wore. During most days of the week, colleagues were dressed almost exclusively in dark suits with white or light blue shirts complete with unassuming ties. Due to its rigid specifications, this corporate dress code had strong inclusionary and exclusionary implications (Crewe 2007). Anyone with a similar style of dress, specifically managers of client companies, was considered a potential member of the inner circle that fashion established. Anybody dressed very differently, such as blue-collar workers, low-level service employees or people wearing shorts and flip flops at the airport, was probably not. Moreover, corporate fashion served as a marker of submission to an unspecified entity that surpassed us and in whose name we were supposed to conduct ourselves (Bourgois 2003: 141–61). The rigidity of such aesthetic specifications verged on the absurd, such as when I sat down on one evening flight home and noticed that the other five men in my row of seats were about my age, had similar haircuts and seemed to be wearing a business shirt of the same light blue colour as I was. In this instance the interplay between the corporate bodies we served and our physical bodies was very close indeed (cf. Douglas 2003). Some of my colleagues considered it liberating not to have to worry about fashion, not least because it simplified packing for future trips. Since almost all suits could be matched with all shirts and ties, the uniformity of our corporate attire did not just invoke functionalism, but it instantiated it.

Of course, fashion's function as a marker of individual personality and status never fully disappeared. To the trained eye, beautiful ties, tailor-made suits, snazzy bags and branded trolleys gradually took on increasing significance in defining their owners. The longer my colleagues and I worked in the business, the easier it became for us to read whether a particular suit, belt or collar was luxurious or common, daring or ordinary. At their core, however, the aesthetic specifications of clothing stressed restraint, order and the effacement of the individual, a fact that became all the more obvious on weekend nights out in Berlin, where techno fans, punks, hipsters, emos and drag queens displayed how variegate and playful fashion and the use of the body could be. Here is how Susanne, a consultant from Munich, describes how the corporate aesthetic of hierarchical difference and endless repetition led her to question her own existence as a consultant:

> Once I was working with a colleague at a company near Düsseldorf. We used to take the [Thursday night] flight back ... to Munich, which is the main consultants' flight. It is totally absurd [in that I] once sat in business class in row 22 because the whole plane was booked as business class. So this nice colleague and I were queuing at the pretty cramped security check-in .... It felt quite bizarre for us to be surrounded by people with [expensive] Rimowa[5] trolleys, nice leather bags and suits. For me this was a key moment. Upon taking a look around myself, I was thinking that somehow, when I take a step back, I do not really want to be a part of all this. Somehow I do find these consultants strange.

Thirdly, apart from institutional affiliation and an abstract aesthetics, the 'field' was defined by the pervasive use of money. The creation and maintenance of the corridor of mobility and abstraction in which my colleagues and I moved required vast amounts of very real, very cheap and mostly locally 'fixed' service sector employees. Taxi drivers had to commute between airports and offices, cleaning staff kept hotel rooms and office spaces inhabitable, catering employees fed us, builders, electricians, plumbers and IT staff maintained the built environment, and a vast number of suppliers and service sector employees coordinated and scheduled all of these activities. Every member of this vast series of interactions related to us either directly or indirectly through the use of money. Prostitutes sipping on drinks in the lobbies of luxury hotels in Düsseldorf, Paris and Rome may have been initially less essential in this system, but their systematic resurgence points to the fact that commerce was potentially boundless, and that even love, companionship, intimacy and sexual desire would become monetized in the long run (Hart and Hann 2009: 2).

The monetization of life continued into the consultants' free time. Several of my colleagues bought clothes at airports while waiting for their flights and used the hotel gyms in order to stay fit. Our employer had a contract with a laundry service that would pick up our dirty clothing in the office on a Friday and return clean shirts and suits for the following week. Our in-house postal service would take care of sending mail to friends and family and store whatever goods we had bought online during the week. On weekends, consultants would increasingly eat out, hail taxis and engage in numerous expensive forms of entertainment. Some would take this logic to the extreme and buy expensive bottles of alcohol in clubs, while others kept it more conservative, aiming to invest in property or save for their children. Yet, especially in the context of Berlin, a city in which around a fifth of the population lives below the poverty line (DPG 2015: 3), it is safe to say that all of my colleagues and I spent much more money than the average resident.

As much as money was an alternative medium of communication in these instances (Hart 2000), it was just as important as a shield from violent interference (Cohen 2001; Graeber 2012). It is by now fairly well established that airports, for example, serve as machines for producing strongly 'normalised' behaviour in which deviance is highlighted and invites intervention (Maguire 2014: 125). Offices, luxury hotels, taxis and restaurants were also among the most effectively policed spaces that could be found in an urban environment. Guarded by the equally kind and threatening smiles of receptionists, flight attendants and corporate security staff, my supposedly 'global' field site was effectively shielded off from the wider population, making it often more self-centred and self-referential than many of the localities it claimed to transcend. My colleagues and I got used to having our symbols of non-interference ready at all times, whether they were passports, travel tickets, office badges, Wi-Fi passwords, cash or credit cards. Effectively conjuring these symbolic door openers, so as to overcome constant stops to our movement was not just necessary – it became a marker of professionalism and charisma when carried out with an air of negligent nonchalance. Money was so important for entering and moving through this 'corridor' that consulting companies advanced some of their recent recruits, such as myself, a few thousand Euros for the first weeks of work, enabling them to pay taxis and hotels until they received their first salaries and travel expense reimbursements.

The delineation of this field site speaks to ongoing discussions about the nature of 'the field' in anthropology more widely. Inspired by the increasing public awareness of modern-day globalization in the 1990s, anthropologists have productively questioned whether or not translocal phenomena could successfully be studied through local research (Marcus 1995). Rather than following initial calls for multi-sited research for the study of multi-sited phenomena, however, some anthropologists have made the case to retain and critically engage with geographically bounded field sites, both as a reminder of the unavoidable partiality of ethnographic knowledge and as a tool for challenging established conceptual totalities of all sorts (Candea 2007). Thus, instead of operating with ideal types in mind and looking for their instantiations in the world, it has been suggested that anthropologists use the world's 'messiness, contingency, and lack of an overarching coherence or meaning ... as a control for a broader abstract object of study' (ibid.: 180). Authors such as Cook, Laidlaw and Mair (2009) have extended this critique of analytic holism, arguing that geographical factors, frequently salient in discussions of 'the field' as space and place, should be wholly discarded. They contend that in order to establish a field, anthropologists should not focus on geography but on the theoretical questions that guide their research.

Arguably, these debates have been helpful in their appeals to epistemological caution and their emphasis on the constructed nature of field-site boundaries (cf. Lazar 2008: 39–49). However, either in declaring the geographic aspects of a field site to be arbitrary in the sense of bearing no necessary relationship to the object of study or in declaring geography altogether obsolete in defining what 'the field' may be, they leave us with a fundamental question: Where and when are we in the field? If geography does not matter, then what are the main criteria that may allow us to define it – tentative and partial as such definitions will surely be.

On the basis of the observations made above, I understand 'the field' in this book as the times and spaces in which a socio-epistemic relationship between anthropologist and research subjects takes hold. While this relationship may be riddled with confusion and potential equivocation (Heywood 2015), this is the best guidance I have to know when and where I may have been in it. In my case this relationship was fundamentally marked by institutional affiliation, aesthetics and the widespread use of money as a communicative and exclusionary medium. If we were willing to conceive of the 'field' as the time and space of a specific socio-epistemic relationship, we might be able to grasp the degree to which the choice of it may or may not be arbitrary. The criteria for where, when and with whom research will take place will certainly remain arbitrary in the very broad sense in which politics, kinship, economics or religion may be studied almost anywhere and at any time. However, as soon as anthropologists develop a more specific theoretical concern, for example an interest in the kinds of temporality that European service sector employees might develop, the fit between the time and space of research and the question it is supposed to answer will cease to be random.

Structure of this book

The following six chapters develop the argument that the work of consultants is primarily 'abstract' in nature. Chapter 1 is a background chapter that provides a short history of the consultancy sector, before outlining how management consultants fit in the forms of German class distinction. It argues that the economic success of management consultants follows an increasingly stark division between operational labour and management in large-scale corporations. While this division constitutes the condition of possibility of management consulting, it does not explain the success of professionally provided consulting services in their current institutional form (either as part of free-standing consultancy companies or as a subset of services offered by large accounting firms). This is shown to originate in a long history of corporate financialization and state activity. The chapter makes reference to the autopoietic qualities of abstract labour, a theme that will arise again in Chapter 4.

Chapters 2, 3 and 4 describe three main products of consulting work, namely speed, power and knowledge. Chapter 2 shows that management consultants work on social relationships, as they are frequently hired to speed up corporate activity, whereby they act as one of the drivers of capitalist acceleration. Since speed is hard to sell directly, management consultants foster an intense temporality in the people they work with, one that foregrounds the temporal nature of all things and stresses temporal finitude. As part of selling speed, consultants need to develop this temporality themselves. Alienation here takes the form of 'temporal angst', that is, the feeling of being trapped in time, as well as a blindness to the long-lasting and the potentially infinite aspects of human existence. The chapter shows that abstract labour, in its removal from physical production processes, lends itself to high-speed work and that it takes a strong toll on the bodies of the people involved.

Chapter 3 investigates how power operates in management consulting. It shows once more that in the projects that I have witnessed, consultants were not primarily 'knowledge workers' who dealt in providing information to clients. Instead, they frequently worked to create and foster the legitimacy of client managers. This was done by referring to two contradictory aspects of knowledge and by positioning themselves either as 'insiders' or as 'outsiders' of client companies. This made consultants socially liminal beings who ran the risk of being seen as a polluting other, a problem that drove their strong focus on rhetoric and partially explained their controversial role in society at large. The chapter foregrounds the lack of managerial legitimacy as one of the main tensions within large-scale corporations.

Chapter 4 describes the knowledge work that consultants carry out by examining how Microsoft Excel models are built, how their outcomes are translated into PowerPoint slides and how such slides are presented to clients. It argues that this labour is abstract in the sense that it confronts employees with the epistemic problem of not having a concrete referent against which to test the validity of their analyses. It is equally abstract in the sense of being fundamentally opaque, a quality that arises from the consultants' seamless mixture of rhetoric and episteme. The end of the chapter outlines why the notion of the absurd may be a useful heuristic for the study of Western elites.

Chapters 5 and 6 investigate the consultants' motivations for submitting with surprising willingness to an intense and highly abstract labour regime. Chapter 5 argues that in situations of constant epistemic, emotional and affective detachment, the self becomes a principal site onto which labour is exerted and that consultants consider corporations as primary sites of self-improvement. However, this focus on the self stands in stark contrast to their existence as commodities. Consulting companies deal with the tension between these two aspects of personhood by trying to align them via a number of 'moralistic technologies', an attempt that is only partially successful.

Chapter 6 establishes that abstract labour lends itself to the construction and use of 'profitable uncertainty'. It is brought about by postulating potential worlds, insisting on the freedom of certain economic subjects and assuming that their actions could have a relevant influence on the world. 'Profitable uncertainty' is here described as a pervasive condition held to apply to client companies, as well as to consultants themselves. The chapter ends by describing the uncontrollable excess which accompanies it.

The conclusion further refines the nature of abstract labour by comparing the work of German management consultants to that of British social anthropologists, whom I had studied for 12 months between 2015 and 2016. It points out three fundamental differences between the two, namely the purposes of both kinds of labour, the ways in which they create and overcome their abstract nature and the time frames under which they operate. Its overarching argument is that German management consultants subsume critique to the purposes of business, while anthropologists are in the business of critique.

CHAPTER ONE

Background:

A Brief History of Management Consulting

The following short history of management consulting will show that its success goes hand in hand with an increasingly stark differentiation between management and operational labour in large-scale corporations. The increasing degree of abstraction of managerial activity is the condition of possibility for consulting work. Yet, it is not sufficient to explain the organizational particularities of consultancy firms. After all, managerial support and advice can be provided through a vast variety of institutional forms, ranging from state-funded institutions to industry- or firm-specific research and training divisions. Far from being a natural outcome of the rise of managerialism, contemporary consulting, in its current institutional form, will therefore be shown to be the result of a long history of corporate financialization and state activity, which began in the United States. The chapter also situates the work of management consultants in contemporary national class dynamics. In making these arguments, this chapter will point out that consulting constantly creates the conditions for its own demand. It highlights the autopoietic qualities of abstract labour, which will be further investigated in the following chapters.

The beginnings of management consulting

The question of when exactly the history of modern-day management consulting begins depends on how authors define the profession. Kipping (1999: 195) and Canback (1998: 4) trace its roots to the last quarter of the nineteenth century, when US 'experts' in the fields of engineering, accounting and advertising first started offering independent advice to companies. Fink (2014: 15) as well as Ernst and Kieser (2002: 47) do the same, by commencing their historical reviews of the industry with the foundation of the consulting company Arthur D. Little, in 1886. The Boston-based company started by working in the chemical industry, where it provided clients with quality control assessments for productive processes. They enabled clients to check whether the goods they procured were of a high enough quality and helped them fight competitors in patent infringement lawsuits. The focus on quality control was paired with a series of cost-reduction projects in which Arthur D. Little would evaluate the cost-efficiency of different bleaching techniques in paper production or investigate how the process for keeping dried paint insoluble could be rendered less expensive (Kahn 1986: 28–9). Initially, their focus lay mostly with the engineering part of production.

Even during these early days, when consulting work was still mostly concerned with quality control and engineering issues, its focus on cost reduction came hand in hand with attempts of realigning the labour force. This was done according to Frederick W. Taylor's socio-scientific principles. Taylor held that inefficiency 'in almost all of our daily acts' was America's main problem and promised that systematic management, based on clear rules of behaviour, active training of workmen as well as managerial guidance would constitute an apt remedy (Taylor 1998: iv). In a similar vein, early management consultants like Arthur D. Little promised clients to combine 'the perfection of products' with 'the improvement of processes' (Kahn 1986: 27), visibly blending corporate concerns for people and things as expressions of costs. By engaging in quality control and cost analyses, early-day chemical and engineering consultants were already concerned with processes of standardization, as well as the socio-scientific production of commensurability, which still marks their line of work today. While the fairly close engagement with production processes meant that that their work was initially still fairly concrete in nature, their early concern with production costs already hints at the greater degree of abstraction that management consulting was to acquire until today.

The condition of possibility for the rise of management consultants was the increasingly complex nature of American corporate capitalism. Since the first half of the twentieth century, US companies have transformed from small, owner-run, single-product firms into large, dispersed and decentralized corporations with a broad portfolio of products and production activities. As part of this transformation, administrative tasks were increasingly separated from production (Chandler 1998, 2004; Sassen 2001: 97–101). 'Strategic management' was invented as an independent activity for salaried managers, whose main job was to monitor overall corporate performance and to decide how to allocate resources in the long term. Production, in turn, was equally redefined. It was now the task of operating divisions that were structured either according to product lines or according to increasingly dispersed geographical areas in which corporate activity took place (Chandler 1998, 2004; Lazonick 1993: 27–36). The drastic division of administrative tasks from production, often among several steps of corporate hierarchy, opened the possibility for 'administrative experts' to offer their services to management. Thereby, consultants increasingly played the role of mediating agents between blue- and white-collar workers. Throughout the beginning of the twentieth century, however, consultants could position themselves more and more as experts of administrative work itself.

This is why, in contrast to the management historians mentioned so far, McKenna (1995, 2006) argues that the history of modern-day consultancy companies really begins only in the 1920s and 1930s, when the advice industry gradually shifted its focus from the scientific management of the shop floor to a reorganization of white-collar labour. By the late 1920s, American consulting companies had both grown and diversified. A. T. Kearney had been in existence for thirty years, and firms such as Edwin Booz & Company, McKinsey & Company and the former Stevenson, Jordan and Harrison had by then all been founded (Edersheim 2004: 17). By now, they focused on corporate reorganization more widely and increasingly employed cost accountants or professionals with a background in law and banking. Consultants became increasingly confident that it was possible to improve managerial tasks, regardless of the activities that were to be managed. Their work thereby became more and more abstract, as people, objects and practices under concern grew both conceptually and often physically distant.

While the division of management from production thus laid the groundwork for the activity of management consulting, it does not explain the institutional establishment and continuous growth of organizations specializing in it. Several authors have attempted to explain the success of this particular corporate form, with reference to the entrepreneurial virtues of the founders of consulting firms (e.g. Fink 2014; Kahn 1986; Edersheim 2004). While these well-educated, well-connected and rhetorically gifted white American men were certainly intelligent and industrious, their characters and business decisions can tell us little about the collective rise and the sustained boom of the consultancy industry over more than a century. This ongoing industry-wide success has its roots in the broader political economy, notably the ascent of economic financialization, and a mixture of state legislation and state demand.

During the 1930s, the Great Depression was a major driving force for American management consultancies. It had caused many corporations whose customer base was breaking away to face mid-term bankruptcy, unless they drastically cut costs. Management consultancies were happy to step in, analysing where savings could be made, legitimizing lay-offs to management and staff, and allowing management to share part of the blame for lay-off decisions. Crucially, the Great Depression also allowed banks and insurance groups that held industry bonds to take control over loan-defaulting companies. As members of so-called 'bondholder's committees', they now owned a series of Depression-ravaged manufacturing companies. They needed to make these companies profitable again, but did not know how to organize industrial business activity (Fink 2014: 17). Management consultants made it their job to either restructure industrial activity or 'at least wring some value out of [company] remnants' (Edersheim 2004: 16). Thus, they grew as the result of the increasing financialization of industrial activity, serving as debt advisors for creditors, who had taken corporate control but did not know what to do with it. These origins point at a long history of rise of finance. They show that the currently much-discussed spread of corporate and private debt and credit obligations is in essence a more extreme version of a longer capitalist drive for financialization, which dates back at least to the early nineteenth century (Lazonick 1992; Polanyi 2001: 10ff; Thrift 2005: 5).

During the 1930s, the state was a second critical force behind the rise of contemporary management consulting. The 1933 Glass-Stegall Banking Act boosted the newly instituted consulting business by outlawing banks from providing lucrative corporate advice. At the same time the 1933 US Securities Act imposed strict auditing requirements to all corporate financing activity (McKenna 2006: 17–19). Unsurprisingly, the new-found management consultancies thrived in this mixture of state-induced demand for auditing and excluded competition. The 1930s anti-monopoly legislation under the US American New Deal strengthened them further, by prohibiting corporate executives from sharing information through trade associations or industry cartels. This enabled consultancy companies to become exclusive providers of benchmarking services and other forms of inter-firm knowledge exchange in the United States (ibid.: 20). Contrary to their frequent invocation of free market values, the origins of current-day management consulting are thus closely interwoven with acts of government decree.

Consolidation and growth

From the 1940s to the 1960s American consultancy companies became well established as advisors of CEOs in the fields of business organization and market analysis. Some of them, who had counted one or two dozen consultants in the 1930s, grew to several hundred employees by the early 1960s (Kipping and Kirkpatrick 2005: 8). The role of state demand is usually underestimated in this development, and contemporary observers tend to act surprised at the close involvement of consultancy firms and government entities (e.g. *The Guardian* 2010; *Der Spiegel* 2013a). However, early on in US history, war efforts had already significantly boosted government demand for consultancy services. The tremendous increase in US public spending on the mass mobilization of people and goods during the First and Second World Wars meant both an immediate and a lasting push to management consulting firms. Particularly Booz Allen & Hamilton and Arthur D. Little thrived on co-organizing the American military-industrial complex (David

2012: 76–8). A sustained rise in US post-Second World War public defence budgets provided them and their competitors with further consulting contracts in the following decades (ibid.). Additionally, the companies' closeness to the military established a 'revolving door' for military personnel and consulting executives (e.g. Kahn 1986: 57–8). It founded the close connection between management consultancy companies and state entities, which still marks this line of work today (e.g. Transparency International UK 2012: 3).

The sustained involvement between consultancy firms and government entities is linked to the increasingly managerial understanding of politics on the side of US government officials (Arnold 1976). Early non-military use of management consultants by the US federal government was explicitly meant to adopt a 'general efficiency approach' that was assumed to prevail in private business (David 2012: 79). From the late 1940s until the late 1970s, management consultants were thus involved in improving the workings of the US healthcare sector, the US Post Office, the Department of Transportation, The National Science Foundation (NSF), Internal Revenue Service (IRS), the US Olympic Committee and a series of urban development offices, to name but a few examples. During this time, the establishment of business schools and the expansion of the business press fostered the view that management was a craft on its own, regardless of content. This conviction was crucial if consultants wanted to find employment with companies and state officials in vastly different sectors of the economy (ibid.).

During the late 1950s and early 1960s, management consultancies began a rapid expansion to Western Europe (Kipping 1999: 209). While their goal had initially been to serve European divisions of American companies as part of a post-Second World War overseas investment boom, they quickly built a regional basis among European corporations, who wanted to 'protect themselves' from US competition by tapping into their expertise (McKenna 2006: 172). As a shield against global competition, management consultancies spread the decentralized multidivisional model of corporate organization. They became the principal conduit for American managerial capitalism in Europe during the 1960s and 1970s (ibid.: 190), disseminating a business model that distanced management from production, and lent itself to the provision of their own services (Ernst and Kieser 2002). Their work thereby increased the likelihood of its own future demand by diffusing a corporate form in which they themselves could thrive. Consultants thus engaged in an act of economic autopoiesis that is typical for regimes of abstract labour.[1]

The themes of managerialism, financialization and state involvement also marked the consolidation and expansion of management consulting. In the 1960s, when American consultants thrived on following established recipes abroad, two further developments facilitated their growth. First, their international expansion roughly coincided with what Thrift has called the rise of 'soft capitalism' (Thrift 1997, 1998). Spanning across the boundaries of public and private institutions, soft capitalism is marked by new discourses of management that stress – among other features – corporate knowledge production, routinized innovation and heightened self-reflexivity. These new-found virtues were supposed to guide the collective totality of a firm, as well as the individual existence of manager and worker. Thrift has linked this change in the nature of capitalism to a 'cultural circuit of capital', a 'machine' consisting of business schools, management consultants and management gurus (including publishing houses and a management-oriented media) who have learnt to use fear of uncertainty and desires for self-improvement as the basis for highly profitable business activity (Thrift 2002: 19, 2005). Soft capitalism continues until today, allowing consultancies in the 1980s and 1990s to bridge stagnant market conditions in Europe. At that time, most major companies had already taken on the multidivisional corporate model, as well as recipes for greater white- and blue-collar efficiency, so consultancies relied more heavily on projects concerned with improving 'corporate culture' as the new essence of soft capitalism (cf. Chong 2012).

Secondly, management consultancies began to focus in earnest on IT projects. They did this, riding another wave of state support. As part of US post-Second World War antitrust legislation, IBM had been prohibited from offering computer-consulting services in the 1950s (McKenna 2005: 20ff.). The rapid rise of computing technology, and the hurdles from competition set up through state legislation, thereby opened up a wide field of corporate advice in which management consultancies prospered. Rather than concerning themselves with the actual set-up of computer systems, they focused on the associated managerial problem of establishing a fit between IT and general business activity (Davenport 1998;

Westrup and Knight 2000). Chong (2012), who has provided us with a first ethnographic study of Chinese IT consultants, shows that the nexus between their work and state activity has remained close until today. IT consultancies in China continue to tap into government projects of 'modernisation' and macroeconomic reform (ibid.: 12–16). In her example, they continue to be part of explicit state attempts at economic renewal, partially geared at emulating Western corporate role models.

Finally, consultants did well out of the effects of the shareholder revolution, which was a 'massive shift in cultural understandings of the corporation from the 1950s to the present time' (Ho 2009: 123). This revolution culminated in the mergers and acquisitions waves of the 1980s and 1990s. At its most basic, this shift consisted in redefining the purpose of a corporation from a multiplicity of socio-economic objectives – such as providing employment, producing desirable goods and services for customers and paying taxes – to the single most important goal of maximizing shareholder value.[2] The origins of this shift lay in a mixture of state regulatory measures and technological change. Changes in government regulation since the 1970s enabled the large-scale transfer of shares, from individual households to huge institutional investors, such as pension funds, mutual funds and life insurance companies, who could now exert pressure on management. Moreover, they allowed these and other investors to put money into much riskier products than previously possible, and to increase their share-buying power through 'leverage', that is, by accumulating vast debt obligations for investment purposes (Lazonick and O'Sullivan 2002; Sennett 2006: 37–8).

While these developments frequently resulted in substantive job losses and greater work precariousness for employees (Lazonick and O'Sullivan 2002), they were beneficial to top management, investors and management consultants. They profoundly changed managerial work by rendering managers accountable both for company results and for the ways in which these results were represented to potential investors and the public (Froud et al. 2006). Consultants prospered in this new situation. While in 1980 less than five firms with more than a thousand consultants existed, there were more than thirty in 1997 (Ernst and Kieser 2002: 2). They could foster their old roles as unbiased mediators between business and finance and they could take on an additional, largely symbolic function. In their strong and extrovert adherence to the demands of finance, their sheer presence in a company now constituted a message to shareholders that their desires would be met. Managers could thereby send a positive signal to investors simply by hiring consultants. Consultancy companies thus embraced shareholder value, with most of them developing and spreading proprietary metrics for how to measure and generate it properly (Froud et al. 2006: 45–6).

The speed with which consultants take on new organizational discourses, even so-called 'management fads', is often described in terms of adaptability (Thrift 2005: 12). They seem to embody the very 'flexibility' that they demand from clients and the general labour force (Boltanski and Chiapello 2011: 20; Martin 1994: 145). While this is certainly true, this brief historic overview of management consulting shows that they equally co-cause the conditions that drive their business. While the shareholder value revolution had its origins in state legislation and technological change, consultants contributed to its rise, nurturing a social phenomenon in which they could prosper. Once again their history points to the autopoietic qualities of abstract labour.

The autopoietic nature of this particular kind of work does not mean that it is bound to be eternally successful in its historically specific institutional form. Instead, consultancy companies are currently under pressure from several sides. On the one hand, there is an ascent of specialized consulting firms, which claim to provide more concrete forms of expertise. They may focus on individual aspects of corporate activity, for example installing and improving of IT or accounting systems,[3] particular industries like the global sports industry[4] or the international development sector.[5] These competitors to generalist firms that specialize in strategic management consulting include the increasingly large consulting divisions of accounting firms. They also comprise so-called 'in-house' consultancies, which have been created within large manufacturing companies such as Siemens or Lufthansa, who cater to top management of both their own firms and others.

A second source of pressure results from clients' mounting demands that management consultants not just draw up plans, but ensure their implementation as well (Armbrüster and Kipping 2002; *The Financial Times* 2013). Implementation oversight pushes down prices, since it takes place over long periods of time, for which daily management consulting fees are usually too high. It is also deemed much less glamorous than more abstract management consulting, as it involves regular interaction with low-level managers and blue-collar workers. This undermines widespread notions of social elitism on which management consulting continues to rely. Finally, it foregrounds the permanent problem that expensive plans written in the comfort and socio-epistemic seclusion of boardrooms may not be easily applicable in production. The 'friction' between abstract labour and production makes management consultancies open to critique (Sturdy 2011: 527; Tsing 2005).

Interestingly, both of these challenges fundamentally question the strong division of managerial and non-managerial activity. While traditional strategy consulting is built on the conviction that management work itself can be improved regardless of content, specialized consulting companies sell their 'closeness' to specific processes or particular industries as an asset. Equally, increasing demands for implementation presuppose a closer engagement with production than has previously been the case (BDU 2015: 8). In both instances the abstract nature of management consulting, which can often be an asset turns out to be a limitation. In the light of these structural problems, short-term reductions in demand, such as during the dot-com crisis of 2000 and the 2008 global financial crisis, may put traditional consultancies at risk (Christensen, Wang and Van Bever 2013; Niewiem and Richter 2004). While crises do allow them to generate new projects, their financial performance is generally stronger in environments of economic growth, in which the cost-reduction projects of some industries and the expansionary goals of others can be combined (Armbrüster and Glückler 2007).

Management consulting in Germany

In Germany, management had long been considered integral to production. German managers had developed a preference for technological rather than organizational ways to improve their business (O'Sullivan 2002: 275) and until the mid-1970s the spread of new management ideas had mostly taken place via publicly funded institutions, such as the German Productivity and Innovation Centre 'RKW', to which unions were as much affiliated as corporate managers (Faust 2000: 68–30). However, when German corporate executives focused on the internationalization of business activity in the 1970s, 1980s and 1990s, they turned to

US consultancy companies for advice. The latter had successfully positioned themselves as the exclusive providers of global business knowledge. Against a German crisis of established institutional knowledge mediation, they epitomized a mixture of new capitalist virtues such as mobility, acceleration and flexibility with which the phenomenon of globalization had become associated (ibid.).

Yet, management consultants also remained true to their social function of stepping in as the long arm of management when it deemed unpopular corporate reforms necessary. Thus, they established themselves in the German public sector as part of the early 2000s labour market reforms of the centre–left coalition of the German Social Democratic Workers' Party (SPD) and the Green Party. Consultancy companies Roland Berger and McKinsey were used in the design and implementation of the notorious labour market reforms called 'Hartz 4', which lowered unemployment benefits and loosened labour rights. Other major consultancy involvement in Germany's public sector during the 2000s included reforms of the German military, postal service, telecommunications service, transport and public sector IT, to name but a few examples (e.g. Leif 2006). In 2014, public sector consulting in Germany was estimated to make up around 9 per cent of industry revenue (BDU 2013: 10). This makes it the third largest market for consulting, after manufacturing (34 per cent) and finance (24 per cent) (ibid.). The increasing involvement of consulting companies in drafting government policy has met with a strong public backlash, criticizing consultants' high fees, lack of accountability, frequent use of jargon and scarce experience, as well as the government's overall lack of interest to build expertise within its own ministries (Die Zeit 2004; Leif 2005, 2008). In spite of public concern since the mid-2000s, the German government has continued to work closely with consultancy companies (Armbrüster, Banzhaf and Dingemann 2010), even when looking for ways in which to manage the recent large-scale influx of asylum seekers (*Der Spiegel* 2016). The German weekly newsmagazine *Der Spiegel* calculated that government ministries under Angela Merkel paid roughly EUR 1bn in consulting fees between 2009 and 2013 (*Der Spiegel* 2013a).

The work of management consultants must be understood against a new German desire for elitism. It can be observed in the country's recent higher education reforms (THE 2016), in recruitment practices of the private and public sector (e.g. FAZ 2012; *Der*

Spiegel 2014) and even on the country's major dating websites.[6] Consultancy companies have succeeded in positioning themselves as part and parcel of this new elitist discourse, mostly via recruiting practices, in which they target prestigious universities (Friedrichs 2009; Herles 2013), a practice which reflects the recruitment strategies of Wall Street (Ho 2009). Management consultancies are bound to these universities in at least two ways. On the one hand, they tap into their prestige by mentioning the academic provenance of their staff in project pitches and on their intranet when assembling project teams (Chapter 4). On the other hand, they find fairly ambitious students at these institutions who are used to an elite status, which they do not want to lose when leaving higher education. In this double reliance on an elitist education system, management consultancies recruit disproportionately at the recently instituted private universities in Germany, and at the most selective universities of the United States and the United Kingdom. They also conduct recruiting events with Germany's 'National Merit Foundation', an institution founded in 1925 that provides financial support only for the country's 'highly gifted'[7] students (Kunze 2000).

The notion of elites would come up time and again in interviews with consultants. Rooted in fifteenth-century connotations of referring to people who have been chosen by God (Williams 1983: 112–13), the term refers to a vaguely defined, yet all the more encompassing quality of, personhood, which may or may not be observable in all aspects of social life. It may refer to productive activity as well as to consumption habits, to ideal standards or lived praxis, to physical attributes as well as to intellectual sophistication, to personal agency or position in a social structure. Since the term elite is so broad, its unqualified use provided it with an all-or-nothing quality that left little analytic room for describing in detail which aspects of social life actually justified its use in a given situation, that is, at which points someone with elite qualities began and ceased to be part of the elite. This ambiguous yet totalizing nature of the concept was frequently made use of by those I interviewed. Some of them strongly rejected it, saying it was basically meaningless. Others subscribed to it at times explicitly, but often implicitly by referring to themselves as being either especially intelligent or particularly quick at work, exceedingly hard-working or exceptionally efficient, close to power or refined in their tastes. Often these self-descriptions were of a circumstantial nature, made in relation to other groups that consultants would want to differentiate themselves from.

As a result, consulting work has received a substantial amount of interest from the popular media as well as artistic circles. The notorious play entitled *McKinsey is coming* (Hochhuth 2004) deals with different social and psychological aspects of unemployment and puts the symbolic role of consultants on display. While no consultants feature in it, the mere announcement of their arrival is seen as synonymous with job losses in the name of rising share prices. The movie *Age of Cannibals* (Naber 2013) has provided a highly satirical, view of their work. Staged as a chamber play, which takes place in luxury hotels of unspecified developing countries, it depicts the daily life of consultants as a mixture of cut-throat cynicism and a perfect removal from the world outside their hotel. In the movie, the outside world is depicted only as a minimalist, abstract painting behind polished hotel windows. While Hochhuth's play echoes popular German fears of job losses after labour market reforms in the early 2000s, Naber's movie challenges the removal of management from both production and wider social life. The recent movie *Toni Erdmann* (Ade 2016) has created a more nuanced and more realistic view of their work. The critically acclaimed film provides a highly intimate understanding of consulting, as a profession that provides an aspiring middle class with access to the world of the rich, even if this comes with an increasing alienation from pre-existing social relations.

In addition, an entire subgenre of first-person accounts written by former consultants (or consulting recruits) that focus on the absurdities of their working lives have turned into best sellers among German readers. Undercover journalist Friedrichs, for example, famously accused consultancy companies of institutionalized hubris (Die Zeit 2006; Friedrichs 2009). Weiden (2011), a management consultant for over nine years, has provided a humorous account of consultant mannerisms, mocking their desire to communicate through PowerPoint slides as well as their frustration with the fact that client realities do not correspond to the content of their slide show presentations. Through an equally personal but much darker lens, former consultants Sauer and Sahnau (2002) caricature consulting work as nothing but an overpriced scam, while former consultant Herles (2013) criticizes managers for hiding behind consultants and consultants for being conformist careerists. Journalist Leif (2008) deplores the lack of transparency of consultancy work in the public sector. He also points out the fact that in privatizing parts of the German military, consultants recommended additional advisory services, driving up costs in a self-perpetuating motion (ibid.: 2005). These critical works stand in strong tension with the ongoing economic success of consultancy companies in Germany. They also clash with praises by the business-friendly press that often hail consultants as the masters of the business world (cf. *Manager Magazin* 2014; Rasiel 1999; Rasiel and Friga 2002).

It was against this highly polarized discourse surrounding consultancy companies that I met a cohort of 24[8] newly hired colleagues who all started their job together with me in September 2011. Most of us were in our late twenties, and only a third were women. All of us were white and less than a fifth had a foreign-sounding last name. Moreover, we had all obtained high marks at university, around 80–90 per cent were recent graduates and the majority of my future colleagues had spent at least one year studying abroad. They had mostly studied at Russel Group universities in the United Kingdom or at Ivy League institutions in the United States. A disproportionate amount of my new-found colleagues had been members of the German National Merit foundation and all spoke English fluently (and at times several other foreign languages). Moreover, I was suprised to find out later that two of my future team members were of aristocratic descent.

Our group reflected German class stratifications in various ways. We had the kind of cultural dispositions that would allow us to interact with the country's managerial strata, for whom class-specific habitus was key (Hartmann 2000, 2004). Just in case we needed further refinement, our employer gave us a book on proper manners in the business world, as part of our training. While most of my colleagues would have a degree in business and finance, several also had a background in engineering and medicine, with the occasional social sciences or humanities graduate in their midst. Naturally, there were not many foreigners or people from non–middle-class households, since in Germany people with a migratory background continue to enjoy very little social mobility (BPB 2012). Income inequality after tax has increased over the past decade (Krause 2015) and wealth inequality in Germany remains strikingly high, at a Gini coefficient of 0.78 (Grabka and Westermeier 2014). In addition, at 22.4 per cent, the country has the highest gender pay gap in the European Union (EU 2012). And yet, none of these issues was likely to affect us. Hardly anyone among us knew exactly what kind of job we were about to begin, but what we did know was that it was an 'achievement'[9] to have made it through the application process, not least because our mentors and senior colleagues unanimously congratulated us on it.

The following chapters will argue that part of the chasm between high praise and harsh critique of consulting can be explained with reference to the abstract nature of the work that is carried out. In being removed from the concrete, opaque in nature, and in making reference to discourses of rationality, consulting work manages to obtain high salaries and access to political elites. Its class position is thus not accidental, but part and parcel of the job that consultants carry out. However, this removal and opacity also opens them to critique for being too removed from productive processes and thereby not as valuable as their pay cheques may suggest. Thus, the entirety of consulting work can be questioned with relative ease, both by the popular press and by those people who are either negatively affected by it or who do not share its basic normative tenets. The following two chapters will describe this in some detail.

Conclusion

In conclusion, this short historical overview has shown that the activity of management consulting followed a growing distance between managerial and operational activities. As an institutional form, consultancy companies were the result of a long history of corporate financialization and state activity. As a cultural phenomenon it began in the United States and expanded to Europe during the second half of the twentieth century. This chapter has also shown that consulting has autopoietic qualities, in that it co-created the conditions for its own demand. Lastly, it has alluded to the fact that the employees who find themselves in consulting jobs tend to come straight from university and reflect on the whole a privileged class position. Against this historical background, the following chapters will describe management consulting in practice.

CHAPTER TWO

Selling Speed:

Capitalist Acceleration and Temporal Angst

Even during the first days on the job, and as part of our corporate training, my colleagues and I would learn that one of the defining contradictions of consulting was that we were meant to dominate time, while simultaneously being perfectly subservient to it. On the one hand, we were taught to work with Gantt charts, that is, visual representations that meticulously delineated the expected completion of future work processes. We remained constantly aware of project deadlines, timelines and appointments, carried out time-and-motion studies in which corporate workflows were measured with a stopwatch, regularly described client employees in our slides and spreadsheets as 'full-time equivalents (FTEs)', and learnt how to calculate the 'net present value' of corporate investments, that is, the fictive present monetary value of future investments made over long periods of time. In all of these activities, my colleagues and I made time an explicit matter of our concern, showing that we mastered duration, foresight, sequencing and rhythm like few other people in few other professions.

This raises the question why, on the other hand consultants seemed to be subservient to time to an extreme extent. Many if not all of my colleagues professed that days and weeks felt simply too short to get their work done, and they often sweated over writing spreadsheet analyses and presentation slides until they reached their physical limits. While at work, they were frequently struggling with sleep deprivation and rapid weight gain. In fact, our more established colleagues had mentioned to us only half in jest that upon becoming a consultant one would gain around 5 kg in weight. A close colleague of mine had once broken her nose trying to walk through a glass door after several days with very little sleep, while another one fainted repeatedly because of constant fatigue and an unhealthy diet. When illness struck, many of my colleagues and interviewees did not feel they could take time out from work. As a result, three of them suffered from eardrum ruptures when they continued to fly with heavy colds until cabin pressure had become too much for them. One, who did not think she could ignore pressing deadlines in spite of a bladder infection, developed an inflammation of the pelvis, while others suffered from stomach ulcers and seemingly endless colds. A stress-related nervous breakdown, a depression that turned into hospitalized paranoia and a heart attack were also among the very sad developments I witnessed in the field. While some gendered exceptions to the tendency of overworking among management consultants may exist, in that male employees occasionally fake work activity (cf. Reid 2015), this was not the rule in my field site. Instead, the ethnographic issue I was confronted with was why management consultants should simultaneously be dominant over, and servient to, time to such an extreme degree.

My answer to this conundrum is that consultants sold speed to corporations. One of the principal products of their labour was to accelerate the production processes and working lives of others. In order to do so, consultants needed to establish modes of analysis and kinds of relations that constantly evaluated labour with reference to its temporal attributes. Thereby they spread what is here called an 'intense temporality', that is, a relationship to time (Gingrich, Ochs and Swedlund 2002) that constantly highlighted the temporal aspects of life and focused on temporal finitude. As part of their catalytic function, they needed to serve as exemplars of temporal dominance, thereby developing this intense temporality themselves. This drove both their long working days, through which they tried to achieve within the time of a project what others would deem impossible, and the permanent urgency with which they operated. The downside of selling this intense temporality is that it brought with it a specific form of alienation, one that did not just stem from temporal incongruities, say between their bodies and the temporal constraints of a project, but also from a feeling of being trapped in time, as well as a blindness to the long-lasting and the potentially infinite aspects of human existence.

In providing a description of how speed is sold in a corporate environment, this chapter speaks to the curious fact that an increase in wealth among workers under capitalism does not lead them to work less (e.g. Thompson 1967: 95; Rosa 2013). In spite of their privileged class position, the daily lives of consultants were dominated by feelings of impatience and the almost constant effort to ensure a purposive use of time. Various explanations have been given as to how this treadmill effect of capitalist modernity is brought about. Eriksen (2001) and Boyer (2013: 5) have recently highlighted rapid improvements in communication technology and increased flow of information as one of its drivers. These factors clearly mattered in my field site, where all employees were meant to be constantly virtually available to their bosses and peers. However, the disproportionate speed and length of the workday still exceeded that of many other users of similar technologies.

As the paragraphs below will show, the temporality of management consultants was more closely related to the nature of capitalist production. Postone has famously linked social acceleration and capitalism, arguing that capitalist value creation is static and that each advance in productivity compels all competing producers to follow suit (1993: 289–90). Harvey has made a similar point, holding that there is an 'omnipresent incentive for individual capitalists to accelerate their turnover time vis-à-vis the social average' as a main driver for the acceleration of economic processes and social life in general (1992: 229–30). This chapter adds to these insights by showing that in the work of German management consultants speed was no longer just a by-product of capitalist value production, but had become a commodity in and of itself. As part of this 'original accumulation'[1] of time under capitalism, the human activities that were already part of capitalist production were constantly being put under renewed scrutiny (cf. Marx 2005). In the corporate context of the German middle class, speed was not sold as a biochemical substance (Pine 2016), but consultants tried to conjure it by establishing an intense temporality, that is, a relationship to time marked by urgency, which found expression in their analytic metrics, organizational structure and work practices. As labour is being rediscovered as a key human activity for the creation of temporal congruence in capitalist modernity (Bear 2014a, 2014b), this raises the question as to what the consequences of speeding up other one's work might be. Anthropologists studying corporate settings have insisted on the multiplicity of time (Adam 1994) showing temporal incongruities between financial spheres of circulation and material production (LiPuma and Lee 2004: 37, 2005: 420–2), between corporate employees and idealized others (Miyazaki 2003, 2013: 103), and between the historical and the 'attritional' temporalities of unionists and political activists (Lazar 2014). They have equally pointed out that economic reasoning may drive at different aspects of temporal ordering, evacuating either the near future (Guyer 2007), the past (Abram 2014) or the contemporary (Holmes and Marcus 2006). While these multiplicities persisted in my field site, the most noteworthy effect of selling and exemplifying speed was that my colleagues felt as if they were trapped in time. They bemoaned that their private lives were now getting 'booked solid[2]' and that it was increasingly hard to 'squeeze activities into their days[3]'. This pointed to the loss of less immediately purposive conceptions of time, in which long-lasting and potentially infinite aspects of human existence could be given greater prominence.

This chapter begins with a brief description of project work for a paper mill[4] outlining that speed was one of the principal products that our team of consultants sold. Subsequently, it will describe a series of organizational features and work practices that established creating an intense temporality among ourselves, as a precondition for selling it to others. Lastly, I will highlight the nature of alienation in this particular temporal context and the class-dependent ways of dealing with it.

Selling speed

In April of 2012, I began working on a consulting project in a paper mill. Giulio, the partner responsible for the project, had described our work over the phone to me as a 'diagnostic', stating that it was our job to look at the mill's work processes, identify what worked well and what did not, and pinpoint the mill's 'growth potential'. As one of our main internal documents summarized it, our basic question was 'how can the mill improve its operations (e.g. reducing costs, improving productivity) in order to further contribute to corporate competitiveness?'. This abstract question was to be answered by our team in just slightly over two weeks. I first met Giulio late on a Sunday night at an airport near the mill. He was in his early thirties and struck me as a friendly, forthcoming and highly energetic man. We had arrived a day before our project started so as to be able to begin work in the mill fresh on Monday morning. During the long late-night shuttle ride to our hotel, Giulio explained to me and two other male consultants in their late twenties that mill management expected our team to find at least EUR 30m[5] worth of 'potential'. Fifty per cent thereof were to be found in labour costs. As our shuttle made its way past the mill and towards our hotel late in the evening hours, he ominously repeated the words 'got to find that potential' to us.

In the light of the short time horizon of the project, every hour of it counted. Our international team had daily morning meetings, during which everyone reported the work they were about to do, as well as daily evening debriefs, summarizing the 'improvement potential found' over the past few hours. My colleagues were visibly stressed, eagerly hammering into their computers and disallowing chatter that was not work related. They minimized lunch breaks and dinners and generally continued work after dinner until late at night. Giulio was known to work on all weekends to make the project a success, and we slept an estimated average of six hours per night. In this manner, we were to prove to mill management that we could carry out this diagnostic much faster than they themselves or any of our competitors would be able to.

Apart from being a marker of our professionalism, speed also mattered as a source of profit within the mill's productive processes. One way of 'finding potential' was to examine the work of forklift drivers in its largest warehouses. My team got a tour of the mill, interviewed the managers of different storage facilities and observed the work routines of forklift drivers. We noted meticulously where and how enormous paper reels were moved from the production line to storage areas, when and how often trucks came in, and how long it took to load them. The results of these observations were summarized in a template that Giulio had provided. It figured a diagram into which an estimated average for each main activity of forklift drivers was entered. Forklift activities were then colour coded into the categories 'value added' (green), 'enabler' (yellow) and 'non-value added' (red). Our assumption was that if the red category of activities was 'cut out', either by retraining staff or rearranging the warehouses, the same amount of work could be done with less staff, saving the mill the amount in thereby unpaid salaries and increasing profits accordingly. In this process, work activities were converted into time and imagined to be sped up. The difference between current and imagined temporalities was then expressed in a percentage change, (i.e. the same work could be done in about 80 per cent of the time it currently took) which could be translated into people, whose salaries constituted 'improvement potential', that is, profit. Thus, by timing the work of forklift drivers, one could establish, for example, that *ceteris paribus* 'warehouses 2 and 3 show potential of over 51 per cent'.[6] Similar analyses were carried out throughout the paper mill, in their research and development labs, raw material storage faculties and at points of interaction with suppliers and transport companies. In each instance, recommendations of how to speed up work processes were converted into potential monetary gains.

In the interviews I conducted with consultants from different companies, it became clear that they were often hired to speed up corporate clients in various ways. As Martina, a junior consultant with a background in finance, put it: 'I believe that [we are] sometimes [called] because of time. It is much easier to take decisions for people external to the company and it simply happens a lot faster. This might sound silly but in some cases getting things done half a year later simply costs an awful amount of money.' A former project boss of mine – who had a penchant for militaristic metaphor – put it more bluntly, '[Consultants are] troops that you can send in somewhere. They work hard and they work long hours and they will whip my own troops forward. A little bit like a rapid deployment force,[7] when you expect resistance and do not want to burn yourself or your own men.' Another colleague, who was interning as a consultant, expressed in shock that we were 'like the grey gentlemen in Momo', fictional characters in one of Germany's most notorious children books, who used mathematics and rhetoric to make people work harder and steal their free time (Ende 1986). Finally, the point that consultants worked as agents of acceleration was made most poetically by a senior consultant's wife, who mentioned with an air of melancholy that we worked 'only so as to make the world spin a little faster'.

From the point of view of clients, this was equally true. For example, Dr Marke, a senior member of the strategy department of a major German manufacturing company, stated in an interview:

> I find it incredibly fast to discuss a topic with [management consultants] and to have the first slides on it already on the following day. This is what they are very good at ... . You do not wait for long but you can simply run for it and see the board with [the documents]. This is an advantage because your own company often does not have the time and the people to do this.

Dr Marke added in the same conversation that he was aware of the downsides relating to this style of work, namely that consultant analyses he had seen had not been of the highest quality, privileging structure and speed over analytic rigour.

A permanent state of exception

As the example above has shown, the catalytic function of consultants is based on establishing an intense temporality, that is, a relationship to time that foregrounds the temporal attributes of most if not all activities in a corporation, while simultaneously highlighting temporal finitude. On the one hand, this was done via the collective understanding among management consultants and their clients that the former were called when clients were considered to be in situations of turmoil (Roland Berger 2014), drastic change (McKinsey 2014) or other important kinds of far-reaching structural change (Bain and Company 2014). Management consulting was thus understood to take place in a state of exception, in the sense that decisions could part from established norms (Schmitt 2005) and high daily fees of consultancy companies could be justified. Social scientists tend to describe such states of exception with respect to the forms of authority and relations of sovereignty that they reflect and enable. With existing social norms largely on hold, the state of exception allows sovereign people and groups to put into place radical economic policies that may have previously received little to no official popular support (Ong 2006).

However, states of exception also have far-reaching temporal implications. Among clients, they were assumed to be limited in time, in opposition to the long-lasting and potentially permanent nature of normal economic activity. The contracts they negotiated with consultants were thus budgeted on a so-called per diem basis, where each consultant costed a predefined daily amount of money and project deadlines with clearly delimitated outcomes were set from the start. Consulting was thus generally marked by a strictly set deadline, at which ties with a current client would be cut and final analyses had to be rendered. Their finitude was enshrined in the Gantt charts, prescheduled meetings and 'milestones' presented at the beginning of each project. From the perspective of the client, the exception stopped when a project came to an end, while from the perspective of the consultant, it was in fact permanent (Agamben 2005: 2), interspersed only by further exceptions when particularly pressing meetings loomed. Consider how consultant Eva remembers the time when she had to 'work on the edge'[8] during one of her projects:

> We were [with the client] from Monday until Thursday from 8 am until 9 pm. Then we went to the hotel and worked mostly until midnight or 1 am. During peak times often until 4.30 am. Midnight was our average, which still allows you to sleep for six hours but most frequently it was 1 am or 2 am. There was also a phase during which we worked until 4 am.

On the one hand, the exceptional circumstances of clients meant that a normal understanding of work requirements did not apply. Instead, exceptional times required quick responses and big promises from the start, as to how and when they could revert to normal. Thus, upon selling a project, senior consultants had an incentive to claim that extraordinary amounts of work would be possible for their teams, both to justify the vast amounts of money spent on them, and to prove that they were capable of mastering the exception and using time better than anyone else. This heightened the 'promissory atmosphere' of project work (Strathern 2011) in which future activity was established as being both challenging and temporally limited from day one.

Interestingly, this emphasis on temporal finitude persisted with respect to the consultants' own careers. My colleagues and interviewees had specifically temporal understandings as to where they should be on the consulting career ladder now and in the future. One should be able to run one's own sub-projects after about one to three years, lead a project after three to five years and become partner after around seven years.[9] This high degree of temporal specificity concerning expected job promotions is still a rare feature in capitalist corporations. It more closely reflects the tightly temporally regulated workings of educational institutions, which might be one of the reasons why consultancy companies prefer to recruit recent university graduates. The consultants' progress was thereby not primarily assessed on the basis of their salaries, the size of their bonuses or the access they had to exclusive meetings and work spaces. The way it was chiefly made sense of was whether or not they lagged behind their peer group, that is, the group of people with whom they had started their job. Biannual promotion rounds were held during which one was expected to advance to the next level. The most successful consultants were promoted early, while the less successful ones were promoted late, and hierarchy was expressed in how 'fast' one had made it to a particular position. Regular emails to the whole firm that announced who had been promoted in a specific round thereby fostered a competitive disposition between company employees through the use of a temporal idiom.

Consulting was also a state of exception in the sense that common degrees of temporality did not apply. Consider how consultant Susanne described her work, when talking about the key characteristics needed for the job: 'The standard saying [on projects] was things are burning, things are burning, things are burning everywhere. [This is when you need to] exude calm and sobriety with the client and with your team.' She points out the paradox that projects were routinely conceived of as being exceptionally urgent. Meetings could not be postponed, analyses that clients had asked for had to be available right away and delays of any kind were interpreted as a lack of professionalism. The consultants transmitted this understanding to the lower echelons of client staff. For example, when they asked members of Sales or HR departments for internal company data they made clear in emails, phone calls and personal encounters that they would need these data as soon as possible. Employees who did not deliver quickly enough were regularly reminded of the urgency of the situation, until data requests were 'escalated', that is, passed on to their superiors. Consultants thus acted as representatives of upper management to whom any delays in work activity needed to be justified. Thereby the state of exception was spread from the top of a corporation down to its lower levels.

As the descriptions of bodily breakdown at the beginning of this chapter have shown, the permanent urgency of management consulting was often unsustainable. This was reflected in the 'steep pyramid structure' of consulting companies, in which a large number of junior consultants worked for a few years at the bottom and only a handful of profit-sharing seniors operated at the top. This structure was necessary as it ensured high salary increases with each promotional step, even in macroeconomic environments of declining demand or increasing competition (McKenna 2006: 193; Hill 2013). Yet, it was also required to enable a vast amount of new recruits to uphold the catalytic function of management consultancies and to keep only people like Giulio, who was able to keep the pace over years on end (at the time of writing, that is, five years after this project, Giulio has become partner). Again, recent graduates from top universities made for particularly apt recruits in this case, not primarily because of their skill, intelligence or experience but because they were ambitious, respected hierarchy and had been trained into working long hours towards clearly defined deadlines.

Common degrees of temporality also did not seem to apply with respect to the consultants' own career paths. Here, management consulting constituted an exception in the sense that colleagues and interviewees conceived of their own jobs mostly as a break from normal life. For most, if not all of them, consulting was understood to last only a couple of years, serving as a springboard into something else. It was a liminal episode of their lives and a training ground for later, when they either wanted to make it into the upper management levels of private corporations or wanted to use the money and experience gained for starting their own businesses. Often they also just wanted to pass the time until they would know what they really wanted to do in life. This idea of consulting as a liminal and experimental period of life was promoted by consultancy recruiters, who actively presented their profession as a means of learning what other jobs and professions were out there. In all of these cases consulting itself was to be a catalyst of one's personal career, speeding up what would otherwise take longer. Time was fundamental in all of these considerations, and finitude was one of its main characteristics.

Temporal exemplars

Buying and selling speed required the exemplary instantiation of temporal dominance in daily work practices (cf. Robbins 2015). During the first few weeks of working as management consultants, my colleagues and I took part in a series of training camps meant to prepare us for the job. In each of these, the emphasis on speed and on constantly finding a purposive use of time stood out. We were asked to solve business case studies in small teams, as part of which we were systematically given far too much literature and information to digest in far too little time. Our trainers reminded us that we would never be able to solve the cases in the time provided unless we structured our work efficiently within our teams, and they regularly entered our offices to remind us that we only had a few minutes left until we needed to present our findings. Other exercises taught us to 'communicate *top-down*', that is, to state only the outcomes of our work, rather than its processes or shortcomings, when asked what we were working on. Trainers equally had us engage in role play in which one of them pretended to be a distracted and visibly hectic CEO, to whom we had to present project results over just a few seconds that we shared in an imaginary elevator or in an imaginary taxi.

Living and exemplifying an intense temporality remained essential while on the job. Consulting was seen to require physical presence with the client, so my colleagues began the week between 4 am and 5.30 am on Monday mornings, caught a taxi to the airport and boarded one of the first flights of the day between 6 am and 7 am. It was industry standard to be impeccably dressed and to travel with an absolute minimum of belongings, as anything other than hand luggage would slow down check-in and checkout processes at the airport. Thus, every Monday at around 6 am, the airports of Düsseldorf, Frankfurt, Munich and Berlin turned into seas of men and women in dark suits, aged between 25 and 35, who made their way with a mixture of fatigue, routine and impatience through security checks, business lounges and boarding queues.

One could feel the tension rising during these early hours of the week. Many consultants were already on their smartphones before the flight either to check-in online or to write first emails and text messages to their colleagues (cf. Ho 2009: 179). A few of them had their laptops open to work on particularly urgent PowerPoint documents, emails or quantitative analyses while waiting for the plane. Upon arrival, the consultants would be the first to rush out and catch a taxi to the client's office buildings where their colleagues and members of the client company were already waiting for them. By now everyone continuously read and wrote messages on their mobile phones and laptops in the taxi between airport and the client's office, letting their team know where they were, when they would arrive, inquiring if any work had already come in and looking over first documents.

Late on a Monday evening we typically took another taxi to a nearby hotel where my colleagues and I often worked until we went to sleep. This continued throughout the week, usually until Thursday evening, when everyone returned to their home cities, often leaving for the airport at the last possible moment. Friday was known as office-day, during which teams worked from their home towns. They tended to end early, usually between 6 pm and 8 pm, and many consultants found themselves relatively relaxed, as they could work away from the direct supervision of bosses and clients.

This intense temporality did not seem to decrease the further one climbed up the company hierarchy. Project leaders were known to be overworked as they were constantly facing clients, while also being held responsible for project success in the eyes of senior partners. The latter were in charge of several projects at a time, which meant they would fly three to five times a week to see each project at least once. They depended heavily on their secretaries for managing their 'back-to-back' calendars and they would at times get furious if this was not done correctly.

From the perspective of consultants, their intense temporality was a key marker of distinction between them and their clients, as the latter were generally considered slow. This was particularly true for middle management and for lower white-collar employees, whom junior consultants would work with on a daily basis. These groups were frequently derided in conversations between colleagues for coming to work late, leaving too early and being generally unable to keep up the pace.[10] It was also true for client companies as a whole, often labelled in interviews as unattractive potential employers because one would stagnate, sitting on the same chair for years on end. Consultants likened them to oil tankers which take a very long time to change direction. Colleagues also used a temporal idiom to mark themselves as superior to their clients. One of my *team leaders* called it 'magic time' when she produced a large number of analyses and slides and ran many seemingly productive meetings in a row. Our intense temporality thus positioned the client as a temporal other, not merely through allochronism, that is, the deliberate denial of coevalness by locating others in another time (Fabian 1983: 32) but also by defining their differing kinds of temporality as a source of weakness. Clients clearly recognized this temporal discrepancy. At times they would do so with admiration, commenting on how impressed they were at the speed and the times of the day at which we were still working. On other occassions, they would joke about us spending nights at the office and mention with a mixture of compassion and mockery how they received emails from us both late at night and early in the morning. In the latter instances, they presented their own temporality as one based on their own life-choices, rather than as an inability of living up to objective temporal demands.

One of the ways in which the consultants' intense temporality was expressed was a loss of patience. When asked how the work had changed her overall, interviewee Andrea stressed:

I believe work has rendered me a little more impatient. ... That must be due to the fact that we are used to working under pressure and to having all kinds of *deadlines*. When you are under stress the unnecessary things, like a queue at the airport or a dysfunctional boarding pass are a little too much. It is the small things that you did not expect that become the last straw that breaks the camel's back.

This was observable on a daily basis: colleagues walked fast and often interrupted one another. Upon entering an elevator, they would always press the button that closes the elevator doors so as to gain a few seconds and they started using their smartphones whenever they had a moment to spare. It was common for them to be on the phone (mostly via headset) while driving, dealing with taxi drivers or checking in and out of hotels. In conversations, they quickly wanted to get to the point and at airports, restaurants, hotels and taxi stands they had very little tolerance for having to queue.

Impatience was also increasingly notable in people's private lives. Junior consultant Michaela, for example, explained in an interview,

> My mother ... does not know how to communicate *top-down*. When she tells me what she did yesterday, then I ask her to say the same thing with only half the words, now again with half the words, now again, and now it is ok. You simply value your time very differently and you get upset about periods of unused time. ('Leerlaufzeiten')

Time management and temporal angst

The intense temporality of management consulting increased the risk of getting overworked, a problem frequently discussed during work breaks and weekend get-togethers. As a remedy, consultants were taught during job initiation trainings that *time management* ('time management'/'Zeit managen') was going to be a key skill for them. Poor *time management*, in turn, was held to be the cause of overstraining oneself. The notion equally came up regularly in work performance evaluations in which having good *time management skills* was one of only a handful of official prerequisites necessary to make it to the next level in the company hierarchy.

Various *time management* techniques existed. Senior and junior colleagues of mine were masters at writing *to-do* lists and at re-prioritizing their work on an hourly basis. They regularly communicated what they did to the rest of their teams so that nobody would do what the other had begun, and before taking a quick lunch or a coffee break, they would ask colleagues to finish different tasks for them so as to have something fresh to work with after their break. Here, I will discuss two such '*time management* techniques' in detail. The first is known as 'giving *pushback*' ('pushback geben'), an activity which some considered an art form. It consisted simply in refusing to carry out particular tasks while still conveying personal enthusiasm and willingness to help to the person requesting it. Partners, secretaries, research staff and consultants all quickly picked up how this had to be done. They would love to help out but were unfortunately on a very urgent project; they would like to look into something, but other tasks were currently much more pressing; they would think that doing an additional bit of analysis was a great idea, but they were currently 'totally under water' – that is, flooded with work.

Refusing job requests in this kind and keen yet also very firm fashion was considered a key skill for the job. Giving *pushback* was so important that it was explicitly mentioned in internal documents for newcomers and regularly discussed at work. Project leaders would often make jokes about how they gave *pushback* to partners and clients, showing that they were willing to take risks for their teams and joking about the trickery that it involved. *Pushback* was part of *upward management*, that is, of exerting influence over clients and bosses, seen as always wanting consultants to do more work for them, and it was usually done with the goal in mind of gaining some free time or of rendering work more relaxed.

I once overheard what I considered a particularly well-constructed pre-emptive *pushback*, when a colleague of mine told her boss the following sentences over the phone: 'It is almost 3 pm on a Friday now. I am going to do the following from here on out [mentions two more tasks]. Is there anything else that we must absolutely get done today so as to get out of the office by 6 pm?' By setting the temporal context in this way, my colleague reiterated the ideal of leaving the office at an early hour on a Friday evening. She also reminded her boss of the activities she still had to complete until then, so as to eventually limit the amount of additional tasks that she might be given. In this way, my colleague politely refused any additional job requests ex ante unless they were incredibly urgent.

The skill of giving *pushback* not only lay in refusing work in the right kind of tone, but also lay in judging the importance of particular tasks so as to refuse or de-prioritize the right ones. One good way of going about this was to do an analysis and to present findings quickly, after around one hour into the task. If the project leader, partner or client in question insisted on going further, then one could always do more, yet, frequently, a first shot at an analysis might already be considered sufficient. If so, one had saved or gained time[11] by not doing too much. Another way was to emphasize the limited amount of time that one had in the conversation with partners and clients and to ask which exact tasks were expected of oneself within this timeframe. That said, there was no hard and fast rule for giving *pushback* well. It depended heavily on gauging which tasks the people in charge expected and at what point they might consider them insightful or convincing enough. Consultants therefore needed to rely on their knowledge of the social constellations of the people involved, their emotions and communicative styles and of the temporal nature of their projects (cf. Zaloom 2012). The management of one's own time thereby turned out to be a fundamentally social exercise.

Success at this socially and emotionally charged balancing act of gauging which analyses and which levels of complication were required in a task was frequently supposed to be brought about with by a second *time management* technique, known as the '*eighty-twenty* rule'. Junior consultants were often reminded not to get lost in the details of their work but to *eighty-twenty* it instead. Several different interpretations of this rule existed among my colleagues. Some would hold that during the initial twenty per cent of the time needed for a task eighty per cent of that task would get done. This indicated that one could think about moving on to do something else after the first twenty per cent of the time. Others would argue that during the first eighty per cent of the time needed for a task almost all of the necessary work associated with it would get done. In their understanding, they could leave out only the last twenty per cent of the time estimated at the outset.

In both interpretations, the rule seemed somewhat unhelpful, since finding out how complex and detailed a task was, was in fact part of the task itself. Frequently, consultants simply could not know in advance how long it would take to get reliable data on a particular market, how much time they might require to clean up some *raw data* that they had received from a client or after what time a client might become convinced that working in one direction was better than working in another. In all of these cases then, they would not know when they might or might not have hit a certain percentage of their work. The idea of doing a task *eighty-twenty* therefore could not apply in a strict sense.

Part of the reason why this was impossible was that an *eighty-twenty* approach to work was originally not concerned with time at all. The prominent management theorist Joseph Juran had made reference to it in an influential handbook on corporate quality control (Juran and Godfrey 1999). Coincidentally, he had provided the example of a paper mill, where twenty per cent of product types accounted for eighty per cent of the costs associated with defective paper production (ibid.: section 5.21). In another surprising logical jump, Juran's figures eighty and twenty were inspired by work on wealth distribution carried out by the Italian economist Vilfredo Pareto (Juran 1994, 2005). Pareto had shown that wealth tended to be distributed unequally, at a stable ratio in different times and countries (Persky 1992; Kaplow 2004; Lockwood 2004). While Pareto's work on wealth inequality had in fact come up with a ratio of sixty to twenty per cent, where sixty per cent of national income is earned by the top twenty per cent of income recipients (Persky 1992: 183), Juran had associated Pareto's work with a ratio of *eighty-twenty* instead.

Ever since, the so-called 'Pareto Principle of *eighty-twenty*' has become known throughout the business world. It has been extended from product quality control to a great variety of other business issues. This did not even stop when Juran published an article entitled 'The Non-Pareto Principle; Mea Culpa' (1994), in which he declared that linking his rule in product quality management concerning a 'vital few and a trivial many' to Pareto's work on income distribution had been a great mistake. The article undermined much of the empirical basis of the *eighty-twenty* rule but by then it was too late. Nowadays, a reader interested in management studies can still learn about the importance of *eighty-twenty* in books such as *Pareto's 80/20 Rule for Corporate Accountants* (Parmenter 2007), *The 80 20 Manager: Ten ways to become a great leader* (Koch 2013) and *Top Market Strategy – Applying the 80/20 rule* (Rush Kruger 2011). The rule is also cited explicitly in the literature dealing with self-improvement, regardless of whether it is concerned with sales performance ('eighty percent of sales will come from twenty per cent of your customers' [Barchitta 2013: 23]), weight loss, ('80 percent of your weight loss success will come directly through your nutritional choices and 20 percent will be aided by your activity level' [Bednarowski 2013: 43]) or relationship advice ['the stubborn issues that are really hard to resolve are nearly always 80 per cent about the past and only 20 per cent about today' (Marshall 2011: 29)].

In spite of the consultants' manifold attempts at *time management*, their goal of getting free time was systematically missed. I do not believe that my colleagues aimed at failure as an endpoint in these instances (Miyazaki and Riles 2007). Instead, their hope at a non-exceptional work regime was upheld, in spite of daily evidence to the contrary. Consider the defence of a twelve-hour workday as a viable option by experienced consultant Christine:

> On average [I end my workday] probably around eleven thirty pm. ... Ten pm is an early evening. I think that this is wrong and I believe we do not work better if the general expectation is [that] we [should] always work until midnight. ... I believe that for many – or for me at least – working until twelve pm and starting early in the morning is pretty much the limit of what can be done over a longer period of time. I could not work always until four am. There are people who can, but whatever. And since you work so close to the limit you have no time to think about how useful what you do really is. If your goal was to work only until eight pm you could think much more clearly about when to stop, when to make the *cut* and whether it might be necessary to do this or whether you work so much because you have been inefficient.

Partners also tended to defend the normative ideal of working twelve hours a day (from 8 am to 8 pm) even if junior consultants complained that it hardly ever materialized. Thus time management techniques served as one of the avenues through which the hope of making the job sustainable in the long run was upheld (cf. Miyazaki 2006).

I would like to suggest here that this is in part due to a tragic aspect inherent in the notion of *time management* itself. Like the analytic approaches, organizational features and work practices described above, *time management* constructed all activities principally with reference to their temporal attributes and presupposed that time was limited. It thereby made reference to death as the mother of all deadlines (cf. Bloch and Parry 1982; Willerslev et al. 2013), in the sense that all activity would at some point be over and also that everything we did aimed at its own finitude in the first place (Heidegger 2006: 245). Consultants were thereby further conditioned into disregarding the infinite aspects of all things temporal. *Time management* was thus tragic, in that it co-created what it is supposed to counteract.

Moreover, it located the responsibility for how time was spent in the individual subject. Many of my colleagues and interviewees complained in private conversations that, upon pointing out to their bosses that they were overworked, accusations of mismanaging their time were likely to follow. As one of them remarked laconically, 'When you work too hard and when you do long hours [they simply tell you that] you are shit at prioritising.' Consider how one of my interviewees, Tim, who would have severe work-related health issues a few months after our interview, put it:

> 'Well, a former *Team Leader* ..., once said to me: Tim, as a consultant you are always in *survival mode*' ... because somehow you quickly have to get information, process things fast to understand them and rapidly decide what is important. In this *setting* you are always a little bit hunted. He also said that if you are in it for a longer period of time you do not even notice it so much anymore, but that's how it really is and how people from the outside see it. I have just been on holiday for six weeks and many people have told me that I seem very relaxed in contrast to how they used to perceive me. I myself also noticed a really silly thing: Somehow this bruise on my arm that had not healed in four months healed within a month of holiday, *which tells me a lot*. I think this teaches you to rigorously prioritise.

In the light of the intense temporality with which consultants operated, a key form of alienation, here understood as an unfruitful appropriation of self and world (Jaeggi 2014: 256ff.), was the feeling of being trapped in time. Taken together, the constant focus on temporal aspects, finitude and the individual subject formed a peculiar sort of existentialism, where temporal *angst* or *angoisse* became the daily norm (Crowell 2004; Sartre 1970: 2). My colleagues were not just concerned with the temporal politics of work (Verdery 1996: 39), nor were they primarily anxious about the contingent nature of future social relationships (Stafford 2007, 72), or temporal incongruities (e.g. Miyazaki 2003; Borneman 1993; Vogl 2010: 126). They struggled with their potential inability of living up to temporal constraints as such, as they seemed objective, inescapable and exceedingly important. Every aspect of their lives, whether it was a weekend visit to the cinema or a telephone conversation with their parents, was now construed with respect to its temporal attributes. This kind of temporality stood in polar opposition to the long-term time horizons of ecology, religious belief or the timelessness of, for example, Balinese temporality, in which death has been shown to be rendered less relevant through the emphasis of depersonalized and eternal symbolic orders (Geertz 1973: 389–91).[12] Such alternative temporalities were made invisible by the work regime analysed here.

The opportunities of dealing with this kind of alienation were specific to the class position of the consultants in question (Carrier and Kalb 2015; chapter two). When they felt that they could not keep the pace anymore, that the temporal constraints of their lives became overwhelming, or that the full dedication of their lives to their workplace was not worth it, they could find another job fairly easily. All of them had high incomes, excellent CVs, were still young enough to be hired elsewhere and disposed of the necessary habitus to begin working in the Berlin *start-up* scene or in more relaxed and stable employment arrangements in established public and private sector institutions. This opportunity, to change temporality when one reached its limits, was not open to people of lower class positions (cf. Pine 2016). Management consultants thus turned out to spread a temporality that they themselves were only rarely capable to uphold.

Conclusion

Time, as most writers on the topic emphasize, seems particularly inescapable (Munn 1992, 93). There is no thought about time outside of it, and no matter how we try to relate to it, we are always in an important sense in it (ibid.). Yet, time is also exceptionally absent from our lives that it has led anthropologists and philosophers to doubt its independent existence. Edmund Leach famously argued that we talk of measuring time, as if time were a concrete thing, waiting to be measured; but in fact we create time by creating intervals in social life (Leach 1971: 135).

I have here followed Gell (1992) in trying to hold assumptions about the nature of time itself at bay as much as possible, while focusing on how consultants relate to it through a series of analytic approaches, organizational features and work practices. I argued that all of these were expressive of an intense temporality, that is, a relationship to time that stressed the temporal nature of all things and highlighted temporal finitude. This constituted the precondition for selling speed, here discovered as a source of income in contemporary capitalism. As part of spreading this temporality, they needed to live it themselves in an exemplary way, an activity that led the masters of time management to feel trapped in time and pushed them to their physical limits. Consultants often dropped out of this unsustainable temporality after just a few years, a privilege that was not available to many other employees in the German economy who lacked alternative job opportunities.

What can these observations tell us about the abstract nature of labour, as found among consultants? While many anthropological studies of time have focused on the material requirements of products and tools in economic activity, ranging from the rhythms of agricultural production (Dobler 2016) to the use of raw materials and machines in artisanal shops and factories, the time frames of consulting seemed largely removed from these constraints. The link between the length of a project and actual productive processes, for example the temporality of paper production and the two weeks that our project in the mill lasted, was at times tenuous, and at others fully arbitrary. In spite of this, the shared understandings that consultants operated during exceptional times and the need to instantiate temporal dominance as part of selling speed meant that temporal constraints were experienced as hyperreal. Their concrete effects on the bodies of management consultants were hard to miss and showed that even the most abstract forms of labour did not lack in reality for the people who carried them out.

CHAPTER THREE

Economies of Legitimacy

A little over a year into my job as management consultant, I was sitting opposite my colleague Lucien, in our office in the heart of Paris. 'I know nothing about insurance; absolutely nothing' he remarked while crouching over his laptop. Lucien, a junior consultant hired in France, was writing a PowerPoint slide, meant as a rough plan for our client for how to sell more private travel insurance products in Asia, over the next five years. It depicted a number of activity categories along the Y-axis (such as 'ensuring market access', 'developing a sales team', 'preparing legal issues') and the years during which they had to be implemented along the X-axis. Into this grid of activity categories and years, Lucien wrote what needed to get done and when. His points were 'all high-level stuff', he said, and included mostly broad statements such as 'map top local brokers and wealth managers in target countries', 'start building dedicated global sales team (2–4 FTE)' and 'define timeline for legal and regulatory steps'. While writing these points, he repeated how ignorant he was about insurance activity. He had occasionally made admissions over the previous weeks and months, mentioning how little he understood when meeting individual clients or laughing at how unsystematic some of the assumptions of his spreadsheet calculations were.

More often than not, Lucien's assertions of his own ignorance were accompanied by a smile, conveying a sense that much of his work was somewhat fake. I took his smile to mean that he did not know what he was writing about, but that it could be considered funny that he managed to convince others of his 'expertise'. His success as a consultant may have seemed absurd to him, as he had no prior project with the insurance business and seemed to have little knowledge of how insurance companies operated beyond what he considered 'common sense'. Instead, Lucien seemed to have been placed on our team of consultants for sociocultural reasons, rather than for any specialized knowledge. He was the only French member on a team consisting of three Germans (including myself), working with the European subsidiaries of a German insurance company.[1] Since we spent most of our time either at client offices or in our own office in Paris, Lucien could interview the French insurance staff and help the members of our team book offices, taxis, flights and hotels.

At other times however, Lucien's seemingly facetious comments about his own ignorance appeared to suggest an air of genuine wonder. He seemed to marvel at his ability to be successful at his job, in spite of his ignorance of the subject matter. In day-to-day work, Lucien did convey a genuine desire to help his clients. He was personally close to some of the insurance managers he interviewed and genuinely happy when he could present them with useful insights. His sense of obligation to them was grounded not simply in personal affection, but also in the high salary that we charged for our work. On the rare occasions when Lucien took an evening off, he professed feeling guilty because he 'was not adding value' to our clients during this time. It therefore seemed that in his comments concerning his own ignorance, Lucien also admired the fact that he did in fact add value to the client, despite having only a superficial idea of how insurance companies operated. He was amazed by his own productivity, so to speak.

The ambiguity of Lucien's remarks echoes wider attitudes towards consultancy work described in Chapter 1. Popular books about the profession often dismiss it as an elaborate ruse, in which a lot of rhetoric covers up lack of commitment and expertise. At the same time, the German press regularly acknowledges that consulting companies have gained a stable presence in the country's largest companies. After all, 2015 marked the most successful year in the history of management consultancies in Germany, with overall revenues of EUR 27bn and an estimated growth of 7.5 per cent (BDU 2016).

The growth of management consulting therefore raises the question of how people who may be quite ignorant about a topic can write plans that will eventually lead to the investment of several millions of euros. Is management consulting ultimately a scam, in which young men in suits pretend to know about topics about which they are actually oblivious? Do clients not spot their ignorance? Are clients in fact complicit in a wider game of smoke and mirrors in which they use consultants simply to enforce what has already been decided? While these questions are certainly interesting in their own right, this chapter will try to investigate the wider point that underlies them, namely the concern for the social legitimation of work. It will ask what kind of work is considered legitimate in a corporate setting and how processes of legitimation operate.

Similar to the previous chapter, this one argues that, in contrast to much of the literature about them, management consultants are in fact not primarily 'knowledge workers'. This may come as a surprise to analysts of the sector, who often represent themselves as the structural answer to corporate information deficits (e.g. McKenna 2006; Thrift 1997, 1998). It may also be startling to potential clients and young job applicants who may have read on consultancy recruiting websites that they engage mostly in 'problem-solving' or that their product is 'their ideas, the solutions to many of the world's most complex challenges' (Bain & Company 2014a).

And yet, as much of the discussion of abstract labour has already implied, knowledge will here be shown to be one of several means employed in the wider effort of consultants to provide management with legitimacy (Mosse 2005a). Contemporary managers frequently lack legitimacy, as they operate in strongly hierarchical institutions and frequently interfere in the work of their subordinates but remain incapable of leading via the performance of exemplary mastery (Spittler 2016: 126ff.). A key function of consultants is thus to legitimize the managers who hire them and who try to alter work activity within their companies. Only if they do so do consultants have a chance at being hired again in the future. They are thus to be understood as 'management consultants' rather than 'business consultants', in that their work needs fundamentally to serve a managerial subsection of a company. Its usefulness for the entirety of a business, on the other hand, is marked by much greater contingency.

This legitimating work that I observed was abstract, in that it allowed managers to establish relations with vast amounts of people that were marked by an emotional and affective disengagement from them. The analyses, plans and presentations of consultants were meant to alter the labour of corporate employees, yet neither consultants nor managers were supposed to become intimately connected to them in any way. Instead, consultants were meant to rigorously channel their emotional and affective ties to the substratum of management that was most directly involved in paying their salaries. Thereby, consultants themselves constituted a technology for the establishment of detached relations by the managers who hired them (Candea et al, 2015; McDonald 2015). They provided management with descriptions of staff that enabled high-level decision-making without too much personal engagement with the employees in question.

As part of this work, management consultants equally needed to legitimize their own position in the company. Both efforts of legitimation were interdependent, in that clients who were legitimized by consultants were inclined to accept their abstractions, while only consultants whose abstractions were seen as legitimate were in a position to strengthen their clients. As will be demonstrated, consultants achieved legitimacy by skilfully using their position on the socio-symbolic boundaries of corporations, which were frequently sites of considerable ambiguity (Golub 2014; Welker 2009; Welker, Partridge and Hardin 2011). They positioned themselves either as 'insiders' or as 'outsiders' of the companies for which they worked. This made them socially liminal beings (Sturdy, Schwarz and Spicer 2006; Sturdy et al. 2009), who alternated between different sets of expectations concerning the social obligations they had towards the company in question. Their constantly liminal position increased their risk of being seen as a polluting other, a problem that consultants addressed by cultivating personal charisma and by alternating between a positivist and a perspectival understanding of knowledge.

Consultants as outsiders

How did Lucien get into the position of writing an insurance sales plan for Asian countries if he knew almost nothing about insurance work or about Asia? We had been working on this new project for only a month. Our client, a large private insurance company, was looking to expand its business in one of its core insurance markets, which was growing at a fast rate. The question we were tasked with answering was how best to do so, in terms of both which markets to address and which institutional set-up would be necessary.

Lucien and I addressed this question by doing some market-sizing work, in which we compared our insurance client to its main competitors. In order to do so, we used business performance numbers provided by our client and compared them to those in the annual reports of competitors, which were available online. When we did not find such annual reports, we relied on estimates, which were provided by our research staff. We also made regular, if less frequent, use of our company's research teams, whose task was to provide consultants with information that might be deemed useful in client work. The researchers who were based in Germany, India and the United States had access to several company and market research databases, while also compiling some of their own information on different markets, companies and product trends. However, getting information from them was usually difficult, as research staff often took too long to find out exactly what we needed. At times they were also reluctant to share information with us, as they had a lower tolerance for rough-and-ready quantification, not least because they did not feel the same amount of pressure in their day-to-day work.

Once the sizes of the main competitors had been estimated, Lucien and I were asked to establish the 'sales potential in Asia', that is, sketch how numerous and rich potential customer groups in Asia's biggest countries might be. Thus, we gathered information on the number of employees in particularly large firms, estimated their number of expatriate workers on the basis of our insurance client's own share of expats, projected how many of these our client might be able to insure, multiplied that with an average insurance premium and thereby arrived at a market size for this particular insurance product. As on countless other occasions, these calculations were riddled with difficulties. Employee numbers were readily available, but our estimates of expatriate shares were hard to justify, as was their market share. The members of my team had little patience for calculative mistakes, but a high willingness to stop worrying about epistemic uncertainties regarding calculation assumptions when numbers needed to get presented. Time and again fellow consultants stressed both at work and in interviews that they would 'not *boil the ocean*', that is, not overanalyse topics.

Once these efforts at 'market sizing' and establishing a 'sales potential' had been completed and agreed with clients, it became our job to develop a plan for how to sell insurance over the next five years. We contacted two members of the client company – managers in their mid-fifties – who served as our official points of contact for questions on sales and marketing. Lucien visibly liked both of them. He had taken them out for lunch and he often mentioned how much he enjoyed listening to their colourful anecdotes about the difficulties of selling insurance products and about never overpaying claims of any kind. Our contacts likely did not take Lucien or me very seriously as a source of advice on how to do their job. However, they seemed to take to us in an almost paternal way and visibly enjoyed teaching two interested youngsters about how their job was done. Moreover, they knew that our boss – the German partner on our team – was close to theirs, so they tried to share with us exactly the kind of information that would work in their favour. For example, they had long before our arrival argued that the United States was a market with huge sales potential. Now that we had been given the task of assessing the situation, they made sure to repeat to both Lucien and me how much money could be made in the United States, if only they would be given the chance to try.

Both Lucien and I were influenced by their accounts and gave the idea of selling insurance in the United States greater consideration than we would have without them. However, we also took their information with a grain of salt. While the insurance market in the United States was comparatively large, we were not convinced of the actual sales potential, as competition seemed fierce. Andreas, the German *team leader* of our group, was also uncertain and Paul, the partner responsible for our project, decided after several analyses and discussions that going to the United States would not be our line of reasoning. His main client, who was paying for the project, had significant doubts about it and Paul, who had been in the business for over a decade, was also convinced that the United States was too difficult a market to deal with. While the sales potential might be substantive there, he deemed the competition and legal risks to be too high. We followed his reasoning and presented a few PowerPoint slides making these points to the head manager at the insurance. Shortly after the meeting, our two sales contacts were evidently upset. They had not been present at the meeting but had already obtained our presentation from their boss and greeted Lucien and me with the words, 'Now you really did kill the US for us with those slides.' While their critique was harsh, it nonetheless came with a tone of reconciliation, as one of the two remarked that they would probably go to the United States anyway. As he pointed out, 'When you are gone and things quieten down, we will give the US another try.'

The ethnographic material presented so far shows that consultants legitimized knowledge by presenting themselves as outsiders. For Lucien and I this was true in many respects. We were not part of the client's company, had not worked in insurance before, and since we were over twenty years younger than both our key contacts, they considered us relatively new to the business world as such. Management advice was usually based on the idea that it was advantageous to provide an outside perspective to economic actors. This idea was frequently highlighted by the German media (e.g. *Der Spiegel 2011a*; *Süddeutsche Zeitung* 2014) as well as by strategy consultancies themselves. Thus, Boston Consulting Group (BCG) Germany wrote on its website: 'At BCG, teams of consultants are explicitly put together so as to mix different disciplines and levels of seniority. Consultants with industry experience can contribute their expert knowledge while university graduates bring a rather fresh and unbiased perspective to client concerns' (BCG 2014a). The McKinsey US website made a similar point, by publishing a book excerpt by Nobel laureate psychologist Daniel Kahneman entitled 'Beware of the inside view.' In the excerpt, the author contrasted an 'inside view' of anything or activity to their 'outside view'. While the 'inside view' was characterized by focusing on specific circumstances and searching for evidence in personal experience, the superior 'outside view' was defined by directing attention towards a class of similar cases (Kahneman in McKinsey 2011a). For example, when guessing how much longer a work project might take, one could either extrapolate on the basis of what has been achieved in a project so far (i.e. the 'inside view') or look at other people who have carried out a similar project (i.e. the 'outside view'). Kahneman contended that the 'outside view' was generally more reliable. He wrote, 'If the reference class is properly chosen, the outside view will give an indication of where the ballpark is' (ibid.). It thereby provides you with the most basic information, while the inside view merely helps to 'adjust your estimate' (ibid.).

Two kinds of outsider knowledge

Our social position as outsiders came with a specific understanding of knowledge, in which a 'fresh perspective' should be economically desirable. It denoted a perspectival understanding of knowledge in which economic activity could be seen from a variety of angles and was, in fact, better understood, when more perspectives were engaged on it. In the Western canon, this understanding of knowledge can be dated back to Leibniz's theory of substance or 'monads', which perceive the world in a perspective peculiar to themselves (cf. Russel 2004: 1187). It is also obvious in Nietzsche's oeuvre, in which the author calls 'perspectivism the founding principle of life as such'. He claims that 'perspectival seeing is the *only* kind of seeing there is, perspectival "knowing" the *only* kind of "knowing"; and the *more* feelings[2] about a matter we allow to come to expression, the *more* eyes, different eyes we use to view this same matter, the more complete our "conception" of it, our "objectivity" will be' (Nietzsche 1996: 98).

In the German economy, this perspectival understanding of knowledge grounded contemporary fears of growing 'betriebsblind' (literally 'company blind' or 'work blind'), a risk that consultants, their clients and the German press referred to on a regular basis (e.g. Bower 2008; Die Zeit 1976). Germany's most renowned dictionary called *Duden* defined the term as follows: 'Blindness for mistakes or lacunae that emerge in one's area of work due to long lasting membership' (Duden 2014). Underlying this particular fear of 'blindness' was the belief that routinized work activity led people to know their job so well that they began to carry it out automatically. They were thereby expected to take ever more aspects of it for granted and to lose the 'critical perspective' on what they did. Knowledge was here perspectival and its perspectives were predominantly shaped by work routines. Once a blinding and – it was assumed – dysfunctional work routine had been established, employees would need help from an outsider, not because they did not know their job but because in a sense they knew it all too well. Once people accepted the three major claims outlined above (1) Knowledge is perspectival in nature. (2) Work routines predominantly define this knowledge. (3) Establishing a work routine limits available knowledge), they might accept that their work required occasional checks from outsiders.

Yet, the outside view had a second component to it, which was surprisingly different in the claims it made. It denoted a positivist understanding of knowledge, where interacting with an outsider promised new pieces of information, which could be fruitfully incorporated into client work routines. In these cases, knowledge was deemed to be obtainable and transferable regardless of perspectival issues. This is what Lucien and I were doing, when working with the outside research staff and Partner Paul on our project. In this case, the consultant was not considered blind to his or her own experience but was expected to grasp and transfer knowledge to the client. Lucien and I were here not seen as individual workers, but as nodes in a wide network of people, all of whom could transfer information to a client. This view was highlighted in sales *pitches* in which the high daily charges for consulting work were justified with the vast network of partners, experts and researchers that was held to stand behind each consultant.

In European history of thought, this view of knowledge is frequently traced back to a positivist tradition – either that of Auguste Compte, or more explicitly that of the later Logical Empiricists – associated with the 'promotion of a rigorously "scientific" epistemology [as well as a] supreme self-confidence about its own objective, systematic and ahistorical outlook' (Scharff 2002: 2). In the business world, this understanding of knowledge is currently undergoing a revival, as part of a corporate turn towards 'big data' in which the dream of amassing and understanding vast amounts of information from outside a company is given a new dimension (Boellstorf 2013). In many ways, this understanding of knowledge implied that clients were stuck within the confines of their own institutional affiliation, a situation that was to a large extent grounded in the state's legal system. The German law for the Restriction of Competition, for example, disallowed 'agreements between businesses, decisions by company associations and concerted practices, which aim to or have as an effect the prevention, restriction or distortion of competition' (BMJV 1998). Consultants were thus one of the institutional mechanisms that overcame this legal restriction without being unlawful. They tried to transfer knowledge from other companies, other sectors, other countries and other times (by using senior consultants with past experience) within the confines of the law. As one partner put it during a training session, 'We are like the Internet. We make all companies better by transferring *best practices* from one to the other.'

According to this logic, consultants and their clients ascribed to a threefold claim that was substantially different to the one above. They held that (1) knowledge was positivistic in nature; (2) institutional affiliations (rather than work routines) predominantly defined this knowledge and (3) establishing an institutional affiliation limited available knowledge. When these claims were accepted, an outsider's view may become desirable for clients not because the clients knew their job too well, but because they did not know it well enough.

As an institution, Strategy Partners seemed to be convinced that both conceptions of knowledge were correct. On the one hand, they hired surprisingly young staff right off university and sent them on the job with little substantial training (cf. Sennett 2006: 97). On the other, they went through great efforts to somehow 'bundle' the knowledge that their staff acquired in different projects so as to use it in client work. Our Facebook-like website on the company intranet listed past trainings and projects we had worked on, linking each consultant's profile to those of all her former colleagues. This way it would – in theory – only take a few mouse-clicks to find somebody who might know about a particular topic and to write them an email or give them a call. Consultants were also connected through live-chat systems as well as regular telephone and videoconferences on business topics. Moreover, the intranet featured a vast repository of PowerPoint *decks* from past projects, which were meant to be used by less experienced staff so as to get *up to speed*.

While intra-firm knowledge exchange was actively encouraged, it was limited by two main factors. First, experienced consultants were often deeply involved in their own project work and could not spend too much of their time helping other teams. For example, Lucien and I were convinced that market-sizing exercises such as the one we had to carry out for a subgroup of Asian countries would have already been made dozens of times. While our *team leader* did gain access to a series of PowerPoint slides concerned with similar such estimates, it was not possible for us to trace who had made which calculation or which calculative logics had been applied. Our *Team Leader* Andreas therefore suggested that we start our calculations from scratch as that promised to be both faster and more reliable than chasing up other consultants.

Second, the knowledge written down in simplified PowerPoint slides or *spreadsheets* was usually impenetrable in hindsight and therefore hard to reuse on subsequent projects. This was partially due to the opacity of the technology itself (see next chapter) and partially due to the legal stipulations that prohibited corporate collusion. Due to these stipulations and to confidentiality agreements signed with clients, the summary documents we could share within our firm after each project had to be *sanitized*, that is, made to present mostly vague and conceptual information. Using these documents was rendered all the more difficult because junior consultants who were in charge of building models had often left the consulting profession as a whole by the time their expertise was needed again. Internal estimates were that we renewed about 20 per cent of our consulting staff every year. In interviews I carried out with consultants of various companies, they all tended to criticize that attempts at sharing knowledge through written documents frequently failed. The most stable source of knowledge according to them was the partners, whose nebulous but self-assertive expertise impressed many junior colleagues.

Yet, we were not just epistemic outsiders, but also social ones. This had the fundamental advantage that we could carry through socially controversial projects. In our case, we would help design a merger of subunits that would find considerable resistance in the insurance company itself, but seemed to make sense from the perspective of top management. In this regard, our social position as outsiders or largely 'unencumbered selves' (Sandel 1984) exacerbated the 'social production of indifference' attributed to bureaucratic work more generally (Herzfeld 1993). Consultants usually acknowledged their own structurally created indifference and justified it by claiming that they ensured the continuity of the corporations they were working for. This is how one interviewee from Munich put it:

> We are often seen as *bad boys* and in fact we are often hired by the top so as to push through decisions that have already been taken or have already become clear. This is not necessarily adding value. In a way we serve to facilitate decisions. [In this

case people can say] 'but consulting firm XY said we should [do this]' so it will get done. This begs the question of whether it is a good thing that a top manager refuses to say [himself] that 30% of staff should be laid off.[3] I don't know. I was recently working for a renewable energy client, who was deep in the red. The client had to get restructured because revenues had broken away. Everyone in that company knew they were only making half the revenues but still had the same amount of staff … . This cannot work sustainably, since they had been making continuous losses for five years … . Sooner or later the decision must come that people will have to go, so a consulting firm will eventually be hired to find out where, and to put its name behind all of this.

One of the *team leaders* I interviewed put it more succinctly:

In general you do the dirty work. This much is clear. In my case, this is also due to my focus on org[anisational projects], which usually involve change. Human nature is thus that we not like change or do not do it spontaneously without there being a need for it.[4] [Therefore] it is inevitable that I am more or less called whenever teams are literally forced to shovel shit. This is simply how it is.

Clients frequently valued exactly this social position of consultants. Consider how this senior public sector official sees it:

I believe that [strategy consultancies] could help many ministries, especially in two main areas: Everything that is truly related to strategy development … concerned with large and very [politically] relevant portfolios …. Here it is helpful to get somebody external into the process because our ministry simply does not have the knowledge and our [more specialised sub-organisations] are overly bound up in their own business interests so that they do not actually give objective advice. The second area is about reducing bureaucracy. While [in this ministry] things are now at least getting done electronically [laughs], … many other ministries still use paper files. There are still many processes that are overly complicated and time-consuming.

The public official appealed to consultants because their position as outsiders means they were less 'bound up' in social relations in general. Even if the information needed for writing political strategies did exist somewhere in the ministry, it would take a socially 'unbound' outsider to judge its truthfulness and assess its importance. Furthermore, while the general consensus at having to reduce bureaucracy may exist across the public sector, the practical work of assessing whose work is truly needed and whose is not is one that no manager can carry out without losing much of her employees' support in the long run. High-level bureaucrats might thus appreciate institutional outsiders as much as private sector managers do, turning consultants into a tool for their 'virtuous' detachment from the institutions of which they are in charge (Knox and Harvey 2015).

Working with 'outsiders' in socially difficult situations might seem effective at first, but it also increased the likelihood that plans would not be adopted. As shown above, clients unwilling to comply with our plans and analyses were always tempted to just sit things out, wait until we would leave and get back to business as usual. This was also the professed 'principal fear' of many of my colleagues and interviewees, namely that their plans would 'disappear in a drawer'[5] and never be implemented. Surprisingly, lower-level consultants had no formal way of finding out if and how their recommendations would be converted into practice or not. They would leave their client at the end of a project and hear about it again only if it came up in casual future conversation with partners or clients.

Consultants as insiders

While the outside view that defined the management consultancy business model certainly deserves much of our attention, I would like to emphasize that this chapter, as well as the next one, provides a host of examples of how consultants 'gather and re-use' information from within client companies. Rather than just bringing in knowledge from the outside, Lucien and I spent a lot of our time creating slides for our upper management that reified information provided from *Controlling* and *Sales* departments. When we considered insurance sales in the United States, senior consultant

Paul, who was an 'insurance insider', did steer us into one direction. Yet in many other instances, we took up the advice of our *Sales* contacts on which countries in Asia might make for interesting markets and on how to start selling insurance products there. In my own experience and from what the majority of my colleagues and interview partners told me, consulting work was indeed mostly concerned with synthesizing and transforming knowledge that was already available within different parts of a client company, but that rested unattainable for top- and middle management. Macroeconomic accounts frequently neglect this critical function of consultants and focus excessively on how these companies bring in information from the outside. In this and countless other instances, however, our analyses relied to a large extent on the knowledge of middle management, whose experience was put into slides and presented to the head of the project.

But we were not just epistemic insiders, we were also social ones. When our team first began working in Paris, we immediately scheduled a *meeting* with the person who would guide and oversee our work efforts for the insurance company in question. Her name was Claudette, and she was a French woman in her early thirties who – as our German *Team Leader* Andreas had found out by looking her up online – had made a stellar career in the French public sector, before moving to the insurance company in question. Lucien once again took upon himself the role of cultural translator, explaining to us that hers was a typical elite trajectory in France, where successful public sector work stood in high esteem and facilitated direct entrance into the higher echelons of private sector management. Andreas seemed only partially impressed by this. It must have initially been hard for him to accept how remarkable her professional development really was, since he was overall dismissive of public sector work, reflecting the more contemptuous attitudes towards it that are prevalent in the German private sector.

Andreas also laughed at the sight of some of Claudette's online pictures, in which she looked overly traditional, wearing heavy jewellery and dark lipstick that made her appear much older than she was. He had an acute sense of women's physical appearance that influenced the way he worked with them. He occasionally looked up pictures of female colleagues online, and on our intranet, so as to judge their looks. Most if not all women who walked past our *team room* visibly distracted him and he remarked time and again with a peculiar mixture of moral outrage and personal excitement that our French female colleagues wore outfits that would be considered far too daring in a German work environment. Lucien, Paul and I reacted to such remarks with considerable reserve.

Our first *meeting* with Claudette took place on the upper floors of a swanky Paris office tower. Paul, the partner on our team, Andreas, Lucien and I had come early, whereas Claudette appeared a good ten minutes late. The *meeting* could not start without her and the time waiting for her was filled with anxious email writing on our smartphones. During the wait we sat down again and as soon as she entered the room everyone rose to their feet to greet her. After a round of polite introductions, we sat down and Paul outlined the general market position of the insurance company as well as the performance of its different business units and subunits. He presented Lucien's and my market analyses with great confidence before going on to describe our upcoming project work. He explained that our goal was to assess several insurance markets, redefine the business activities of a particular insurance division in the light of these assessments and subsequently provide a sketch of the organizational implications that the expansion to these markets would have. In his presentation, these steps followed one another both temporally and logically, as the definition of business activities would define the future organization of the unit. To put it in even broader terms, work practices and organizational structure were to stand in a necessary relation with one another, marked by temporal anteriority (practice precedes structure) causality (practice causes structure) and metaphor (practice serves as a blueprint for structure).

This staging of our project activity both contradicted and reflected the verbal explanations that Paul had given to our team in private. In contradiction to the slides that Paul presented, Claudette's boss had already taken the decision that two subunits of the organizational entity in question should be merged. He did not need a profound analysis of business activity in order to know that this was necessary. Claudette acknowledged verbally that she knew about this decision, but she certainly did not insist on spelling it out on paper. She was aware that this was a politically difficult subject, since merging the subunits would mean that one of their head managers would ultimately lose much of his current power.

At the same time, the presentation also reflected what Paul had told us in private. According to him, Claudette's boss really had a point in merging the two subunits, because they seemed to be disturbing rather than supporting or complementing one another. Some of their administrative work, so the story went, was done in parallel and could probably be done using fewer 'resources'. The subunits also seemed to share only an absolute minimum of information and competed with one another on the same markets. Paul therefore understood the merger of both units to be an act in which work structure was in fact getting *aligned* with work practice. Moreover, while the merger of two subunits was already a done deal, it truly was unclear what the final product of that merger would look like. Our job was thus to provide at least a rough indication of the make-up of the newly merged entity.

Unlike many other partners, Paul was much less inclined to use gossip as a means to relate to clients. Instead, he casually mentioned several meetings he had had with members of the insurance company, signalling to us as much as to Claudette that he was well connected to her boss and knew her company like the back of his hand. In fact, Paul explained that he had been consulting 'for this particular client for around a decade', making him more senior than much of the middle and upper management we worked with. He certainly knew the place better than Claudette.

During our first meeting, Claudette did not leave a positive impression on our team. She spoke English with a very thick French accent, much of the content that we presented was clearly new to her, and she did not provide much *input* on our planned future analyses. Her main contribution during this first *meeting* was to stress what exactly her boss – whom she frequently mentioned – was interested in. She became most lively towards the end of the presentation when we were planning future meetings, specifying who should and who should not attend them. When we subsequently left the office, Andreas, who considered himself an expert on the insurance business, remarked disparagingly that Claudette had seemed very fixated on the logistical aspects of work rather than its analytical content. He called her a 'Prozesstante' (literally 'Process-aunty'). He also pointed out how short her dress had been and that businesswomen in Germany would not wear such revealing costumes. To him, Claudette had failed to present herself as a professional and respectable member of our project.

Gender played a major role in this negative impression. Management consulting has remained a men's business in Germany, where, in spite of active recruitment policies aimed at young female consultants, the share of women partners remains strikingly low. At Boston Consulting Group it lies at about 9 per cent (in Germany and Austria), at Roland Berger at roughly 8 per cent, at McKinsey Germany at around 6 per cent and at Bain & Company at 4 per cent (for Germany and Switzerland) (Töpper 2012 as cited in Tomenendal and Boyoglu 2014). As several of my female interviewees told me, this was largely due to social expectations that women should look after their children. Thus, when giving birth to a child, they faced the choice of either being bad consultants, who took too much time off, or being bad mothers who sacrificed their children's well-being for their careers.

However, subtler gender dynamics were equally at play. Metaphors used in consulting such as 'growth', 'monetary flows' and 'market' have been shown to rely upon gendered notions of fertility (Braun 2011: 64) and consulting discourses remain particularly masculine in tone, in part as a response to the very ambiguous nature of the work practices involved (Marsh 2009). This makes it hard for women to insist on gendered stereotypes as tools for their own advancement, a technique that has in the past been fruitful for women on Wall Street (Fisher 2012). In consulting, as in corporate culture more generally, patterns of domination continue to be frequently based on understandings of desire and sexuality (Pringle 2005). Thus, during my time as a consultant, I learnt about only one relationship between consultants in which the woman had the same rank as the man and about four in which more highly ranked men had shown a sexual interest in lower-ranked female consultants or secretaries. The latter were accompanied by a considerable amount of unverifiable rumour and gossip about how partners systematically tried to get with young female interns, recent recruits or secretaries. What this gossip pointed to was the double expectation that women in lower ranks would use their sexual attractiveness to attract higher-ranked men and that women who were considered attractive by male consultants were usually of a lower rank than them. Claudette broke with both of these expectations, thereby troubling conventional understandings of professionalism.

Consultants as liminal beings

Surprisingly, the initially negative view that my team had gained of Claudette changed over time. While jokes about her frequent references to her boss and her broken English were numerous during the first weeks of the project, Paul and Andreas gradually began speaking about her in an increasingly respectful tone. Claudette grasped within only a few meetings which analyses we presented to her, how these were linked to one another and what should logically follow. While her English remained poor, her stance towards our team became more assertive the better she understood the nature of our project. Paul and Andreas actually valued this assertiveness. They equally began to acknowledge that Claudette was a skilful politician, since she insisted on inviting the most relevant people during our future meetings, avoiding outright éclats by ensuring that no *meeting* would bring actual news to any of its participants. Claudette, Paul and Andreas were all equally keen on ensuring that the content of every *meeting* would be discussed with each participant beforehand. Clients needed to get taken *on board* and everyone constantly had to *align* on how to proceed in the future.

Consultants thus oscillated between inside and outside, not just in terms of knowledge work but also when building social relations. Andreas, Lucien and I were different kinds of outsiders in this regard. None of us knew Claudette or had contacts within her company so as to find out about her. Lucien who was more familiar with French culture could at least teach us how to properly interpret the online information about her. This information was so limited, however, that her physical appearance and brief performances in team *meetings* became the principal means of building social relationships with her. In many ways, Claudette was initially the real outsider to this project. She was new to the company, new to insurance work and new to the private sector in general. Her frequent references to her boss were only partially effective in strengthening her social position. However, she was skilful enough to use her work with us so as to quickly improve her standing in the company, becoming an 'insider' over time. Towards the end of her project with us, Claudette was promoted, not least because she had known how to use our analyses to quickly learn about her own employer, its different insurance markets, and about the worries and hopes of her bosses.

Paul on the other hand was initially the closest to being a company insider. His work with this particular insurance surpassed that of most employees in terms of time, knowledge and contacts. Claudette was equally aware of this, knowing that she could tap into Paul's insider status in order to quickly become better at her job. This constellation in which a new manager collaborates with an experienced consultant is in fact common practice to enable managers to function in positions they know little to nothing about. Here the conventional constellation where managers are insiders and consultants are outsiders is reversed. Towards the end of our project, however, Paul was once again relegated to an outsider position. We ended the project by writing a proposal for another one, so as to seamlessly continue our work with this client. However, the proposal was not successful. As a result, our key cards to the insurance offices were handed in, our printers and scanners were packed up and shipped off and the outcomes of further project *pitches* would have to be awaited. Ties with the client had officially been cut. While confidentiality restrictions do not allow current-day members of Strategy Partners to confirm whether or not their work with the insurance company continues, it is safe to assume that it does. Paul's ten-year involvement with them had shown that their business ties had in fact become permanent.

While our structural position was thus never wholly clear, this ambiguity of being insiders and outsiders worked to our advantage. As partial insiders, we could gain Claudette's favour and impress her with our expertise. As partial outsiders we could do what nobody else could socially afford and be held responsible for a merger of business units that would have negative consequences for some.

'Superior' liminality

So far, this chapter has argued that consultants are fundamentally liminal beings as they skilfully move between two competing understandings of knowledge and between different social positions. Yet what does the term 'skilful' actually entail? Surely outsiders and ambiguously placed groups in all kinds of social settings are often seen as representative of disorder and pollution (Douglas 2001; Turner 1991). Being neither insider nor outsider, consultants therefore had to ensure not to decline into the status of a 'polluting other'. They could easily be accused of being insiders who fake outsider status to receive a higher salary, or outsiders pretending to be insiders to gain people's trust. This constant danger of being seen as polluting others was heightened by the abstract nature of our labour, which remained fundamentally opaque for most insurance employees who met us. However, it also enabled it, as we were fundamentally working on the ephemeral object that is intra-corporate social relationships.

In moments of disillusionment, some consultants such as Tim had strong doubts themselves about the legitimacy of their work:

> I found [my own levels of ignorance] disturbing, until I realised that it is all a big game we play with one another. Of course the clients know that we do not know [things]. However, it is much more pleasant to act as if we did, so that [their] head of division can eventually get exactly the recommendation he desires. After drinking a bottle of wine together, a client once said to me 'We use your *best practices* so as to push through our own *policy*.' After that, everything was clear to me [laughs]. Another [client] was *overly excited* to receive a new traffic light instrument[6] because he could fire people with it. Each time my reaction to our colleagues was: '*This is not what I signed up for.*' I tell myself that whoever pretends to want innovation only because he plans to fire people is an evil human being.

Tim's view highlighted the absurdity that arose when what was often considered knowledge work descended into a farce that only served the reconfiguration of social ties. By his account, Tim was not valued as a source of valuable and necessary analyses anymore, but he had been degraded to a mere instrument of the client, who did not take him seriously but used him for his own ends. If this was in fact a constant risk, then how exactly did consultants need to move between company inside and outside in order to be successful beyond simply receiving a pay cheque? Let us turn to the above-mentioned *meeting* once more to look for answers.

The first *meeting* with Claudette was mostly run between Paul and her, with occasional interjections by Andreas. Paul was leading us through our printouts of PowerPoint slides because he had 'sold the project' to Claudette's absent boss and was officially in charge of its success. One of the first slides of his presentation featured an overview of our team, that is, pictures of six white, clean-shaven men in dark suits and light shirts, wearing ties. Four of these were actually members of our team, while another two partners were officially part of the project but only rarely contributed to our day-to-day work. A professional photographer had taken these pictures during one of our initiation training sessions. She had asked us to come to a training day in a suit and tie, had made us lean with our left elbow on a small column and had told us to smile. By leaning ever so slightly on the column, our bodies were positioned at an angle that ascended from left to right. This feature of the pictures became most evident in our home offices, where rows of pictures of all office members were usually posted on a wall somewhere. In its repetition of similar elements (i.e. the people in suits) this arrangement highlighted the structural aspects of the photographs. Below our pictures that Paul presented, the slide mentioned that we all had expertise in relevant fields, either with the client or in finance (Lucien) or in this specific insurance market (myself). Paul had a unique presentation style that in that he was far less lively or aggressive than most other partners I got to know. Instead, he spoke in a reassuring, almost patriarchal, tone that implied that everything he said was basically common sense, or – as my German colleagues frequently called it – 'gesunder Menschenverstand' (literally, 'healthy human understanding'). This style stood in stark contrast to his small physique and otherwise youthful, almost boyish appearance and occasionally nervous body language.

Andreas was eager to speak as well, since his future promotion from *team leader* to junior partner would mostly depend on an assessment of his ability to build social ties with clients.[7] He had mentioned this fact frequently to us, yet in this and future meetings he largely left the floor to Paul. As a tall man, Andreas was closer to the physical ideal of an *alpha male* which several of my male and female colleagues had mentioned as the implicit ideal of consulting work. Yet, with his quiet and almost shy nature, he lacked Paul's self-assertion, a weakness that was especially evident in client meetings. Andreas had proven his *leadership skills* time and again by showing that he *delivered* all sorts of analyses and documents on time. However, he now needed to prove that he had the personal characteristics it took to generate his own contracts with clients in the future.

Lucien and I equally were under quite some pressure to speak at least once, but we did not during this first encounter. My first *team leader* had taught me to ensure 'having *air time*', that is, 'speaking up' in meetings. His advice to me was always to say something when a partner was around. He specified that I should not 'say anything absolutely stupid', but that I should 'say something, even if it is not brilliant'. His guidance was in fact critical for a successful career in consultancy, as those colleagues who ignored it would eventually suffer the consequences. *Team Leader* Sofia, who will be introduced properly in the next chapter had pointed out the same in the past. Speaking freely in meetings was part of being self-assertive. Coaches passed on this lesson to young female consultants at gender-specific training days (cf. Fisher in Fisher and Downey 2006). Women were held to be generally more careful and silent in meetings than men were and – so they argued – would have to make an extra effort to impress. One female colleague, who had been urged to leave her job because it had been decided that she would not be promoted, told me over coffee that she had been far too slow in understanding how important 'having *air time*' in front of partners really was. She had always thought that 'doing her work and doing it well' would be sufficient. It was already too late when she understood that the partners, who decided on her career trajectory, would just see her for just an hour a week. With too little time to check the quality of her work in detail, it was during this hour that she would need to say something, anything[8] so as to leave them with a positive impression of her.

Further reasons existed for speaking up. One partner, who wanted me to say more during formal meetings, explained to me in a *feedback* session that we cost our clients thousands of Euros per week, so we always had to 'show them something' in return. He explained that, just like me, he had initially been quite careful with words, but that he had learnt to speak up in client meetings over time. He suggested that a good exercise for me would be to set myself a target for future client meetings. I could decide before the next meeting to speak up at least five times. Alternatively, I could resolve to constantly disagree with a client, simply so as to see what would happen. He added that such behaviour would not always be possible but when a project was 'relatively stable' he suggested

I definitely give it a try. 'What is going to happen?' he asked rhetorically. In the above-mentioned *meeting*, however, Lucien's and my silence was not a problem. We were expected to leave the floor to Paul and Andreas initially, because in these early stages of the project they would need every available opportunity to *bond* ('bonden') with clients. Consultant–client relationships were widely regarded to be crucial for determining whether or not a project would become a success.

The conclusions that can be drawn from our first *meeting* with Claudette are easily summarized with reference to Aristotle's rhetoric. The Greek philosopher had defined 'rhetoric' as the ability to see the available means of persuasion in a given situation, focusing on three main elements, namely the subject that does the persuading, the content of her speech and the listener who is to be persuaded (Aristotle 2007: 37–9; also Kennedy in Aristotle 2007: x; Rapp 2002). With reference to the speaking subjects, their persuasive power or charisma lay in a variety of elements. As mentioned above, their structural positions and gender roles were certainly influential. However, the pressure on everyone to speak during the first *meeting* and the odd suggestion of taking on different personas point to a specific practice through which consultants cultivated charisma. Speaking up in a self-assertive manner, in spite of a possible lack of knowledge, was a symbolic act, which would show that we adhered to values of aggressive boldness. It would be indicative of our 'willingness to take decisions',[9] the absence of which was widely regarded to be the main problem of client companies. Furthermore, it would show clients that we were energetic and involved, something that top management always seemed to value. This verbal self-assertion could take bizarre forms at times. One partner I worked with, for example, was notorious for interrupting almost everything his colleagues said, finding ever-new expressions for doing so, such as 'Can I just slide in here …', 'If I may briefly …', 'Very briefly let me …' and 'If I could just one more time …'. He was known to talk at people rather than with them. This technique could obviously backfire. Thus, a very senior partner was rumoured to have lost his job because he had been so aggressive with clients that they refused to have him at *meetings* again.

Speaking up was part rhetoric, part epistemic technique. Consultants considered discourse itself to be valuable, regardless of whether our views were very well founded or not. The mere act of uttering opinions, anecdotes, hunches and ideas was deemed to establish a discursive field that facilitated project work and helped to approximate truth. Both in front of clients and in internal meetings consultants greatly appreciated this attitude. Their communicative ideal was one where almost every thought was communicated, either verbally or in writing. Thinking for one's self was necessary, but it was not valued as being particularly conducive to *teamwork*, and it was easily associated with overly intellectual behaviour of little practical relevance.

Apart from speaking up, much of the persuasive power was to come from our physical appearance. As described in the Introduction of this book, consultants adhered to a rigorous dress code of dark suits or outfits, white shirts and blouses and simple dark shoes. Facial hair was not the norm and neither were piercings, visible tattoos, being overweight or any other form of bodily peculiarity. The fact that our bodies were meant to serve as persuasive devices was partially made evident by the fact that we travelled to be with clients as much as possible. It was also apparent in the pictures we presented to Claudette, which had been standardized in a way that conveyed dynamism and élan. Moreover, we had dressed up for Claudette in the basic attire expected in insurance management, including ties, which we would take off as soon as we worked from our own office space. Moreover, we paid close attention to body language, getting up when Claudette entered the room, moving towards her to greet her with energy and a smile, and following her physical clues throughout the *meeting*. In previous corporate training sessions, we had been taught that the vast majority of meaning exchanged between people was communicated non-verbally and that attention to non-verbal cues was essential in our line of work. If the client drifted off, it might be advisable to get up and explain something directly against a projected slide or with the help of a flip chart. If the client's body language communicated scepticism, it might be time to ask them how they felt about presented content, and when in doubt about how to conduct ourselves, we were supposed to 'mirror' client movements.

The standardization of our physical appearance points to a third aspect of personal charisma worth highlighting. Being a consultant meant having to deal with a vast amount of different people, usually from a white German middle-class background.

One needed to interact with busy secretaries, secretive accounting staff, sceptical employees and demanding managers all at the same time. This required a mixture of politeness and a lack of personal extravagance. Most of all, it meant submission to the will of partners. The analyses they asked for needed to be delivered and they needed them to arrive on time. A basic rhetorical skill in consulting was thus to personify the most basic common denominator: being someone whom most people would like and who would provide the required work in a punctual manner. In looking for such principally diligent and pleasant individuals, consulting differed from the more aggressive and even more macho 'maverick individuals' cultivated on trading floors (Zaloom 2006b: 113).

Charisma in consulting was thus a mixture of self-assertive speech, a bodily appearance that combined standardization with dynamism and a basic disposition to submit and to please. In its original sociological use, Max Weber had made no reference to charisma in the context of economics. He had linked this 'gift of grace' to prophets, warlords, plebiscitarian rulers, demagogues or political party leaders (Weber 2004: 34–5), yet he excluded corporate leaders and company bureaucrats from it. Consultants, however, were indeed obsessed with charisma. They frequently had discussions about it, often couched in the language of *leadership skills*. Here is how one *team leader* described it in an interview:

> Outside appearance gets more important the higher you rise in the ranks. You have to do good work but you also have to present it well. [You must] convey in a convincing manner that you have done a good *job* and persuade a lot of people that everything has been great. ... It can be down to personal charisma. For example, we had one Partner who just entered a room and people would listen to him. They would think 'Yes, he is tall and dashing.' The *Team Leader* on the project was short and round. The Partner however was skilled at interrupting people, turning their words around and taking the edge off things. This is an important skill and has a lot to do with charisma, which is hard to grasp. Maybe [the clients] would find out in two weeks that the idea [he presented] was shit, but in the moment, it sounded great.[10]

Apart from charisma, another source of persuasive power lay in the analyses that Paul presented. The almost mechanical logic of his reasoning worked together with the focus on numbers and stringent aesthetic of PowerPoint slides analysed in the following chapter. In addition, Paul's presentation evoked a vast repository of invisible knowledge that each member of our team had supposedly accumulated as part of their 'past experience'. It was referred to on our slides and in Paul's remarks concerning his decade of experience with the client. Finally, many of the convincing aspects of Paul's message lay in his frequent references to pragmatism. In tone, content and body language, Paul would reassure all of us that, in spite of the infinite complexity of the problem at hand, a reasonable solution could be found. While he had constantly pushed Lucien and me to refine our company and market analyses, and while he remained sceptical of our results, this scepticism was downplayed in his presentation.

Thereby, Paul artfully combined two competing notions of truth. On the one hand, our team had a strong sense of truth as correspondence between world and concept. The current and future organizational make-up of the insurance company was supposed to match up to a set of entities in the world. At the same time, however, Paul knew how to shift from this understanding of truth to a pragmatic one in which he valued those bits of information that would work for the purposes he had in mind. In presenting our findings, he applied a pragmatic approach which valued information with respect to its practical consequences (James 1995: 18ff.; Zeitlyn 2012: 534). To Paul, as to most other senior consultants, numbers were always shaky, analyses incomplete and predictions uncertain. Yet his frequent references to common sense naturalized 'a relatively organised body of considered thought' as something that 'anyone clothed and in their right mind' knew (Geertz 1983a: 75). He could happily make this strategic move, because to him, as to many of my colleagues, the main problem of most companies did not lie in imperfect information. It lay in poor communication and coordination within, which could lead to inertia. Thus, Paul had learnt how to make the jump from one conception of truth to another with relative ease and at just the right point at which most clients would consider it necessary. Nevertheless, the tension between the two conceptions of truth was never fully resolved. Claudette knew this as much as we did, so she had to rely on additional clues to decide whether or not the plans we presented to her made sense.

Reflecting Paul's pragmatism, almost all management consultants I met were somewhat proud of not being actual experts at anything. Instead, they made a point out of 'telling things as they really were' and of knowing how to stop overanalysing at just the right time. Their self-esteem derived from the reduction of all sorts of complexity to a few accessible bullet points, which seemed 'experience near' (Geertz 1983a: 57). This was not restricted to the work done in the presence of clients, but it was applied in consultants' own daily work as well. Lucien, when writing the sales plan for Asia, for example, might not have known anything about the insurance business, but he managed to get a lot of 'common sense' points on paper.

Consultancy representatives and industry analysts would often make the point that consultant expertise relies on gathering the in-depth knowledge of other parties and summarizing them in a commonsensical way. In order to explain Lucien's work, they would assume that his clients, senior colleagues and members of the Strategy Partners research units provided him with knowledge about the wider insurance sector ('sectorial expertise') and about sales strategies more generally ('functional expertise'). In fact, this understanding of the division of consulting work constitutes a fundamental part of the business model of all major consultancy companies. While the client provides the details, so the story goes, the consultancy firms contribute sectorial and functional expertise.

While this makes for a convincing business model, it is not at all what happened in practice. Lucien had essentially improvised the plan in question on the basis of his 'common sense'. He could not ask his clients about it beforehand as he did not want to appear perfectly clueless and was of the opinion that having something written down on paper generally facilitated *teamwork*. Neither our research staff nor Paul and Andreas had a clear idea of how to write such a plan. They knew much more about actual insurance products and would have had to improvise a *roll-out* for insurance products in Asia as well. Surprisingly, when Lucien checked the product of his 'common sense' plan with clients, they made only a few amendments to what he had put down. Perhaps they did not know how to roll out sales either. Or they may have found value in simply thinking something through on the basis of the parameters of 'common sense' that they shared with us. Or they may not have cared because their hope was to carry on business as usual once we left. Andreas told me months after the project was over that much of the drawn-up mergers and sales expansions had been delayed in our absence, so it seems that the two sales managers had good reason to react to our plans in a relaxed way.

The most immediately observable result of our project affected Claudette. Her disposition was a third and final important element in the *meeting* described above. As a woman in a male-dominated world of insurance work, she had a strong interest in being taken seriously and in asserting her authority. As a sly newcomer to the world of insurance companies, she was happy to rely on our support, provided it would work in her favour. It is hard to say with certainty whether Claudette was or was not impressed by Paul's initial presentation. Yet, one indication that she was somewhat pleased was that she and Paul eventually carried out another project to support her in her new role after she had received a promotion.

Conclusion

Like the previous chapter, this one has argued that in contrast to much of the literature about them, management consultants were in fact not primarily 'knowledge workers', but that they mostly worked so as to reconfigure intra-corporate social relationships. A key element of this was to provide the managers who hired them and who tried to alter work activity within their companies with legitimacy. As part of this effort, management consultants needed to legitimize their own position in a company, something they achieved by alternating between different understandings of knowledge and by presenting themselves alternatively as client company insiders or outsiders. Their resulting liminal position increased their risk of being seen as a polluting other, against which consultants used a host of additional legitimation techniques aimed at becoming 'superior' liminal beings. The chapter has thereby shown how power operates on the amorphous and frequently ill-defined boundaries of large business corporations. At the time of writing this chapter, Paul, Andreas, Lucien (and I) have all left consulting. While Paul and Andreas now work full-time for insurance companies, and have become wholehearted industry insiders, Lucien is not quite sure where his professional life will take him next.

This chapter has also shown a way in which the social labour of consultants was abstract. It enabled management to establish relations with vast amounts of people, which were marked as much by formal dominance as by emotional and affective disengagement from them. Consultants thereby constituted a technology for the establishment of detached relations for the managers who hired them. As part of this, they rigorously channelled their own emotional and affective ties to the substratum of management that was most directly involved in paying their salaries. The following chapter will outline the notion of abstract labour in greater depth by showing that the knowledge work that is part of consulting is principally defined by the absence of a concrete referent.

CHAPTER FOUR

Abstract Labour and the Absurd

While the previous two chapters have established speed and power as two of the products of management consulting, this chapter will focus on how consultants sell knowledge. Anthropologists have shown that corporate entities are invested in ideas, models and frameworks that engender social transformations of all sorts (Mosse 2005: 3). The efficacy, and in part also the nature of these ideas, relies on a series of external factors such as the ways in which they are socially and culturally embedded as well as the material carriers through which they are expressed and communicated (Latour and Woolgar 1986; Latour 1993). Therefore, this chapter will describe the knowledge work in consulting by focusing on two of its most important technologies, namely Microsoft Excel and PowerPoint. The two computer programs have become so pervasive in the corporate world, and sometimes even in the private lives of employees, that they warrant much greater attention than anthropologists have so far been able to pay to them. Moreover, proficiency in these two technologies and the presentation of their results is considered the 'bread and butter', that is, the actual craft of consulting. The chapter thus describes how consultants build spreadsheet models, translate calculations into slide shows and present these to clients.

It argues that management consulting is predominantly abstract in nature, in two main senses of the term. First, consultants and their managerial clients exchange knowledge for money, yet they constantly face the fundamental problem of not having a concrete referent against which to test the validity of their analyses. Consultants try to analyse entire companies or business divisions, yet they do not know most of the people in them, they have hardly any understanding of their social relationships, and often they only superficially grasp the material set-ups under which people in a client company operate. This problem reflects the wider managerial condition of contemporary capitalism, but it is heightened for consultants, since they tend to work on fairly short-term projects in almost constantly changing business units, companies and even industries. I therefore consider consulting to be paradigmatic for wider trends of increasing managerial division and complexity. In this environment, the abstractions used to make sense of the referents under analysis (i.e. the representations of businesses, business units, individual work practices, etc.) often turn into the main object of interest, thereby blurring the difference between referent and representation (Keane 1997).

Secondly, this chapter shows that consulting is abstract in the sense of remaining fundamentally opaque. On the one hand, this is due to the technologies that consultants use: spreadsheets and presentation slides seamlessly combine elements that pertain to episteme with those that are rhetorical in nature, and both technologies remain closed-off to outsiders since they need to be explained by their authors in order to be understood. On the other hand, consultants themselves can be considered agents of opacity since they work in seclusion from those people whose working lives they analyse, and because they are trained not to share any information about their jobs indiscriminately.

The argument as to the abstract nature of their labour is based on recent studies in the anthropology of corporate forms. While works within this field have privileged individual aspects of knowledge creation, such as the role of numbers (Zaloom 2003, 2006: 141–61), narratives (Holmes 2009) and aesthetics (Riles 1998: 378, 2001: 16, 2011: 54), this chapter takes on their important insights, but shifts analytic focus back to the more basic challenge of establishing convincing descriptions of entities that remain fundamentally unknown. In part, this is because consultants draw with great liberty on numerical analyses, narrative techniques and aesthetics as long as they believe that they will thereby arrive at effective descriptions of client companies.

Present abundance and expected dearth

Six months into my job as a consultant I was sitting in the *team room* of my second project, together with two colleagues. We had come together somewhere on the ground floor of a German public health insurance company to work on an 'organizational project'. These kinds of projects were principally concerned with a client company's structural make-up, rather than with its market position or product mix (*strategy*) or the operational efficiency of day-to-day workflows (*operations*). The room's insipid character stood in stark contrast to the imposing, modernist beauty of the offices of our own consulting firm, where my colleagues and I had been recruited and trained and where we tended to work on Fridays.

In Germany, health insurance was compulsory for all citizens and provided mostly by public insurance companies,[1] which covered over 85 per cent of Germany's population (Civitas 2013: 2). They were mainly funded through payroll taxes, which amounted to 15.5 per cent of members' gross wages.[2] These taxes were pooled together with government money in a Central Health Fund, before being allocated to public insurance companies. While these companies could thus not earn money by pricing their services, they were still meant to compete with one another, and their principal means to do so was to increase revenue and profit by attracting a lot of healthy members. More members meant more money from the Central Health Fund and the healthier the members were, the lower the costs of insuring them would turn out to be. A second key aspect of competition was to reduce costs. In theory, insurance companies also had the option of introducing additional services, for which they could charge a premium. However, experience had shown that as soon as they tried to do this, large parts of their membership would quickly change insurer so as to continue to pay the lowest possible rate.

In 2011 and 2012, while our consulting project took place, the German economy was doing much better than expected. Unemployment was surprisingly low and the payroll tax had just been increased, so public health insurance companies were amassing enormous reserves, amounting to around EUR 22bn in late 2012 (*Süddeutsche Zeitung* 2012). Politicians from different parties began to demand that part of these reserves be paid back to the public, while insurance company managers wanted to hang on to the money to mitigate future economic slumps. The companies' basic idea was that during the next economic downturn, whoever held the largest financial reserves could continue to charge the lowest possible membership fee the longest, thereby growing their membership base in what was still considered a consolidating market.

In this climate of present abundance and expected dearth, the top management of the health insurance company we worked for decided to plan future staff levels. They wanted to ensure that their future employee structure would remain low and sent around a request to all main business divisions asking how many employees they would require over the years to come. The division heads promptly reported back, and almost all of them made abundantly clear that they would require considerably more staff than they currently had, increasing the overall amount of a particularly expensive group of employees, labelled 'Specialists' from 2,500 to 2,590.[3] This request clearly did not fit the *board's* plans for keeping costs down in case the economic climate deteriorated, so it decided to maintain the number of Specialists at roughly the current size.

Yet, since none of the division heads would back down from their initial demands, the *board* opted that consultants should deal with the situation. We were to meet with each division head in person to find out where more staff might truly be needed and where they could actually do with fewer employees than they currently had. That way, we would be able to reduce the overall number of requested Specialists to where it should be by reallocating staff from one division to another. The division heads, however, would try to keep their teams as large as possible, since top management judged their productivity with little regard to their staff levels, and because retaining employees fostered their claims to autonomous leadership. Division heads thus contested *board* prerogatives to decide where personnel should go, partially to show their own subordinates how protective they were of them.

Meet the team

Against this environment of internal political struggle in times of economic abundance, my colleague Anne, our boss Sofia and I met in our *team room*. Anne, a kind and empathetic woman in her early thirties, was new to consulting. After having received a master's degree in the field of development at a prestigious British university, she had worked for several years in the United Kingdom and the United States, gathering some experience in NGO project management and fundraising. Wondering how she might make the transition back to the German job market, she had heard about consulting from a friend, and now found herself on her first project, together with Sofia and myself. Anne would not work to resolve the quarrels over future staff as her main task was to oversee the implementation of a recently redefined insurance strategy. However, she shared the *team room* with Sofia and me and since Sofia supervised both of us we felt like a team.

Anne seemed generally brimming with life and had a strong tendency to use English expressions with a heavy American accent when speaking German. She was happy to work in consulting as she had 'always considered herself a *problem solver*', yet she also had an acute sense of the absurdity of some of our daily tasks and frequently laughed at how *random*, 'strange'[4] and ultimately banal life as a management consultant could be. While she acknowledged that consultants had to be *on the ball* a lot and remained constantly *busy*, she laughed at the fact that much of her work consisted of sitting in endless and somewhat boring *meetings* of an insurance company, in order to then write PowerPoint slides until the morning hours. Our work, she argued, was really not *rocket science*, and she often remarked that, when she had first applied to become a management consultant, she had imagined it to be much more technical and mathematically demanding. All that said, Anne was not particularly confident when it came to her own consulting abilities. She often seemed puzzled as to which analyses or *meeting* to prepare next, and, as she later told me in an interview, she had a hard time dealing with the great speed and long hours that she was expected to work.

Opposite us sat *Team Leader* Sofia, a woman in her late thirties who struck most colleagues and me as a predominantly impatient person. Her physical appearance clashed with that of most of her colleagues and clients, since – as a devout fan of punk music – she had short hair, dressed exclusively in black and had a great number of piercings and visible tattoos. Upon seeing her online picture on the office intranet, male colleagues of mine shuddered in awe, expecting her to be particularly tough, not least because she did not conform to gender norms in the same way as most of her female colleagues did. She made up for her unusual appearance with a most exemplary work ethic and a good deal of macho rhetoric, 'drilling'[5] her way into datasets, 'grinding her way into spreadsheets'[6] and swearing frequently. Renowned to sleep an average of only four hours per night, Sofia valued hard work and personal loyalty above all else. Unable to fulfil her dream of becoming a doctor, she had chosen to work as a healthcare consultant, considering herself an expert in the industry. I was less intimidated by the way in which she undermined conventional gender roles than my peers, and actually valued her straightforward approach to work and life in general. Moreover, my initial impression that Sofia had a big heart for the people she knew personally was confirmed a few months later, when Anne had been driven seriously ill as a result of work pressure and personal disposition and Sofia supported her in a caring manner.

With all her self-confidence, Sofia tended to comment disparagingly on the 'strategic mistake' by the *board*, which, in her eyes, had failed to 'decide *top-down*' how many members of staff would in the future be available for each division of the insurance company. Instead, the *board's* 'request show'[7] as she called it had 'predictably' led the division heads to demand disproportionate staff increases. Sofia acknowledged several times that the 'lawn mower approach',[8] that is, simply cutting everyone's number of additional Specialist requested back to zero, was not an option since some of the divisions genuinely needed more staff, while others could be restructured and would need less. However, she also seemed to make this remark with an air of regret, not least because the power to decide on the employee structure ultimately lay with the *board* and not with us.

Before becoming a consultant, Sofia had worked in finance and was visibly proud of the spreadsheet abilities she had acquired there. Initially trained as a social scientist, she had begun her corporate career with rather poor quantitative analytic abilities but after 'scrubbing the numbers'[9] night after night in her past job she now professed to 'love Excel'. On several occasions she shared with us how much she regretted not building models anymore, now that she worked as *team leader*, a role which required her to check the accuracy of models, but not to build them herself. However, on one afternoon early in the project, Sofia made an exception. When Anne had rushed off to a client *meeting*, Sofia told me to come around the table to look at her screen, so as to show me how to build a proper model. Her invitation was somewhat extraordinary in that we usually did not have time for any teaching sessions. What I did not know at the time was that she was about to establish an overview of the entire insurance company that was going to be fundamental for carrying out our job over the weeks to come.

Spreadsheet magic

Sofia's model was basically a grid that listed all divisions and subdivisions of the insurance company along the left and all employee categories along the top (see Figure 1). It was meant to be an abstract representation of the insurance company. This became clear when she subdivided employees into columns entitled 'current', that is, those who actually existed, and 'ought', that is, those that the divisions in question might or might not have in the future. This difference was not just temporal in nature, but it showed that one column was supposed to reflect actual reality, while the other bore fictional qualities. Two aspects are worth pointing out about the kind of representation that Sofia was building: First, value judgements entered the model from the start (Pickles 2017). Sofia had thoughtfully placed the insurance company's most important 'executive divisions' at the very top of the spreadsheet, and she had divided the categories of staff according to pay scales that reflected social hierarchies into 'Executive management',[10] Specialists and 'Employees'.[11] My guess is that this structure reflected her own way of thinking about the insurance company and that everything else would have made it impossible to show and discuss this model with upper management clients.

Secondly, the act of building the model showed that it was initially not concerned with numbers. Instead, its narrative and aesthetic features came first, carrying a great amount of semantic and normative content (Riles 1998). In its very basic and perfectly repetitive structure, Excel underlined the fact that all of its elements were essentially similar. Placing the model's explicitly apolitical title 'Change Matrix' in big letters on the top left meant narrowing down the nature of all content that was to follow. Vertical and horizontal gridlines weakened the model's internal homogeneity at strategic places, without ever undoing it fully. Number colours

Change Matrix

Division	Executive management				Specialists				Employees				Total			
	FTE ought	FTE current	Delta (absolute)	Delta (in %)	FTE ought	FTE current	Delta (absolute)	Delta (in %)	FTE ought	FTE current	Delta (absolute)	Delta (in %)	FTE ought	FTE current	Delta (absolute)	Delta (in %)
Exec OUs	62.00	60.17	1.83	3.0%	128.00	120.34	7.66	6.4%	362.00	361.02	0.98	0.3%	552.00	483.19	68.81	14.2%
Division 1	13.00	12.99	0.01	0.1%	27.00	25.98	1.02	3.9%	78.00	77.94	0.06	0.1%	118.00	103.93	14.07	13.5%
Division 2	1.00	1.00		-0.0%	3.00	2.00	1.00	50.0%	6.00	6.00		-0.0%	10.00	8.00	2.00	25.0%
Division 3	22.00	21.39	0.61	2.9%	45.00	42.78	2.22	5.2%	129.00	128.34	0.66	0.5%	196.00	171.73	24.27	14.1%
Division 4	13.00	12.95	0.05	0.4%	27.00	25.90	1.10	4.2%	78.00	77.70	0.30	0.4%	118.00	103.65	14.35	13.8%
Division 5	1.00	0.70	0.30	42.9%	3.00	1.40	1.60	114.3%	4.00	4.20	(0.20)	-4.8%	8.00	5.90	2.10	35.6%
Division 6	12.00	11.14	0.86	7.7%	23.00	22.28	0.72	3.2%	67.00	65.84	0.16	0.2%	102.00	89.98	12.02	13.4%
Division 7	77.00	76.37	0.63	0.8%	240.00	229.11	10.89	4.8%	637.00	627.07	9.93	1.6%	954.00	856.81	97.19	11.3%
Leadership	12.00	11.99	0.01	0.1%	32.00	35.97	(3.97)	-11.0%	108.00	107.91	0.09	0.1%	152.00	143.89	8.11	5.6%
SD 1	3.00	3.00		-0.0%	10.00	9.00	1.00	11.1%	27.00	27.00		-0.0%	40.00	36.00	4.00	11.1%
SD 2	21.00	20.39	0.61	3.0%	64.00	61.17	2.83	4.6%	188.00	183.11	4.49	2.4%	273.00	245.29	27.71	11.3%
SD 3	12.00	11.95	0.05	0.4%	40.00	35.85	4.15	11.6%	108.00	107.55	0.45	0.4%	160.00	143.45	16.55	11.5%
SD 4	3.00	2.90	0.10	3.4%	10.00	8.70	1.30	14.9%	30.00	26.10	3.90	14.9%	43.00	34.90	8.10	23.2%
SD 5	9.00	10.14	(1.14)	-11.2%	34.00	30.42	3.58	11.8%	31.00	31.00		-0.0%	74.00	60.28	13.72	22.8%
SD 6	17.00	16.00	1.00	6.3%	50.00	48.00	2.00	4.2%	145.00	144.00	1.00	0.7%	212.00	193.00	19.00	9.8%
Division 8	73.00	69.96	3.04	4.3%	143.00	139.92	3.08	2.2%	281.00	279.84	1.16	0.4%	497.00	422.80	74.20	17.5%
Leadership	10.00	9.00	1.00	11.1%	18.00	18.00	0.00	0.0%	36.00	36.00	0.00	0.0%	64.00	55.00	9.00	16.4%
SD 1	18.00	17.27	0.73	4.2%	35.00	34.54	0.46	1.3%	69.00	69.08	-0.08	-0.1%	122.00	104.35	17.65	16.9%
SD 2	18.00	17.87	0.13	0.7%	38.00	35.74	2.26	6.3%	71.00	71.48	-0.48	-0.7%	127.00	107.35	19.65	18.3%
SD 3	22.00	21.82	0.18	0.8%	44.00	43.64	0.36	0.8%	87.00	87.28	-0.28	-0.3%	153.00	131.10	21.90	16.7%
SD 4	5.00	4.00	1.00	25.0%	8.00	8.00	0.00	0.0%	18.00	16.00	2.00	12.5%	31.00	25.00	6.00	24.0%
Division 9	8.00	6.30	1.70	27.0%	30.00	25.20	4.80	19.0%	51.00	50.40	0.60	1.2%	89.00	77.50	11.70	15.1%
Leadership	4.00	3.80	0.2	5.3%	20.00	15.20	4.8	31.6%	31.00	30.40	0.6	2.0%	55.00	45.80	9.2	20.1%
SD 1	1.00	0.50	0.5	100.0%	2.00	2.00	0.0	0.0%	4.00	4.00	0.0	0.0%	7.00	6.50	0.5	7.7%
SD 2	3.00	2.00	1.00	50.0%	8.00	8.00	0.00	0.0%	16.00	16.00	0.00	0.0%	27.00	25.00	2.00	8.0%
Division 10	61.00	56.59	4.41	7.8%	118.00	113.18	4.82	4.3%	229.00	226.36	2.64	1.2%	408.00	343.95	64.05	18.6%
Leadership	18.00	17.27	0.73	4.2%	35.00	34.54	0.46	1.3%	69.00	69.08	-0.08	-0.1%	122.00	104.35	17.65	16.9%
SD 1	9.00	7.70	1.30	16.9%	20.00	15.40	4.60	29.9%	32.00	30.80	1.20	3.9%	61.00	47.50	13.50	28.4%
SD 2	22.00	21.82	0.18	0.8%	43.00	43.64	-0.64	-1.5%	89.00	87.28	1.72	2.0%	154.00	131.10	22.90	17.5%
SD 3	7.00	6.70	0.30	4.5%	13.00	13.40	-0.40	-3.0%	27.00	26.80	0.20	0.7%	47.00	40.50	6.50	16.0%
SD 4	5.00	3.10	1.9	61.3%	7.00	6.20	0.8	12.9%	12.00	12.40	-0.4	-3.2%	24.00	20.50	3.5	17.1%
Company Total	281.00	269.39	11.61	4.3%	659.00	627.75	31.25	5.0%	1,560.00	1,544.69	15.31	1.0%	2,500.00	2,184.05	315.95	14.5%

FIGURE 1 *The final Change Matrix.*[12]

would indicate both their provenance and mutability. Blue-coloured numbers originated outside of the model, rendering them hard to contest from within its logic, while black numbers would invite changes in calculations until they fit our expectations. Automatic red highlights drew reader's eyes to major envisioned staff increases that were considered problematic, while yellow highlights pointed at key results so as to make an otherwise impenetrable sea of numbers meaningful and readable.

Rounding numbers was an interesting case in point. Sofia did not want to describe employees as actual people in the spreadsheet, but as 'FTEs', that is, as the amount of labour time that each of them disposed of (see Chapter 3). This was in line with client documents that our model would be based on. Due to various calculative reasons, some of these numbers needed to be rounded, an activity which blurred the lines between form and content: on the one hand, rounding could simply be considered a visual adjustment of numerical description to make them easier to read. After all Excel only shortened the form of numbers rather than altering their actual calculative values. On the other hand, however, rounding did also alter the quantity that a number was supposed to represent, since in practice, rounded numbers tend to be discussed and thought about in their shortened form. Determining whether rounding numbers in this setting was in fact a quantitative act that altered numeric value or a qualitative one aimed merely at the abbreviation of form may be impossible.

The make-up of the software had a strong effect on the kind of representation that Sofia was able to make. Excel has a pre-inscribed preference for quantitative data because it only unfolds its full potential when it is used to put large amounts of numbers into relation with one another via calculative formulas. Thereby, spreadsheets used in consulting usually became more than just lists compiled for mnemonic ends. Instead, they functioned as arithmetic tools, which could carry out vast numbers of calculations in a much more reliable fashion than pen and paper would allow. As long as digital spreadsheets were filled with numbers, they could thus unfold considerable agency in the sense that they allowed their intentional users to surpass their own arithmetic capabilities (Gell 1998). At the same time, Excel was still unable to summarize large amounts of qualitative data, so by foregrounding the world's quantitative aspects the program did not only reflect a quantitative reductionism that was frequently associated with capitalism (Lukács 1971), but actually reinforced it.

That said, in spite of this in-built preference for numbers, the model that Sofia was building in front of my eyes was as much a technology of representation as it was a technology of enchantment, that is, a means to employ the acquiescence of other people (Gell 1988: 7; Malinowski 1930). In this case it was meant to intervene in the managerial struggles within the insurance company and to prove that we as consultants could solve a socially difficult situation. Moreover, the model was meant to influence the nature of our *teamwork*. Sofia's creating it in front of my eyes allowed us to bond through a gift-like act of teaching, which was all the more valuable as it occurred under severe time constraints. I believe that Sofia, as an experienced, even cunning, *team leader*, was perfectly aware that teaching me in this explicit manner would allow her to create some loyalty and affinity, a fact that was especially valuable during these early stages of our project. Building the model herself equally made it a technology of rule in that its basic grid of variables predetermined the analyses and results that I would subsequently produce. Moreover, building it was an impressive performance of her consulting skills. By hardly using the mouse, focusing on rapid keyboard shortcuts and writing at times obscure spreadsheet formulas, Sofia exhibited a series of abilities that are highly valued in the world of finance (Kaplan 2010; Planet Money 2015), whereby she fostered her position as *team leader*.

At the same time, her spreadsheet model was magical in that it served as an idealized symbolic commentary on the work strategies that we employed (Gell 1988: 8). It instantiated a managerial ideal of the insurance company in which members of staff could easily be understood and manipulated as discrete and passive entities that related exclusively to corporate divisions. Their double nature of discreteness and passivity would enable us as consultants, and our managerial clients to understand, discuss and manipulate its structure until it matched our ideas. Magic could also be found in the technology's implied holism. By including all divisions and all employee categories in its basic grid, the model seemingly provided instant access to the entirety of company staff and structure. Excel often conveyed this notion of a highly reductive holism, in the sense that it stripped socio-material entities of most of their attributes so as to display very large numbers of the entities that remained. These could then be summarized into neat end results or 'totals' at the bottom of a model. In fact, the term 'spreadsheet' stems from pre-digital times when large paper sheets were spread out over office desks so as to provide their readers with a sense of god-like understanding of their corporate environments. Sofia would eventually print her model on oversized sheets of paper and take it to clients, visibly indulging in the god's eye view that this enabled.

A third source of magic lay in the spreadsheet's speed and mathematical perfection. Sofia's model would set very large amounts of quantitative data into relationships with one another and carry out vast series of calculations with superhuman speed and god-like accuracy. In fact, among consultants, Excel was considered never to be wrong, unless humans working with it had provided the wrong input. Once the basic workings of a model had been defined – usually in the form of mathematical axioms programmed into the software, explicit assumptions regarding input numbers and a panoply of arithmetic formulas that set them into relation with one another – all other aspects of it had to follow in a necessary fashion. The perfection of this mathematical necessity had already appealed to the philosopher Leibniz, who considered numbers and geometry to be the loci of absolute truth (Look 2013).

Once Sofia considered the model complete, she emailed it to me and asked me to fill it with the data from other spreadsheets, which we had received from the insurance's *Controlling* division.

In the process of building and refining the model, we had engaged in a first act of abstract labour by producing a greatly simplified representation of an insurance company without having access to the concrete referents it was supposed to represent. We had not met with any of the Specialists in the insurance, we were ignorant of their social relationships, unfamiliar with the material environment of their daily lives, unaware of the basic ideas that governed their activities and we had no embodied knowledge of their daily work routines. Still we were expected to say something meaningful about them. We would soon realize that the fundamental problem that arose in building our model was our lack of knowledge regarding the object it was meant to describe. This defining feature of abstract labour will become more evident in the following section.

Rituals of verification

Upon entering the numbers and remaining formulas to complete the model, I was surprised to see that somehow they did not add up. In fact, in subsequent projects and interviews with other consultants, I would learn time and again that they almost never did. Sofia and I had originally forgotten to include a couple of organizational entities, such as – conspicuously – the *board* that had hired us. But even when we had corrected the obvious mistakes on our part, several numbers still seemed incorrect. Upon summing up different divisions, the results would often not correspond to what *Controlling* had communicated to us in other documents. Either we did not have the right numbers or *Controlling* had not summed theirs up correctly. Our sum-total of all employees in the insurance company, at the bottom right of the model also did not match what we had read in internal documents. It took us numerous calls, emails and *meetings* with controllers and division heads to define what the 'real' numbers were. This kind of work was as much epistemic in nature as it was a ritual (Power 1999; Harper 2000; Herzfeld 1993) since neither the controllers, nor the division heads nor the *board* were ever exactly sure which numbers corresponded to the employees and their activities. They needed to agree on a number, without being certain which employees were currently working, and which ones were not, who might be on maternity leave, whether maternity leave had been counted half or double or not at all, when exactly the available input figures had been counted, who had been added to the workforce since the last count, how exactly part-timers had been accounted for and so on.

In these moments of heightened uncertainty, when our calculations and those of *Controlling* both came into question and were pitted against one another, the numbers of our model became re-personalized (ibid.; Kelly 2006: 92). Individual members of the *Controlling* division who had authored our source files had to come and justify their work to us and to the patron of our project, a *board* member who wanted to stay very involved. *Controlling* had to provide explanations in front of their boss on when, where and how they had got 'their' numbers, and according to what logics they had added them up. The controllers had the clear interest to show to the *board* that they had done their job correctly and that 'their' numbers were in fact more correct than 'ours'. While our Excel model would eventually simulate knowledge without knowers (Barth 2002: 2) such simulations were not yet possible.

This was not the only conflict involved in getting the numbers right. The discrepancy between our model and numbers by *Controlling* pointed out the fact that nobody could say with perfect certitude how many employees were currently working for the insurance company in question. This considerable uncertainty regarding the *status quo* led to additional negotiations with division heads. Some of them had quickly grasped that their demands to increase staff could be seen in different lights, depending on how much staff they were currently assumed to have, that is, which *baseline* numbers were established between *Controlling* and us. If their *baseline* was large, relative staff increases – calculated as the amount of additional employees over existing ones – would look small. If the *baseline* was small, even a few additional employees might look like a huge relative increase. Some of the division heads thus demanded to get involved in the process of setting the *baseline* right, opening the numbers up to discussion even more.

Their negotiation strategies differed quite dramatically, depending on which numbers they believed would matter most. Those who thought that the *board* was interested in relative staff increases claimed that their divisions had originally been much larger than assumed. They challenged the numbers that *Controlling* provided and offered us more recent datasets that showed how much bigger their divisions really were. Others, however, either did not know that the relative increases mattered or had decided to ignore this. They held that their divisions were much smaller than *Controlling* assumed, appealing either to egalitarian notions of fairness (along the lines of: 'my division is smaller than division x, so my staff increases are justified') or to being understaffed for the work demanded of them. The head of HR management, for example, argued with particular vehemence during one of our *meetings* that her division was much smaller than *Controlling* had claimed. She made the point that she had far too little staff for the workload and blocked off any questions as to who did what in her division by creating confusion, urgently browsing documents without ever finding what she was looking for. She showed that it would be a tremendous amount of work to find out what exactly each of her employees was up to. Sofia diligently noted her version of how few members of staff she had and left the *meeting* with a smile on her face. She thought that as a result of this small baseline number, the relative staff increase planned by HR would appear very large and was unlikely to get approval from the *board*.

A third negotiation approach was taken by the head of *Sales and Marketing*, who simply did not care about our numbers and stuck to the FTE increases he had asked for. A large man with a short temper and a preference for three piece suits that he wore like an armour showed through sheer verbal aggression and irritated gestures that he had no interest in partaking in our negotiations as to whether the size of his current or future staff was necessary. He also repeatedly asked us how his work should be done with less employees, without ever specifying what exactly they did. He was well aware that our data-gathering exercise would have established the *board's* performance indicators as normative goals for his division (Anders 2008), and he would have none of it. While we constantly reasserted that the employee numbers we summed up constituted an adequate description of company units, he rejected our numerical approach altogether.

The laborious process of getting the numbers right showed time and again that the basic problem we were grappling with was that our work was abstract, in the sense that none of us could even partially grasp the entities we were discussing. Who knew what hundreds of sales employees spread out over large parts of Germany were up to at any given moment? Who could summarize the daily activities of any of the insurance claims administrators with confidence? Their managers certainly could not, even when they wanted to. Nor could *Controlling*, with whom we actually tried to write lists of general activities of insurance company employees. This exercise quickly proved to be both impossible and in its impossibility politically outrageous for the head of *Controlling*, as it would suggest knowledge that we clearly did not have. The *board, Controlling,* divisional managers and we did not grasp exactly which activities future employees would engage in, how many of them were needed or how important their work would be for the success of individual business divisions or the insurance company as a whole. In fact, the act of trying to find this information even cast doubt over how much staff there currently was.

In the absence of a concrete referent, there was a lot of room for argument around what to do in the future. The web of competing interests between the *board, Controlling,* the different divisions and us meant that establishing the future make-up of the insurance company would be a politically explosive process. It was couched in long and at times passionate arguments about current staff numbers and activities, future workloads and whether or not any of this could be meaningfully summarized. In spite of this, we were supposed to represent all current and potential employees in a way that would enable the *board* to come to a final decision on the matter. As the next section will show, doing this would require a fair amount of rhetoric.

Thinking through slides

Sofia's decision to take a large printed version of her spreadsheet model to clients so as to discuss current and future staff levels directly on the model was highly unorthodox. First, spreadsheets in general were simply too hard to read. When Anne saw our model for the first time, for example, she was visibly overwhelmed by its size and seemingly complicated nature. It was clearly hard for her to grasp how any of its variables related to one another and which fundamental insights should be drawn from it. Just like our clients, she needed to be talked through it so as to find it meaningful. Secondly, showing spreadsheets to clients was considered bad practice because once they understood them they would often challenge the calculative logics we had employed. Therefore, consultants usually used PowerPoint in *meetings*, which as an equally opaque technology, geared even more explicitly at social enchantment.

As consultants we communicated all major ideas in PowerPoint slides and hardly ever used a word processor. Our reliance on slides was such that some of my colleagues used writing paper that featured pre-drawn slide templates. They only needed to sketch whatever presentation elements they had in mind into the template and email a scan of their sketch to support staff[13] so as to get a beautiful set of electronic PowerPoint slides back about an hour later. Sofia, Anne and I used this service on a daily basis since every *meeting* seemed to require a sizeable *deck* of new slides, emailed to clients ahead of time and discussed with them as paper printouts. The simplicity of paper seemed to focus the discussion (cf. Kaplan 2011) and allowed us to respond to client ideas and comments by jotting down notes that would afterwards be 'built directly into the *slides*'.[14] In this process, the fairly simple Excel model that Sofia and I had built turned out to be an almost endless wellspring for slide creation.

Our use of PowerPoint was a major reason why our work remained considerably opaque, for outside observers, insurance company members, managerial clients, and even for us. Sure, PowerPoint had important elucidating effects, allowing us to present analyses and insights of all sorts. However, since the rise of graphs and charts in private companies at the end of the nineteenth and at the beginning of the twentieth centuries, the tension between presentation and persuasion has gained importance in knowledge technologies (Yates 1984) and our slides were no exception to this rule. Consider the basic rules of drawing slides, something that was considered an important skill, maybe even an artform, among my colleagues. Slides were supposed to be simple and clear, without being devoid of content. As Sofia and subsequent *team leaders* would teach me, this could be achieved by giving each of them a single main message and a limited number of additional points. The *message* would be expressed as a so-called *action title*, that is, a short sentence or elliptical assertion about a single phenomenon. It should in turn stand in a direct and obvious relationship to the slide's main body, so that fairly clear meaning could emerge from their interplay. The main body was ideally a single graphical depiction of a quantitative analysis, created with an add-on software embedded in PowerPoint that permitted us to conjure up *pie charts, bar charts, scattergrams, curve graphs* and *waterfall charts* within seconds. Explanatory notes, doubts, questions and premises that surrounded slide content either had to disappear in a footnote or be abbreviated into a few very short explanatory bullet points on the side. Overly detailed slides were teasingly derided as 'German slides' for being too technical and too hard to understand. This joke had evolved in another country office but was happily adopted by German consultants themselves. Even font size mattered, since small print would make the slide appear too 'full', risking that nobody would read it (see Figure 2).

Clarity and simplicity were not ends in themselves. They were seen as means to bring about a seemingly effortless effect of understanding in the reader. Sofia would get very impatient with both Anne and me if she could not discern within seconds what our slides were meant to say. A subsequent *team leader* of mine, known for being fairly high-strung, also tended to look at them for only a few seconds before either approving of them or exclaiming, 'I don't get it. I simply don't get it. It does not jump at me! It does not jump at me!' These quick reactions to the effect of PowerPoint slides suggested that their message should be intuitively clear to the reader, without requiring hardly any effort. They should elicit an almost automatic reaction in an act of 'pragmatic efficacy' (Bourgoin and Muniesa 2012: 30). The agency of slides thus did not lie as much in allowing us to surpass our own capabilities. Instead, it was one that elicited the affectively charged epistemic effect of intuitive understanding (compare Zaloom 2012: 246).

It is hard to overemphasize the importance of aesthetics in this process. They were so crucial that all the consultants I knew could spend several hours a day aligning texts, little boxes, lines and arrows, changing bullet point styles and font sizes, using round symbols instead of square ones, enhancing company logos, ensuring high-quality printouts and so on. Even clipping printed presentations together should be done in a way that was considered 'clean'. My interviewees often complained about having to 'align little boxes'[16] until late at night and even partners were not free from this most mundane activity. While Sofia was simply annoyed with this aspect of her work, Anne repeatedly pointed out how absurd and funny it seemed to her. She especially considered many of our non-quantitative

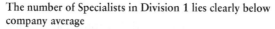

The number of Specialists in Division 1 lies clearly below
company average

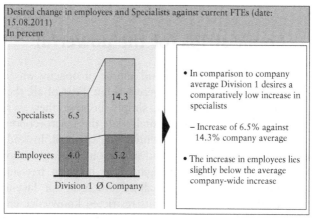

FIGURE 2 *A slide on planned staff increases.*[15]

slides hilarious. Discussions of company goals came with pictures of
a little arrow hitting a target, outstanding questions with a photo
of a businessman scratching his head, *next steps* with an image of
footprints in the sand and so on. The childishness of these images
stood in stark contrast to the presumed importance of our work. The
peculiar mixture of banality and intensity that marked our lives had
an absurd quality for her, as did the exorbitant salary we received for
embellishing slides until late at night.

In hindsight, the surprising importance of slide aesthetics has
turned out to be one reason why this chapter foregrounds the opaque
and the persuasive elements of PowerPoint over its elucidating
qualities. Perfectly looking PowerPoint slides were important
markers of professionalism, and as such, symbolic artefacts as much
as knowledge technologies. Here is how one former consultant
described his job to me over drinks:

> That's what I hated most about the job. Ensuring that all the
> slides looked perfect just so as to make the Partners happy ... .
> But [now that I have my own business] whenever I receive a *deck*,
> the first thing I do is flip through it so as to see if page numbers
> and everything else is well *aligned* ... . That way I see if the guy
> who made it was serious.

His words highlight the wider ambivalence towards aesthetics in consulting, which they considered both frustrating and valuable.

Comic strips for the powerful

Apart from slide aesthetics, a second source of opacity was linked to how presentations (viz. *decks*) were written. First of all, they had specific spatio-temporal attributes, simply because they were not contextualized. Our slide shows usually left the macroeconomic or institutional 'back story' to their content unexplained. Instead, they were compiled so as to be presented in person to people who were already in the know. As an amalgamation between free-standing written document and decontextualized blueprint for face-to-face conversations, PowerPoint *decks* thus restricted knowledge creation and transmission to a small managerial subset of people. Even when slides would get into the wrong hands leaking to other employees or even the public, they would not tell their readers much about the data they were based on or the role they played in overall corporate activity.

Moreover, presentations were written along a strict linear narrative structure in which every slide should logically build on the preceding one. At times they followed predefined story arcs, such as *situation, complication, solution*, in which presentations first outlined a problem, then rendered it more complicated and finally provided a solution to it. A common technique to ensure a convincing presentation structure was to write a 'comic [strip] outline', also known as '*Mickey Mouse* outline', in which miniature versions of slides were very roughly sketched with a felt pen on one or more paper flip charts. As a result, the flip chart looked somewhat like a comic strip, allowing the consultant to check the *flow* of a presentation's narrative and graphical elements in their sequence. *Decks* were usually written by more experienced consultants, *team leaders* and partners, since this was understood to require skill and intimate knowledge of the client. In case clients did not feel like following the strict narrative structure of a presentation, most *decks* ended in a '*backup* section' with additional slides that a consultant could jump to, if need be.

The consultants' references to *Mickey Mouse* might not have been wholly arbitrary as it pointed to the similarity of narrative features between slide shows and comic strips. Both were word-

and-image hybrids where verbal and visual information was present non-synchronously, that is, where the reader 'works with the often disjunctive back-and-forth of *reading* and *looking* for meaning' (Chute 2008: 452). Our presentations were also similar to comics in being mostly pictorial narratives in which words contributed to the meaning of the pictures and vice versa (Harvey 2005: 21). This conjunction of different carriers of meaning created a series of breaks in which greater interpretative freedom was given to the reader. Meaning would here emerge in between text, pictures, different slides and verbal presentations. This made *meetings* based around PowerPoint particularly vague, especially when a gifted presenter such as Sofia ran them and guided clients through the *deck*, picking up cues and interruptions and responding with self-assurance to questions and comments. Her high degree of responsiveness to client reactions was valued as an important consulting skill, known by the name *release your agenda*. It described the rule that consultants were supposed to give up whatever goals and preset ideas they had set for a *meeting*, if they found the members attending it particularly indifferent or concerned. At the same time, Sofia and I attempted to put our points across. Thus we put particular emphasis on the slide shown as Figure 2 when a division's relative staff increase was larger than average, to which its managers usually responded with reference to their increasing workload, or insufficient numbers of currently available employees. In *meetings* where the relative increase of FTEs was small, Sofia and I glossed over it.

A last source of opacity worth mentioning here was that the narrative of a presentation was a form of highly targeted reification in that it was often geared towards informing and pleasing those clients who were directly in charge of commissioning our work. Take the case of our conversations with the different division heads. Naturally, most of the thoughts that they shared with us would fall under the table as each *meeting* brought too much information to pass on to the *board*. So in each of them we duly jotted down their descriptions of staff workloads and estimations of future work intensity. However, only parts of these portrayals would eventually be communicated up. On the one hand, the *board* was simply not interested in detailed descriptions of staff workloads. On the other, both the most senior partner on our project and the main client who had commissioned our work had a strong penchant for quantitative analysis. Both had been trained in economics and finance, and our senior partner clearly despised seeing several purely qualitative slides in a row, excoriating them as 'unfinished'.

Abstract labour and autopoiesis

Sofia was very pleased with the slide shown in Figure 2, since it was easily replicable for each division and still conveyed a vital piece of information needed in the negotiations around staff increases. Thus, the slide made it into many of the PowerPoint *decks* we produced for our *meetings* with division heads and with the *board*. Replicating it was easy, as we could just copy-paste it and adapt graph and descriptions for each division. The ease of its multiplication points to the autopoietic qualities of abstract labour (cf. Chapter 1). Anne, Sofia and I built PowerPoint *decks* for each *meeting* we attended, describing what we were meant to do, which *next steps* needed to follow, which divisions we were dealing with both in their current and future instantiations, how their aspired employee changes added up in absolute and relative terms, what this could mean for the insurance company as a whole, and what other kinds of analyses might be still be possible.

This frenzied production of slides continued on subsequent projects, a fact that was widely lamented by my colleagues, often noted by clients and mocked by popular accounts that claimed consultants engaged in a perpetual 'slide war' (Weiden 2011). On the one hand, the fact that we operated with digital technology simply meant that countless descriptions of any referent could be provided with relative ease. However, I would argue that our incessant slide production was also linked to the abstract nature of our work. First, the absence of a concrete referent meant that a particularly large number of such descriptions were both required and possible so as to describe the 'imagined community' that was the insurance company in ever-new ways (Anderson 1991). Since it could never be observable directly, documents had to be based on other documents, spreadsheets modelled on the basis of spreadsheets, always leaving another way of describing the insurance company open. On the other hand, slides were proof to the client of our work activity. Even if they existed only on screens and at times on paper, they were the one immediate material output that our work had. In the light of the high daily fees charged by consulting companies, clients commissioning our work needed something to point to, an object that even if it was not the legitimate end product of our work, at least documented that that work had been carried out.

In these processes, the sequence of models and presentations throughout the project was far from straightforward. In fact, it is likely that Sofia had already thought of slides such as the one shown in Figure 2 before beginning the process of data gathering. As an experienced consultant, Sofia probably had a number of slide templates in mind when she drew up the 'change matrix', structuring our *Excel* model according to the aesthetic features and desired effects of the end product. Working with a clear end-product in mind was an important skill in consulting, and my most experienced colleagues and interviewees often thought in PowerPoint slides. When they considered new bits of information, they would say things like 'let's do a waterfall on this one', 'just put this in a box' or 'can we do a spiderweb on this?' The difference between *Excel* model and *PowerPoint deck* was thus never quite as stark as the structure of this chapter may have suggested. The difference that was stark was the one between our discussions in the *board* room and what may or may not have been the insurance company at the time.

Project results and the absurd

By the end of the project, Sofia, the two partners and I had spoken several times to all divisional managers, as well as *Controlling* and the *board*. We had analysed company documents and compared the amount of staff of this insurance company to that of others as part of a *benchmarking* exercise. The latter had not provided much insight. It had merely shown that in some instances this insurance company seemed to do a lot of things with relatively few members of staff, while in others, differences in organizational structures were too dramatic to make the comparisons meaningful. Sofia was visibly annoyed by this lack of 'clarity'. At the same time, she never went so far as to question the founding premise of our project, namely the 'fact' that the division heads had requested FTE numbers that were too high. The *board* was convinced of this, so were our partners and so was she. When I once ventured to challenge this premise, Sofia countered with the view that we would never know what 'the objective truth' might be and that all we could aspire for was an 'inter-subjective' version of it. She repeated this thought in a later interview, arguing that it was true for all consulting projects.

Sofia thereby dealt with the fundamental problem of not knowing the referent in question by sticking to the consulting technique called *first-day-hypothesis*. This was a socio-epistemic stance that most consultancy companies applied, in which a hypothesis was defined early on in a project before proving and refining it as part of the job throughout the project.[17] It was at times called 'answer-first approach', 'initial hypothesis' or 'hypothesis-driven approach'.[18] In practice, this idea of a *'first-day-hypothesis'* meant that partners and *team leaders* got together before a project officially started so as to write a story in PowerPoint, which laid out 'the problem', the principal analyses needed and first ideas of what a 'solution' might look like. Frequently then, when a team first came together, it would already have a guiding story sketched out, that needed to be filled or expanded. Arguably, this early construction of a storyline had a profound impact on subsequent analyses. Here is how *Team Leader* Matthias, who had been a consultant for over five years, described it:

> Judging from my experience, the numbers do follow the story. There are other cases too, but typically we tend to live a hypothesis-based approach. This means that you say quite early on what the solution is and what should be done, based on your experience with markets and consumers as well as market circumstances. When the hypothesis-based approach is pursued and when there is a clear and well-founded assumption that one will make a certain recommendation, then it is often the case that the analyses that are made and shown are in fact selected so as to confirm the hypothesis.

This rule was of course not set in stone. In fact some consultants I interviewed subsequently argued that at times the initial hypothesis would be discarded or altered if certain analyses called for it. However, many also marvelled at how often this hypothesis turned out to be true. Business knowledge was thus frequently considered to be embodied in partners and senior consultants, who had encountered a host of different work practices and who could condense their experience in these initial hypotheses, even if detailed analyses had not yet been carried out. In our case, the severe time constraints under which our project was carried out and the agreement between senior partners and *board* members that further staff was not needed made changes to the *first-day-hypothesis* unlikely.

By the end of our project, the *board* stuck to its overall plan of reducing the planned staff increases, making only minor concessions to selected divisions. Broadly speaking, it followed its plan set out from the beginning. Yet, on a divisional level, our work had influenced the *board's* decisions. Our data-gathering exercise, which the head of *Sales and Marketing* had attempted to ignore, was eventually used to decide that his staff demands had been excessive. In fact, the results had shown that his division was not working as well as it was supposed to, leading to a follow-up project to improve *sales* performance. At the same time, our interaction with the head of HR, who had argued that her division was too small, had had unforeseen effects. She had decided to bypass us after our *meeting*, spoke directly with the *board* and – in spite of the large relative increases of staff she had called for – got what she wanted. The greatest loser in this exercise was the *Controlling* division, whose uncharismatic senior manager had once again proven to the *board* that he was not as confident about his numbers as he should have been. In yet another act of autopoiesis, this led to a second follow-up project in which *Controlling* reports to the *board* would be redesigned with our help.

This would mean that Sofia would continue working with this insurance client over the months to come. She had a particularly good relationship with the *board* member who had hired her in the first place and would happily continue to work for this particular client. Eventually she would continue working her way up internal consulting hierarchies, attempting to foster closer relationships with potential project commissioners in the healthcare sector. Anne, on the other hand, would soon begin to seriously struggle with the constant work pressure and stop working as a consultant altogether. As she told me in an interview several months later, the constant speed of the work and the permanent feeling of being somehow inadequate for the tasks at hand would eventually render her less self-secure. Her long-lasting illness that was to follow made me think back to her frequent remarks concerning the absurdities of our work. I had shared that feeling of the absurd with Anne at the time, but I believe that we had responded to it in different ways. She tried to work as a consultant in spite of it until she could not go on. I, on the other hand, used it to guide my ethnographic inquiry, gaining distance to our work by turning it into an object of study.

Anthropologists have long made use of their status as strangers in order to generate insights about the people with whom they live and work (Malinowski 2002; Boas as described by Mead 1973: 13; Geertz 1973). By travelling from one geographical area to another, they experienced the normality of others as strange and – if they engaged in fieldwork for long enough – probably began to think of their own cultural background as strange as well. It is this unsettling experience that has motivated and elucidated much of their inquiry, developing what were initially few scattered interests into fully developed pieces of research. Thereby, ethnographic work has been part of a long history of social research that used locational change as a tool for productive socio-epistemic alienation (Simmel 1908). I use the term 'productive' here because the experience of strangeness in and of itself is not enough to motivate ethnographic enquiry. Strangeness can be shrugged off, laughed at, used as an incentive to change oneself or it may make others seem abject and repulsive. Anthropologists, however, engage with it predominantly by trying to empirically investigate the world.

In its reliance on travel, socio-epistemic strangeness or the de-centring of one's own perspective used to be manifest in the concept of exoticism (Karpferer 2013). Yet, anthropologists have forcefully discarded 'the exotic' as a heuristic category, as part of a healthy and necessary postcolonial attempt at greater self-awareness (MacClancy 2002; Said 2003). What is more, the 'exotic' makes for a poor heuristic device nowadays, as an increasing number of anthropologists have grown up in the society that they decide to study, work in the institutions that they investigate or may be strongly politically involved in their field sites before beginning an anthropology degree (Gupta and Ferguson 1997).

However, this does not mean that the more general experience of strangeness does not remain foundational for intellectual enquiry. Camus (1955) tried to establish the absurd as one of the key experiences of intellectual inquiry in general. He argued that it arises from a tension between world and subject in which humans remain incapable of grasping the full meaning of the existence they lead. The origins of his understanding of the absurd may not be transposable cross-culturally as they are grounded in a strong sense of individualism and an obsession with death as the end of earthly life. The absurd might also not be a guiding instantiation of strangeness in societies in which human beings are considered different by definition (e.g. Stasch 2009). Nevertheless, following the frequent allusions to absurdity in my field site, I think it might find a wide enough applicability within Western contexts to be of use for anthropologists studying elites.

The suggestion that the absurd may be particularly apt for the study of Western elites is based on the conviction that human capabilities are fairly equally distributed. This belief, in conjunction with radical and often suddenly appearing divergences of status and class (Carrier and Kalb 2015), may establish the absurd as one of the key manifestations of strangeness that drive ethnographic inquiry in the twenty-first century. It certainly was a feeling that many of my colleagues and interviewees expressed after entering the world of management consulting right out of college. Nader (1972: 2) reminded us that early American anthropology was the result of indignation over social inequality. I hold a feeling of 'absurdity' to move us into this direction. Its strong affective connotations point to the fact that people will actively respond to this particular instantiation of strangeness in one way or another. At the same time the term is not quite as strong as, for example, 'indignation' which is more closely related to direct political activism (Comaroff and Comaroff 1999: 283). Perceiving the world as absurd is an ongoing, morally and emotionally charged manifestation of strangeness and surprise, and the chapters in this book are in fact based around different aspects of abstract labour that have been considered absurd by several of my colleagues.

Conclusion

This chapter has argued that the work of management consultants is abstract, since it constantly confronts them with the fundamental problem of not having a concrete referent against which to test the validity of their representations. Consultants try to analyse entire companies or business divisions, yet they do not know most employees, their social relationships, work routines, the material set-ups in which they operate or the competing ideas that guide their behaviour. They are thus part of the wider managerial condition in contemporary capitalism in which managers attempt to govern the 'imagined communities' that are business corporations.

Management consulting is abstract in the additional sense of remaining fundamentally opaque. This is partially due to the technology that consultants use. Both Excel and PowerPoint seamlessly combine elements of rhetoric and epistemology. In addition, neither technology is geared at providing clarity for outsiders, since Excel spreadsheets often need to be explained, while PowerPoint documents primarily serve the purposes of verbal presentation. In comparison with fully formed written texts, both technologies deal to a much greater extent in interpretative freedom. Moreover, consultants can be considered agents of opacity themselves as they rarely interact with the people whose working lives they are trying to analyse and alter.

The chapter has also pointed to two additional features of abstract labour. First, it has autopoietic qualities, in that an absent referent can always be described further. Moreover, in the absence of an immediately observable work product, slides meant as summaries of our analyses needed to be produced as they were the only material proof for the work we did. At the same time, it has pointed to the absurd as a useful heuristic for the study of social elites in Western contexts. Provided that an anthropologist encounters her environment with a belief in similar capacities of people, the absurd may be that instantiation of strangeness that arises when we encounter striking inequality or patterns of human behaviour that seem to make no sense and that gear us into some kind of action.

CHAPTER FIVE

Selves and Commodities

While the previous three chapters have outlined the basic features of abstract labour, this one and the next will explore the question why privileged young women and men with plenty of job opportunities would be willing, even eager, to submit to it. After all, we have seen so far that management consulting did not stand in high social esteem in the German general public, the job did not leave a tangible work product, and it required a strict submission to temporal constraints that left barely any time for family and friends. In addition, I would hold that consulting had relatively little romantic appeal. My colleagues and I spent most of our time in unflattering team rooms, writing plans about somewhat mundane questions such as how to reduce the cost of car door production, how to make tobacco advertising more efficient or how to increase the profit margin made on women buying washing powder. It is hard to get truly passionate about the content of these questions, which in turn makes it difficult to establish consulting as a vocation (Weber 2004a).

In the light of these somewhat unattractive features of the industry, this chapter will ask where the appeal of it may lie, providing a boardroom twist to the timeless question 'what makes people work'. Harris (2007) had provided one answer, with reference to the work of Aymara-speaking peasants in the Andes. For them, she argued, work was marked by its positive value as it affirmed human personhood and community. This chapter will ask to what extent this may also have been true in the boardroom context of German management consultants. It will argue that work was here equally important for the constitution of personhood, in that it was seen as a primary site for employee self-improvement (cf. Rose 1999). This mirrors US trends of self-branding (Gershon 2016) as much as German cultural and political notions of self-management (Gingrich 1998; ibid.). In consulting, the 'self', that is, the aspect of personhood that was seen to be actualized, was marked by two main features. It foregrounded the particular aspects of human existence, as well as autonomy in the sense of defining the means and the purposes of one's own activity. As a particularly abstract form of labour, consulting lent itself to ideas of self-improvement. Since consultants mostly worked on intangible social relationships in constantly changing work environments, the embodied self provided them with an observable and lasting object at which their activity could be geared. Moreover, constituting the self as the legitimate end of work activity endowed consulting with a moral force or 'inner strength' that it might otherwise lack (Ong 2006: 171ff.), thereby elevating work to more than just employment.

However, this chapter will also outline the limits of conceiving of consulting in this way. In fact, personhood in this corporate setting turns out to be essentially twofold, in that consultants were always also understood to be 'commodities'. This stood in direct conceptual and moral tension to their 'selves', in that it emphasized the general aspects of their being and constructed them as means to a series of economic ends that were not of their own making. This aspect of who they were in the corporate setting was mostly conceived of as demoralizing, often leading consultants to question whether their jobs were truly fulfilling enough.

Consultancy companies dealt with this split nature of personhood via a variety of 'moralistic technologies', which included self-discovery questionnaires, training seminars and *feedback* routines. These ensured that work practices did not simply express pre-existing moral convictions but instead actively elicited them. They aimed to foreground the compatibilities between improving the self and being a commodity. In the long run, the most successful consultants were those for whom the difference between self and commodity remained relatively unimportant. Others, for whom this discrepancy of personhood became too stark, either developed a cynical attitude vis-à-vis the notion of work-based self-improvement or changed job to find a more balanced sense of personhood elsewhere.

Caveat: Why not focus on salaries?

Before describing the ways in which consulting was part of wider projects of self-improvement, I would like to acknowledge the elephant in the room, namely that consultants work in order to earn money. In a profession in which women and men right out of college could make between €60k and €90k per year before tax, salaries were undeniably a crucial driving force. These vast amounts of money, combined with free telephones, work laptops, air miles, hotel membership points, food and transport expenses, were not available in most other professions, and directly elevated management consultants fresh out of college into Germany's top 10 per cent of income earners. However, I wish to focus here on the wider category of self-improvement as motivating their activity, for three main reasons.

On the one hand, it has long been established in anthropology that people do not react to economic incentives in a spasmodic fashion (cf. Thompson 1971). High salaries can neither explain why my colleagues chose this line of work over better paid alternatives nor explain why they would not simply take the money and work a little less. In fact, most of my colleagues and interview partners stressed that they did not consider their *hourly* pay to be particularly high at all, when compared to the middle and upper management jobs held by many of their clients. They were also convinced that, if they really wanted to get rich, they could work in finance (where they had often gained some previous work experience), and that if they had desired a much easier but still well-paying job, they could have applied to one of Germany's many blue-chip companies or midsize manufacturers.

On the other hand, receiving large salaries often seemed perfectly in line with projects of self-improvement. While some of my colleagues explained that they would use their earnings to build a family home or pay for their children's education, many others seemed to visibly enjoy spending their salaries directly on themselves. Every so often, consultants could take time out between projects, and when they did, Facebook posts, which displayed their exotic holiday locations, beautiful cars and pricey hobbies such as horse riding or diving, were the norm. Regardless of different forms of spending, even the mere act of getting paid a lot in and of itself seemed to matter to ideas of self-betterment. While my colleagues never bragged about pay or bonuses, economic productivity and self-worth have traditionally been closely linked in Germany. In so far as getting paid a large salary was assumed to be positively correlated with economic productivity, receiving it constituted an act of recognition, turning money into a token of esteem. After all, large salaries communicated that consulting somehow had to be an extraordinarily productive activity. Thus, a focus on salaries does not stand in opposition to the argument presented here; it simply leaves out what a salary might stand for in this particular social setting.

Lastly, consultancy companies went through constant and surprisingly elaborate efforts to construct their profession as more than just a means to earn large amounts of money. It is these startling efforts that I will turn to now.

Consulting as self-improvement

During my first consulting project, I worked for a company in the German energy sector together with *Team Leader* Tom. He was in his late twenties, just like myself, but he did not seem this young to me at first. He came from an upper-class family in the South of Europe, and his habitus and extensive experience as a consultant and previously as a private sector investor had endowed him with some of the mannerisms that I associated with men in their mid-forties. Thus, he was known to dress impeccably, he generally talked as if he was describing established matters of fact, he knew how to keep his calm in situations of stress and he was not afraid to joke with or assert his authority over people who were twice his age. This behaviour stood in quite some contrast to his youth, giving him an aura of agelessness and allowing him to gain the sympathy of some of our much older clients, who were all men between 40 and 60.

In private moments, Tom and I established a personal, at times almost intimate, relationship. We had a shared interest in university life, neither of us had children and our common knowledge of pop culture clearly established us as members of the same age group. We often discussed personal matters such as girlfriend concerns, weekend visits to art galleries and Tom's problem that some of his family members who held public office currently found themselves under great media scrutiny related to the European sovereign debt crisis. After days of conversing with clients about business matters and football matches, Tom appeared to enjoy our occasional chats about European politics. As a well-travelled polyglot who had spent his university education in Belgium, he also seemed to appreciate that I had received an education abroad.

During these moments, Tom and I related to one another as selves. He shared with me aspects of his personal history, such as that he had moved away from his former job in finance to have more social interaction with clients and colleagues. He also considered consulting to be a helpful background if ever he wanted to embark on a political career or if he wanted to find work beyond consulting in one of the many client companies that he was getting to know over time. The same was true for me, as I had become a consultant primarily to pay off my student debts and to learn what work in the private sector had to teach me. For me as for many of my colleagues, consulting was a means to improve my financial situation and to learn about previously unknown aspects of the economy. In these instances, Tom and I framed our jobs – as did most of my interviewees – in the light of wider projects of self-improvement.

The fact that we conceived of our jobs in these terms was not coincidental, as consultancy companies relentlessly emphasized that they helped their employees in their personal development. One of the means by which this was supposed to be ensured were mentors, who, according to consulting websites were supposed to guide, inspire and coach employees on their way to the next career step and during the personal development involved with it (BCG 2015a). At Strategy Partners, mentoring was taken very seriously for both junior and senior consultants, yet the role of mentors was highly ambiguous. On the one hand, they were supposed to help their colleagues develop their professional career. When project objectives were not met or when consultants were unclear which project to take on next, the mentor should be their first point of contact. Mentors helped consultants build an 'experience profile' as it was called, which combined expertise and social ties in a specific economic sector with a breath of experience from other industries. By specializing in one or two economic sectors over time, consultants could get to know partners and *team leaders* who frequently worked within them and who would then 'have them on their radar' when assembling teams for further projects. We would thereby make ourselves legible for this flexible project-based work environment (Gershon 2016). At the same time, in an explicit performance of flexibility (Martin 1994), a specialized consultant should also try working in a largely unknown industry at least once, for example, by picking an automotive project after having worked on two projects in banking. Each project should thus ideally be chosen in the light of a clear career pathway oriented towards long-term career goals. The mentor was supposed to help younger consultants in this process, guiding them on the wisest project choices in the light of professional advancement.

At the same time, however, a mentor should help consultants in their personal development. As my own mentor told me during our first *meeting*, his job was to ensure that I would find the work that 'best suited me' in the company. He encouraged me to think about what I wanted, rather than just what the company might want and to proactively make my work as a consultant supportive of the personal goals that I had set for myself. He also stressed that, while our relation could remain strictly professional, he had become close friends with past mentees and that such a development was certainly possible. Consultancy companies thereby actively sought to position mentors as guides on a very intimate level of self-improvement. At times this was made explicit, when employees in advertisements said phrases such as 'by believing in me [my mentor] has made me believe in myself' (Bain & Company 2015: min 1.30). At other times, consultancy companies played with ambiguity by basing career descriptions around very general notions such as 'grow' (Boston Consulting Group's recruiting slogan up until 2015) or 'exploring the opportunities you have' (Roland Berger 2014). These vague notions of personal improvement fostered the widespread conviction that career development should be part of personal progress.

A second way in which consulting was to be turned into a form of self-betterment was the numerous training courses in which hired coaches and company officials repeated to us in a programmatic fashion that our job was not to blindly submit to the demands of partners or senior colleagues, but to actively turn them into something beneficial for our own personal lives. We were told that we should be defiant in choosing projects and we should not constantly bow to the wishes of partners or *team leaders*, whose requests were ultimately infinite in nature. Instead, coaches and motivational speakers reminded us that we were all different people with individual characteristics that needed to be respected. This attitude was reinforced through exercises designed to help us find out who we really were and what we really wanted.

One such exercise was entitled 'I give myself an A'. In it, we were asked to write a letter to our 'future selves', in which we congratulated 'them' for having achieved whatever life-goals we deemed worthy at the point of writing. The letters were then sealed, collected and a few months later sent back to us at work, so that we could check whether we were still in touch with our 'former selves'. On another corporate training, we were given a stack of flashcards denoting abstract values such as 'love', 'family' or 'friendship' and each of us had to choose a limited number of them and consider why they picked the specific flashcards over other options. During one training retreat we even built our hopes for our personal future in Lego. Such exercises were far removed from direct career advancement. Instead, they were meant to allow us to assess our jobs in the light of personal projects of self-improvement. One of my colleagues who left consulting for a career in private equity management assured me that the latter was 'a lot less touchy-feely' and that the answer to any kind of personal development concern there would simply be *you cannot climb a ladder with one hand in your pocket*, that is, a reference to hard work and career advancement that ignored questions of personal improvement altogether.

Many of my colleagues and interviewees in consulting had seemed to take on the idea of self-improvement. In asking them what they enjoyed about their jobs, they mostly answered that they had 'learned so much' or that they had 'such a steep learning curve'. Such answers expressed a host of possible meanings. First, the term 'learning' could refer to the act of gradually acquiring factual knowledge about one or several particular industries. During my time as a consultant, for example, I gained some knowledge about how health insurance companies and paper mills operate, as well as who the 'major players' in the global market for medical device manufacturing were. Whether or not this kind of knowledge acquisition was actually appreciated by all consultants is – to say the least – doubtful. While some of my interviewees did stress that they had begun to learn about new and unforeseen topics of interest, most others echoed the laconic statement of my colleague and friend Jonathan, who remarked over dinner at his flat in Berlin once that '*content-wise* you do not really learn anything at all'. In the rush of constant delivery it was hard to absorb anything of interest, as consultants had too little time to think about their daily tasks as part of wider empirical phenomena or to even develop theoretical questions around them.

Secondly, on a more general level, however, many consultants were convinced that they had gained a more profound sense of how the business world operated. On the one hand, they had spoken to managers of many walks of life and figured out which concerns were important to them and which kinds of habitus they had come to develop over time. On the other hand, they had gained a greater sensibility of the complexities of global industrial capitalism. They had developed a heightened awareness that behind each mundane object that surrounded them there were several industries that employed thousands of men and women who were physically, mentally and emotionally involved in its existence. My colleagues thus often seemed to marvel at the awe-inspiring intricacy of social organization involved in contemporary economic production, a fact that was appreciated by almost everyone I talked to.

Thirdly, and most importantly, the notion of 'having learned so much' pointed to learning about who oneself really was. Take Martina's response to the question of how she has changed personally during her time as a consultant:

> I believe that I have learned a lot over the past two years. It has made me more mature in a way. I have learned much about the effect that my words and actions have on others. I think that you learn how to work more efficiently and that you apply this knowledge. I have also learnt about myself in the sense of what makes me happy regarding the opposition of private life and work life. ... I have learned that work and career alone are not enough to make me happy and that I miss relationships and hobbies when they are gone.

This understanding of the job as the primary means through which to learn about and improve oneself was so important that it trumped high pay as a motivating factor. Several of my colleagues and interview partners agreed that they had opted for consulting because its 'steep learning curve' meant learning a great amount of things in the shortest possible time, and large companies, where alternative careers seemed to loom, were often depicted as less stimulating and less 'challenging'.

First limits to self-improvement

Success in framing management consultancy as conducive to self-improvement was of course not guaranteed. People who rejected consulting job offers and those who left the profession behind often did so because self-improvement was better served elsewhere. One former consultant who had decided to quit her job told me that she was 'very happy to learn a lot' but that she did not mind 'learning it all a little slower' if this meant having some more private time. Another, who did not take up a consulting job offer in spite of having gone through a very demanding internship, told me that she did not believe that what she learnt in consulting could not be learnt elsewhere. Knowledge of how to run successful presentations and workshops or of how to write concise and professional sounding emails, she argued, could be acquired in smaller and much more personal work settings as well. Finally, a young lawyer who had started the job with me and quit only after a few months later to work at a law firm argued that he would learn the same things about himself at the law firm, while also being actually interested in the cases he studied.

Indeed, internal estimates suggested that most consultants left their jobs after just a few years. Most of my colleagues who left their jobs decided to take up leadership positions in Berlin's booming internet *start-up* sector. Interviews with them showed that they were convinced that they could learn lessons there that consultancy work simply could not provide them with, as they now had to lead and motivate employees who were a lot less eager to 'perform' ('performen'), not least because these employees had substantial interests outside of work. Moreover, the ex-consultants now held greater responsibility for the success of whatever *start-up* firm they were trying to make profitable, rendering their work somewhat less abstract. As one of them put it in an interview, now that he was leading a *start-up* he was 'feeling the winds of the market' rather than just talking about them.

Some of the more saddening developments occurred when consulting was indeed successfully established as the primary means of self-improvement, but when individual employees either decided or were told that they were not fit to continue the job. Here character was clearly gambled as part of labour (cf. Zaloom 2006b: 95). Take this interview with Carmen, a former management consultant who had been asked to leave her job after only a few months:

> Carmen: I used to think that as long as I try hard, things will eventually work out. However, I really hit the limits of my own abilities [in management consulting]. ... I had never reached my own limits and I used to always look at people funny when they did not get things done, because for me, that was *easy*. But once you fall on your face, you realise what your limits are and that they are distributed unevenly for everyone. That got me off my high horse.....
> Author: Would you take up your former job again?
> Carmen: I do not want to miss it, yet in hindsight, with what I know now I am not sure I would do it again because in many respects it was simply shit; both emotionally and psychologically. I am an insecure person and I take it personally when my *Team Leader* tells me: Your PowerPoint sucks, do it again ...
> Author: How do you think your life will change with your new job [as an in-house consultant for a German blue-chip company]?
> Carmen: There are hard changes, such as working less and travelling less. I hope I can regain my self-confidence, both in my abilities and in the quality of my work. And I hope to be successful at what I do. It's like failing at Harvard and going to an easier university afterwards, hoping that you will be part of the best there.

Throughout our interview, Carmen's regretful remarks at leaving her former job were accompanied by observations at how her new colleagues were comparatively less well trained, less intelligent and less motivated. She clearly saw her move to her new job as a step down that would 'slow down' her personal development.

Consultants as commodities

A few weeks into my first project as a management consultant, I told Tom the delicate news that I wanted to be taken off our team. It was very late at night and we were sitting in a taxi together, returning to our hotel after a long and somewhat draining *meeting* with clients. During the taxi ride, Tom and I had been discussing how the *meeting* had gone and what we needed to work on next. Then there were no other work-related topics to discuss. I seized the opportunity and told Tom that I wanted to be placed on a different project. My reason was that several thousands of employees were going to lose their jobs as part of it. I argued that while this might well be necessary so as to 'save' their company, it might also not be, and without clarity on the matter I did not want to remain involved.

Tom seemed to understand my reservations but made a strong morally inflected case for me to stay on the team. For him the circumstances under which we were operating were clear. The share price of our client had plummeted and our job was to help management bring it back up again. If we failed to do so, our client ran the risk of suffering a 'hostile takeover' from competing corporations, in which case many more employees risked losing their jobs. He also argued that the share price of our client was reflected in the investments of pension funds, whose growth we were working for. Apart from share price developments, Tom was equally convinced that our client desperately needed 'complete restructuring'. He knew that they 'wasted' a lot of money because of unnecessary administrative work, poor supply management and a generally disorganized coordination of business activities. Tom emphasized the point that the business units we were responsible for needed to become 'lean' quickly (cf. Womack, Jones and Roos 1990), otherwise our client would perish in the long run.

When moral considerations linked to share prices and productive efficiency failed to convince me, Tom argued that it was not our fault that, in this post-Fukushima environment, times were tough in the German energy sector. Client shares had taken a great hit after the nuclear meltdown of the Fukushima-Daiichi Power Plant in March 2011. Japan's nuclear catastrophe had led Germany's chancellor Angela Merkel to carry out one of the most radical U-turns in the country's recent political history. Merkel, who had forcefully argued that nuclear energy was an important 'bridge technology',[1] vital for increasing Germany's renewable energy mix (CDU, CSU and FDP 2009: 29), now declared that she could no longer accept the 'residual risk'[2] inherent in all nuclear energy production (Merkel 2011). As a result, her coalition government had surprisingly sped up the nuclear energy phase-out, much to the detriment of many established energy providers.

I remained unconvinced and after a very honest and personal discussion Tom agreed to have me positioned elsewhere. He did, however, remind me of one thing.

> You know, this is a very prestigious project and many of our colleagues would love to work on it. Sure, you can try to get yourself placed on a different one but in the end you are just a commodity. You can sit on the shelf, wave your arms around and shout 'pick me, pick me', but I am the one doing the shopping and I decide on which project I want to place you. So it is not guaranteed that you will find a better one.

I took the calm and slightly humorous tone with which Tom told me that I was 'just a commodity' to imply that he was sharing a deep and important insight with me. He was neither making a threat nor trying to insult me. Instead, I believe that he had used a moment of trust that we had created in the course of our conversation to enlighten me of a fundamental truth about our profession.

Economic anthropologists have traditionally analysed commodities in opposition to gifts, which has led them to define the former in terms of the presence of markets (Mauss 1990: 5), their reference to prices (Stewart 1997: 151), their greater kinship distance (Sahlins 1972: 196ff.), the absence of reciprocity in their exchange and the relationships between objects that they bring about (Gregory 1982, 1994: 911). Yet, Tom's argument that I and by extension most junior consultants were just commodities presented it as an aspect of personhood, putting it into a new comparative light. Unwittingly, Tom's use of the term commodity harked back to Marx's early analyses of capitalism, where 'labour produces not only commodities; it produces itself and the worker as a *commodity* – and this at the same rate at which it produces commodities in general' (Marx 1988: 71). While Marx asserted early on that persons could be commodities, his idea of the commodity fetish stood at odds with this view, as it relied on a clear conceptual opposition of persons and things. Thus he spoke about a commodity fetish when the 'social relations between men' were confused with the relations between things and *vice versa* (Marx 2005). I take Marx to mean that being a commodity is an aspect of personhood of workers under capitalism, one that it is always surpassed by some form of excess, which means the reduction of employees to their commodity-like aspects is a mistake. On the basis of this, the following paragraphs outline what exactly was meant by the term commodity with reference to personhood. They will show that it highlighted the general aspects of a person and described the person as a means to ends that lay outside of her purview.

When Tom had first decided to recruit me for his project, he had taken the time to research my background on our company's intranet, which featured Facebook-like overviews of all consulting staff. In it, each consultant was represented as a series of similar and thereby comparable features, including a standardized profile picture, the time we had spent as consultants, the trainings we had received, the projects we had been on, links to peers and former colleagues, and the technical expertise we had developed. With all major elements of the site pointing to our potential functional capabilities, these websites were meant to convey to the person browsing them what type of project we would be most suitable for. In addition, Tom also knew my price (something I was oblivious of at the time). As a neophyte, Tom knew that I technically worked for free, since my first months as a consultant meant that I was mostly placed on projects for training purposes without incurring costs for his project budget.

Once on the team, Tom and I also built what can be described as a professional relationship. He taught me how to improve my PowerPoint slides and Excel modelling abilities. He showed me where to find information on our company's intranet and how to prioritize my work properly. He even imparted to me a series of somewhat Machiavellian lessons about proper management consultant behaviour. Thus, he taught me how to carry out useful interviews ('you must know what you want to get out of the interview from the start'), shared with me which clients he considered intelligent, who were 'complete idiots' and who might be 'useful number crunchers'. Every now and then, he even took the time to explain to me when to give support to clients and when to 'let them destroy themselves' in front of their bosses by allowing them to obviate their incompetence in documents or presentations.

In addition, Tom had taught me how to work together as a team. For example, during one of our many conference calls with clients, I had positively acknowledged the proposition of a client that stood at odds with one of Tom's ideas. Tom immediately gave me a follow-up call. Such one-to-one conversations right after telephone conferences with clients were a common technique, meant to ensure that we agreed on the main results of a conversation and immediately defined the work activities that needed to follow. This time, however, Tom began the call with some *direct feedback*, telling me that 'we must never disagree in front of the client'. We should disagree on matters when we were on our own, but whenever clients were present, we needed to 'act as one'. *Teamwork* and the performance of unity were more important in these situations than contributions of content. In all of these instances, Tom was relating to me as an instantiation of my institutional role.

Ultimately, this role constituted the condition of our collaboration and led Tom to teach me how to properly do my work. So, what did Tom mean when he reminded me of the fact that I was 'just a commodity'? I believe that he tried to highlight that my corporate role stood in contrast with and ultimately trumped my characteristics as 'a self'. His example of a commodity, sitting on the shelf, waving its arms around and shouting 'pick me, pick me', pointed to the relative powerlessness of junior consultants within the institution they were working for. Tom could pick them at leisure from the virtual shelf and place them on his projects. This would happen regardless of their will or individual decisions. It also implied the inversion of the means–ends relationship between worker and job. In his example, junior consultants constituted the means to a series of ends that were not of their own making. Their institutional role would force them to bow to the differing prerogatives that existed within the company. It was left unclear whether these were the desires of their teams, of partners or of the company as a whole, but they were somehow connected to how the job was done and would eventually outplay whatever personal goals they might have set for themselves.

Thus, part of being a consultant meant renouncing projects of self-improvement, not necessarily for the sake of self-betterment but simply because it was what the job required. They had to be anethical in the sense of submitting themselves completely, not to the divine (Faubion 2014: 443) but to the work they did as instantiated by the corporate form. Many of the above-mentioned instances of Tom's teachings were indicative of this. Each time he taught me a lesson he both provided me with information on how things could be done and disciplined me with some considerable normative fervour into how things should be done so as to properly fulfil the functions that had been predefined for me. I was now the means to the company's ends rather than the other way round.

On the one hand, this inversion of the means–ends relationship between person and job clearly referred to markets. In Tom's metaphor, consultants were means to the specific end of earning money. In fact, all of the members of our team could be seen as commodities that were sold or rented out to clients, a fact that some colleagues pointed out when referring to our job as mere *body leasing*. They would argue in private that our work was only about the money and that anyone who said otherwise was either deluded or dishonest. The reader might find the point that consultants work mostly for money a bit trite, but it stands in notable contrast to the notions of servitude and managerial support that equally pervaded consultancy rhetoric and thought.

In fact the more senior consultants often highlighted that they considered it 'an honour' to 'serve', 'support' or 'help' clients. Moreover, they hardly ever addressed the monetary aspects of the consultant–client relationships. We had been taught to dodge questions about salaries by clients and outsiders by not ever mentioning exact figures. Instead, we should answer along the lines of 'consultants earn as much as well-earning lawyers'. Clients sometimes asked very openly how much we earned and how much we cost their company, but we were not allowed to answer the first question, and often were in no position to answer the second. The silence around money was such that even lower-level consultants were never officially told how much a client company paid for them. Precise information regarding the make-up of our projects, revenues, costs or profits was simply not made available. All that low- and mid-level consultants knew for sure was that they were 'expensive' and had to work hard because of it. This is why Tom's reference to being a commodity was particularly striking as it implied that all the professed ideas about serving or supporting our clients were mere lip service.

Apart from an inversion of means and ends, the term 'commodity' had the additional meaning of stressing the general over the particular. In business parlance, the concept 'commodity' often referred to the process of 'commoditization', a process by which goods on the market turn from being highly coveted and highly priced luxuries to 'mere commodities' that customers value little and refused to spend significant amounts of money on (Schrage 2007). While anthropologists are keenly aware of commodi*fication* as a process by which objects are placed on the market and thereby receive monetary value, commodi*tization* points to a development whereby market value is diminished. In its instance then, the term commodity is a reference to worthlessness and seeing consultants as commodities meant seeing them as things that were not in fact too valuable. This view was at times echoed by my colleagues in private, when they insisted that anyone could do this their job 'as long as they kept on accepting more work and behaved like a good soldier'.

The loss of market value with which commoditization is associated is not usually linked to a loss in the quality of a thing, a change in consumer preferences or a product's sudden uselessness. Instead, commoditization is said to occur when things can be *replaced* more easily than before. As a recent publication by a consultancy firm argued, a 'commodity trap' describes a situation where even complex products and services are downgraded to 'commodities, with limited differentiation and where competition is primarily price-based' (Roland Berger 2014b). In most other publications on the subject, the problem for why things or products turned into commodities was described as one of 'limited differentiation' (e.g. Forbes 2010; Quelch 2007). It was when a thing became indistinguishable as compared to others that it was truly a commodity. Once again, replaceability was invoked. Hence, Tom's point also seemed to be that in our roles as consultants, we were ultimately replaceable. Several features of our work, such as mentoring, life-advice exercises and personal conversations, might have made us feel as though we were appreciated for being truly unique, yet Tom implied that we were also always general enough to replace one another.

Several features of management consulting emphasized the general aspects of our selves that facilitated personal replaceability.

First, a series of technologies was marshalled to make human replacement happen. In the environment of hyper-mobility in which we operated (see introduction), the physical restraints on replacing one consultant with another had been largely overcome. If five European consultants and equipment were needed at a South African mining project within just a few days, their current physical location would usually not constitute a major impediment in getting them there. This meant that consultants based, for example, in South Africa could be more easily replaced with those from other countries. My colleague's English was mostly good enough to work abroad, the intranet presented us in always the same functionalist format, thereby facilitating the commensuration of who we were with reference to the purposes that our superiors had in mind. These technologies were given symbolic support in that we wore mostly very similar outfits, a fact that was derided by clients who likened my colleagues and me on one project to penguins, indistinguishable to the untrained eye.

Secondly, the idea that managerial work was a craft on its own that could meaningfully be abstracted from its objects meant that most consulting could be done without detailed prior knowledge of the industries in question. If a team needed to work in an automotive *marketing* project, it would at times occur that none of the junior consultants and not even the *team leader* had worked in the automotive industry or in *marketing* before. This circumstance made a project harder, but not impossible. Thus, consultants who were versed in a particular topic could often be replaced with those largely ignorant of it, and there was much less of a need to look for that one expert who had twenty years or more of industry experience.

Thirdly, major management consultancies were organized along structures marked by simplicity and clear hierarchical order, which distinguished their staff along a few steps of institutional positioning. What mattered most of all in the daily work was whether somebody was a (junior or senior) consultant, a *team leader* or a partner. While partners liaised with senior clients, assembled teams and provided rough outlines of what analyses would be carried out, they needed somebody lower in the hierarchy, who actually produced the required analyses and documents for them. If the project was very small, partners could work with just one consultant. If it was large, a junior partner, several *team leaders* and further low-level consultants got involved. This very basic, vertical structure allowed teams of employees who did not know one another to be deployed together and to begin working within just a few hours. A point that several of my employees pointed out was that these commodifying and commoditizing features of our work resembled at least in part the structure of the military.

To sum up, consultants were as much commodities as they were selves and this split in their personhood was marked by two main tensions. The first one was that of inverted means–ends relationships, in which consultants had to submit to requests that were not of their own making (as commodities), while using their job to their own ends (as selves). The second was that consultants were made up of general characteristics (as commodities), frequently of a functionalist bent, as much as of particular ones (as selves). A series of technologies around commensuration, communication and mobility, the view of consulting as an abstract craft and strong, yet simple institutional hierarchies foregrounded the general aspects of consultant personhood, thereby enabling individual replaceability. Being a commodity thus stood in stark contrast to the otherwise popular view that consulting would enable us to improve our highly particular selves.

In the following paragraphs I will describe how consultancy companies dealt with this twofold tension. The argument will be that Strategy Partners tried to turn both selves and commodities into one and the same.

Selves and commodities

The following section will investigate two moralistic technologies that were meant to merge the self and commodity, namely a personality test, called the 'Myers-Briggs Type Indicator' (MBTI) and corporate *feedback*. While the MBTI investigated the seemingly unchangeable aspects of the self, asking how they may be put to use for a corporation, *feedback* tackled the changeable aspects of the self with the aim of altering them in the light of job requirements.

At one of my initial training courses, I was introduced to novel methods of thinking about myself and other people. From here on out, we were supposed to be familiar with the MBTI, a personality test developed in the United States during the 1940s by Katharine

Cook Briggs and her daughter Isabel Briggs Myers. On the basis of over 80 self-assessment questions, it provided a classificatory framework through which to understand self and others.

Modern-day references to the MBTI often emphasize its basis in Carl Jung's book on psychological types.[3] In it, Jung had classified people on the basis of the attitude they took towards objects (Jung 1921: 2). According to him, introverts tended to retreat from objects, while extraverts maintained an active relation to them. Thus, objects usually did not guide the attitudes of introverts but did influence those of extraverts. Jung continued by creating subgroups of introverts and extraverts, distinguishing them in terms of their judgement into 'thinking types', mostly governed by reflexive thought (ibid.: 13) and 'feeling types', who relied more on emotion and affect (ibid.: 9). He also differentiated them on the basis of their modes of perception into those predominantly influenced by the sensations they received (ibid.: 24–5) and those who depended more on unconscious intuition (ibid.: 26).

Jung's theory was not concerned with institutional affiliation or job performance, but rather with classifying human beings in general. Yet, in the early 1940s, Myers adapted his work to the much more pragmatic purposes of personnel selection. She altered it so as to classify people along four character dimensions, namely their perceptual orientation, ways of perceiving, mode of judgement and degree of rationality. Each of these was split into binary oppositions. People who fill out an MBTI personality test thus receive as a result a series of four letters, indicating whether they are predominantly extravert or introvert (E or I), whether they prefer sensual information or abstract thought (S or N), whether they come to judgements mostly through thought or feeling (T or F) and whether they are keen on planning or rather spontaneous (J or P). The proprietary indicator has become hugely popular in corporate environments. After the US Educational Testing Service abandoned it because of unfavourable internal reviews, it was acquired by Consulting Psychologist Press, which has marketed it to a variety of work settings in the business world, as well as to public, educational and religious institutions. Its continuing rise in popularity can be observed in the relative increase of the terms 'Myers-Briggs' and 'MBTI' in the English-speaking literature.[4]

The MBTI was presented to me via email. I received a link to an online questionnaire of eighty-eight questions that I was required to fill in before an introductory training week for early-career consultants. The questionnaire introduced it as an 'instrument [that] is a powerful and versatile indicator of personality type. It is widely used for individual, group and organisational development.' Questions were at times explicitly related to work ('When you have a special job to do, do you like to A. organise it carefully before you start, or B. find out what is necessary as you go along?') and at times extremely personal ('Do you usually A. show your feelings freely, or B. keep your feelings to yourself?'). They also included word pair associations ('Which word in each pair appeals to you more? A. sign B. symbol') and ended with a kind of meta-question ('Would you have liked to argue the meaning of A. a lot of these questions, or B. only a few?).

Arriving at the training, I was given a name tag that had the resulting four letters that defined my personality written on the bottom of it. The coaches who had organized the test took this classification very seriously, explaining that the indicator was a refinement of the work by eminent psychologist Jung and that it described our four most important character dimensions. Unfortunately, explaining these dimensions in detail turned out more difficult for them than expected. The coach explaining the test was confused about whether 'extravert' people actually were in fact loud and forthcoming in social situations or whether they simply 'recharged their batteries' while surrounded by others. She was also unclear whether the test actually described who we were, or – since it was based on self-assessment – who we thought we were, or even who we hoped or feared to be.

I refused to spend the training week with a tag on my clothing that classified me as a certain type of person, a fact that was somewhat problematic as many of the group exercises consisted of dividing us up according to the four letters we had received, giving us different tasks and then marvelling at the perceived differences in group-work results. My peers did not see a problem with these labels, but mostly enjoyed discovering and discussing their personality types. The MBTI seemed to encourage many, if not all, of my colleagues to think about themselves, and about how best they could work together with colleagues and clients who might have an MBTI profile different from their own. Even those colleagues who did not consider MBTI results to be correct appreciated that it made them think about themselves and others in novel ways. In this process, it was repeatedly pointed out that management consultants were far beyond average part of the ENTJ group, meaning that our dominant character traits were being extravert and intuitive, with a preference for thinking and judging. This statement could be read as much as an observation as it was a proud reassertion of who we were collectively.

The general message that thinking about ourselves and others in terms of the MBTI could be useful seemed to be generally accepted. The self-knowledge it brought to light would also improve us as employees. In fact, for several of my colleagues it remained very relevant to their subsequent work. Consider how junior consultant Michaela describes tools and techniques that make consultants good at what they do:

> I even find the *MBTI* very helpful. Right now, for example I am going through a total *clash* because my client is even more 'P' than me. My *Team Leader* is very 'J' and the two constantly get into fights. In this kind of situation, it is helpful when you can stand between the two to explain that you are also very much a 'P' and that you wholly understand how somebody reacts. ... All this is useful so as to be able to take on the perspective of other people.

In her description, the MBTI is as much a tool for cooperation as it is a description of herself. This double role is made explicit by the MBTI foundation, which writes on its website,

> When you understand your type preferences, you can approach your own work in a manner that best suits your style, including: how you manage your time, problem solving, best approaches for decision making, and dealing with stress. Knowledge of type can help you better understand the culture of the place you work, develop new skills, understand your participation in teams, and cope with change in the workplace. [At the same time] knowledge and understanding of the personality type ... can be a tool for personal growth, achieving balance, understanding self, and creating possibilities. ... Your personality type doesn't change over time, but each preference helps you in different ways, and to different degrees, as you move through your life.[5]

The MBTI has received sustained criticism from professional psychologists over the past decades, and most psychology textbooks dealing with the study of human personality make no reference to it (Lloyd 2012: 24). Critics have pointed out the lack of evidence that discontinuous personality types exist (Stricker and Ross 1962), the shaky match between test questions and personality type theory (Pittenger 1993a, 1993b), the limitations of its dichotomous rather than continuous preference scores (e.g. Boyle 1995) and MBTI's low retest-reliability (ibid.). They have also argued that other personality measures are more reliable (Furnham 1996) and that much of its popularity may be due to type descriptions being 'generally flattering and sufficiently vague' (Pittenger 1993b: 51). Even the popular press has reacted critically to its omnipresence in the management world, with *Fortune* magazine (2013) likening it to early-twentieth-century use of phrenology as part of career guidance, and the *Guardian* (2013) criticizing it as an unscientific moneymaking tool.

In the light of the strong backlash against it, one might ask why the MBTI and competing business-oriented personality tests[6] are becoming increasingly popular. The answer provided in this chapter is that these personality tests collapse the difference between middle-class workers as selves and as commodities. In my field site, MBTI squared the circle between the particularities of the self by allowing for sixteen distinct personality types, and the generality of being a commodity, by showing how each personality type could work well with every other one. Moreover, it suggested that the means–ends relationship between individual person and labour was in fact not diametrically opposed. After all, knowing ourselves via the MBTI would turn us into better people and better employees.

Feedback

A second moralistic technology by which the difference between self and commodity was collapsed was *feedback*, a widespread tool of US corporate capitalism (Ong 2006: 179). In the interview above, in which Michaela outlined the tools and techniques needed in consulting, she did not just mention the MBTI. She immediately went on to speak about *feedback* as a feature that set our work apart:

The *feedback* model is also extremely important as very many companies do not have a structured *feedback* process. They have an annual *review*, if that. Hearing during your day-to-day work what you do well or what you might do better is incredibly useful and that simply does not exist in most companies.

Feedback was given constantly in consultancy companies. It existed on an ad hoc basis, in a more formal setting every two to three weeks and after each project. As part of our initiatory training, we were taught through role play how to give and receive *feedback* in a structured manner. We subsequently practised it over several days in small teams of colleagues with whom we worked in groups during the training. The process involved mentioning positive as well as negative observations of someone else's work activity. It had to be specific and it had to refer to activities that could be changed, rather than fundamental personality traits. Receiving *feedback* meant not talking back and resisting urges of self-justification until a later point in time. In theory, *feedback* was given upwards and downwards either through face-to-face conversations or through online questionnaires. While *feedback* was clearly structured, it could nonetheless turn into an incredibly intimate exercise. On a few occasions, tears were shed during our training, especially when colleagues received a kind of *feedback* from one person that they had already received from someone else before. In those moments the exercise seemed to address the most intimate aspects of the self, laying bare weaknesses and vulnerabilities that my colleagues and I usually tried to hide from one another. Even days after receiving *feedback*, colleagues in the training camp would still refer back to it and highlight how eye-opening it had been and how much they had learnt about themselves.

Feedback was integral to the job, in that it influenced the grades that consultants would receive after each project. Project grades were combined into biannual ones, which in turn would decide their future in the company. As long as consultants receive a grade that indicated that they were *on track*, they would make partner themselves within an expected timeframe. If a consultant received above-average grades, this increased her bonus and it may have sped up her path towards becoming partner. Initially, bonuses constituted only a small percentage of salary, yet this changed the more one rose in the ranks. If a consultant received a below-average grade, she was considered to have *issues*, which needed to be remedied or 'worked on' until the next assessment. In the unfortunate case that another poor grade followed, consultants were usually asked to find employment elsewhere.

In theory, German labour law protected consultants from being laid off because of company-specific grading systems. A few months into the job, rumours circulated that colleagues of mine, who had started their jobs together with me, had already been asked to leave, and that they had managed to receive large financial bonuses as an incentive to go. However, in a system designed for constant career advancement, those who failed to move up usually felt enormous social pressure to look for a job elsewhere, so that most people left on their own account and without needing further incentives. Free career advisors and a well-organized alumni network greatly facilitated finding a new job, and everyone I knew got hired elsewhere as a direct consequence of having worked in consulting. This was advantageous for the 'steep income pyramid' structure of the industry in which partners earned considerably more than lower-level consultants (see Chapter 6).

Of course, macroeconomic and institutional factors had an equally great impact on career advancement. For example, Merkel's energy policy turnaround mentioned above meant that there were cost-cutting projects in the German energy sector in the foreseeable future. The career progress of those consultants who specialized in this industry was thus more likely than that of the few often smiled-upon souls who tried to focus their careers exclusively on public sector work. One of my colleagues equally justified her surprising choice for leaving the company just after making junior partner with the argument that there were simply too many consultants on her level who were working in the same sector. Without enough client companies the competition to make it to partner was too tough, as all of this was in the end 'just a numbers game', as she put it.

This, however, was not reflected in the official rhetoric employed in discussing consultant career advancement. Instead, the individual consultant was held responsible for her success and failure. This was obviated in *feedback* sheets, which assessed consultants as persons according to their 'leadership skills' (i.e. *teamwork* ability with clients and colleagues), 'thought leadership' (i.e. quality of their analytic work) and other character traits, such as whether or not they kept information confidential, or showed a great deal of motivation or 'entrepreneurship' during projects. Institutional advancement was thus inextricably bound up with the project of improving one's self. The better the grades we received for these aspects of our selves, the better we did as a company commodity. Once again, *feedback* technology assumed and partially assured that self and commodity would stand in harmony with one another. Similar to the MBTI, the particularistic aspects of consultants were here seen to be classifiable and work was expected from each of us to bring them into alignment with company prerequisites.

In spite of this very elaborate and endlessly discussed system of *feedback*, many consultants did not take it wholly seriously. In interviews they criticized time and again that personal 'chemistry' with *team leaders* and partners was what mattered the most, regardless of how skilled and hard-working they were. If consultants formed good relationships with *team leaders* and partners, then these would ask consultants to work on further projects with them and in return gave the consultants high grades consistently. One colleague of mine, who had been asked to leave her job in consulting, regretted that she had put too much effort into getting her analytic work right and not enough into making the partners like her. According to her own words, she had 'thought that what mattered most was the actual work she did'. She had only understood in hindsight that getting the partners to like her more was at least as important in order to be successful at her job.

Other colleagues and interviewees bemoaned that very superficial 'first impressions' of partners were all that counted. The partners who would ultimately decide on one's career progress did not spend much time on a single project. Instead, they tended to fly from one project to the next, several times a week and seemed to be in a constant rush. Their lack of time meant that work performance assessments were frequently based on just a few very short moments of personal observation as well as second-hand accounts given to them by *team leaders*.

In the light of these shortcomings, *feedback* often failed to successfully function as a moralistic technology. Instead, it was interpreted by many of my colleagues to be just another justification to make people work harder, or to eventually lay them off. Rumours circulated that the collective performance ratings of our company's consultants had taken a deep collective dive during the

2008 economic crisis, forcing many former consultants out of their jobs when there were fewer projects to be worked on. In fact, even during the first training session in which *feedback* was presented to us, an American colleague commented stoically that it was 'just a load of BS'. To him, *feedback* was not explicitly meant to deceive, but that is used with perfect disregard of its truth value, in order to further the immediate goals of those employing it (Frankfurt 2005). Tim, a former *team leader* (Chapter 2), described *feedback* thus:

> Yes, you put a lot of time into it but if you ask me the whole process is a *hoax* to justify that people get large or small bonuses. And to make them feel a little loved. *Let's be real.* Somebody who has been Senior Partner for 20 years does not care at all what a young consultant with two year *tenure* may think of him. … If we really care about *people development* it would never happen that I get a *call* from a senior Partner *director*, starting with the words 'could you guys please use your goddamn brains for once'. Such people would be funnelled out. We should simply say that this is a business, not a family, and that what matters is how much money you bring to it. This is the little truth that no one dares to say, but this is how it is.

The cynical nature of Tim's remarks only becomes fully evident against his personal background. Tim was one of the greatest fans of the 'I give myself an A' exercise mentioned above, calling it one of the best activities he had done during his time as a consultant. Known to be one of the most hard-working *team leaders*, he laboured often even on the weekends, until he got his first heart attack at the age of thirty-three, which led him to quit his job with considerable rancour towards his former employer. Surprisingly, roughly two years after quitting his job, Tim reapplied to work as *team leader* in consulting, as his subsequent job in the Berlin *start-up* sector had turned out to be highly precarious. Tim's view was thus a good example for Sloterdjik's (2013: 37–9) definition of cynicism as 'enlightened false consciousness', in which knowledge of what he considers the dishonest nature of a system does not pre-empt his participation in it. In fact, I take the frequency with which the term 'bullshit' was used as a descriptor of our work to mean that cynicism is a pre-eminent condition, not just in state bureaucracies but in the corporate form in general (Navaro-Yashin 2002: 5; Kendzior

2011; Hermez 2015). In the field site under study, it resulted from the incompatibility of morally charged understandings of employee personhood.

My own interpretation of the tension between self and commodity is a little less cynical than Tim's. Both being a self and being a commodity were necessary attributes of personhood in the corporate environment we were working in, and both needed to be developed to become a good consultant. The intense and all-encompassing nature of consulting work and the moralistic technologies involved in it made this tension all the more striking. That said, the most successful consultants were those for whom the tensions between self and commodity could be largely reconciled, that is, those who accepted the corporate parameters of self-improvement and of self-commodification. One of these people was Tom, who eventually made it to partner and has by now been working as a management consultant for over a decade.

Conclusion

This chapter has argued that one of the main motivations that drive consulting work is self-improvement, whereby the self is that aspect of personhood which is marked by particularity and which is considered autonomous as it defines the means and the purposes of its own activity. This goal stood in direct conceptual and moral tension to the fact that consultants were also commodities, a term that emphasized the general aspects of their being, and that constructed them as means to a series of ends that were not of their own making. Both aspects of personhood entailed competing moral obligations that were meant to be reconciled via moralistic technologies such as the MBTI and *feedback*. The focus on the self as well as on the commodity may be part of attempts at wringing more work out of corporate employees (Muehlebach 2012: 6), yet it is also a response to the abstract nature of this form of labour. As work content remained constantly removed, both on a perceptual and on an emotional level, the work did not manage to function as a vocation or provide an adequate degree of moral fulfilment. As a result, focusing work efforts on improving the self as the underpinning logic for completing one's daily tasks came more easily.

Those consultants for whom the difference between self and commodity was decisive often either left their job or developed a cynical attitude vis-à-vis the corporate project of developing them as anything other than a commodity. Cynicism was here a primary and pervasive expression of workplace alienation which stemmed from competing and irreconcilable notions of personhood and moral obligations. The most successful consultants, on the other hand, may have been those for whom the difference between self and commodity remained truly minimal.

While this chapter has thus provided a first answer to the question of what motivated people's participation in abstract labour, the following chapter will provide a second answer by concentrating on the nature of workplace uncertainty.

CHAPTER SIX

Uncertainty at Work

This chapter argues that abstract labour lends itself to the construction and use of a specific kind of uncertainty, one that results in greater economic activity and is here called 'profitable uncertainty'. While economic observers from the world of insurance and finance have encountered different forms of profitable uncertainty before (LiPuma and Lee 2004), this chapter will show that it plays an important role in consulting as well, and probably in regimes of abstract labour more widely. In my field site, profitable uncertainty was a second major driver for work activity and it was established through three main movements: First, consultants postulated potential worlds, that is, alternatives to the actual, which were mostly considered attractive and attainable. Secondly, they held that economic subjects were capable of making free decisions. Finally, they tried to convince these subjects that their actions could have a relevant influence on whether or not potential worlds were brought about, via the engagement with consulting companies. While the first mechanism created the desire for a state other than the *status quo*, the second and third ensured that the mode of uncertainty established could be monetized.

The first half of this chapter will show that profitable uncertainty is created with respect to clients, the second half that it is also used with respect to consultants themselves. Profitable uncertainty will thereby turn out to be not simply another tool used to create money from nothing. Instead, it is a pervasive condition that is co-created by consultancy companies and that involves clients as much as themselves. The chapter will also show that this uncertainty is hard to control, as it comes with an excess that can lead to stasis in various ways.

While this argument draws on the ethnographic material presented in previous chapters, it is mainly based on the construction and use of a project acquisition letter (PAL). PALs are highly confidential documents used to approach potential clients directly so as to get hired by them for a consulting project. The ethnographic data is complemented with the analysis of publicly available reports by different consulting firms. While these serve client acquisition indirectly by creating a vision of the world and a reputation for consultancy firms that are good for business, they also reflect the consultants' view of how the world actually operates. The second half of the chapter draws primarily on ethnographic description and on interviews with consultants who suffered from strong feelings of uncertainty.

The chapter is meant to complement the growing literature on the corporate creation of uncertainty. Ericson, Barry and Doyle (2000), Kelly (2006: 103) and Weiss (2015), for example, have described how corporate classificatory practices do not by definition reduce uncertainty, but may very well enhance it. LiPuma and Lee (2004: 53–9) have further argued that in regimes of similarly abstract labour, uncertainty is objectified, that is, presented as a universally homogeneous entity, stripped of the ways in which it is socially embedded (see also Reith 2004). This chapter builds on this focus on the heterogeneous nature of uncertainty by asking when and how its instantiation in consulting is economically viable and at what point it encumbers economic activity. As part of this question the chapter investigates how abstract labour and profitable uncertainty condition each other.

Gaps in the analyses

In late 2013 I helped write a PAL to national government officials of a country in sub-Saharan Africa. The government in question had publicly announced that it was looking for consultancy companies to write a plan on how to improve public sector revenue, in particular by increasing tax income. The team working on the PAL had asked all junior consultants of our firm for support via email, and I had been one of the first to reply. With a background in development studies,

I had hoped to work in international development consulting rather than in the German private sector. In return for my help in putting the letter together, the email promised that I would be placed on this attractive project if and when it was to actualize.

Once the letter-writing team had officially taken me *on board*, they taught me in a series of calls and emails that they had worked with different ministries of the same government before, that they considered their past work a success and that the client and we were on good terms. Their strategy was to model the PAL on a series of successful past project acquisition documents, dealing either with similar topics or with the same country. PALs such as this one served as door openers for client *pitches*, on the basis of which projects were acquired or lost to competitors. *Pitches* consisted of personal meetings with potential clients, in which partners explained in a PowerPoint presentation how they envisaged the project's content, who would be involved in it, what it would cost, what the clients' expected gains might be and why the consultancy they represented was best suited for the task at hand. The letter we were writing covered roughly the same ground. In fact, it was a Microsoft Word document in which text was interspersed with PowerPoint slides for a verbal presentation. It had the somewhat dry title 'Examining Potential Government Revenues and Income Gaps[1]'.

When I joined the letter writing team, the partners responsible for this project had already defined much of the PAL's structure. It began by providing a flattering overview of our company, praising the 'global' nature of our work and foregrounding that 'all of our consultants are graduates from leading international universities such as Harvard, Stanford, Oxford and Cambridge'. It continued by outlining that our client had 'ambitious goals' that required 'tremendous investment', which in turn obliged it to drastically 'increase public sector revenues'. The letter highlighted the relatively low levels of government revenues today, which, on the one hand, suggested 'significant potential for [revenue] increase', but on the other pointed to the 'inadequacy of the current sources of income and the challenge that lies ahead'. This double idea of an inadequate present and an attractive future was communicated via reference to so-called 'revenue gaps':

> [Previously outlined weaknesses] result in 'revenue gaps' between revenues that ought to be obtained and revenues that are actually

achieved. The present request for [our study] arises from a need to ... quantify the revenue gap for each revenue category, identify priority categories and quick wins, and ultimately generate detailed policy measures to close the gaps and achieve potential revenues.

The idea of gaps in the PAL would arise time and again in consulting work. Indeed, consultancy companies seemed to specialize in identifying gaps of all sorts. To provide just a few examples, Deloitte hopes to close the 'programmatic gap' in Germany's digital advertising, Bain & Company (2015) holds that 'German banks face a yawning earnings gap', KPMG highlights a widespread organizational 'trust gap in data and analytics' (2016), Ernst and Young see a 'financing gap' in the German *start-up* sector (2015) and PWC, identified in their latest international family business survey, a 'generation gap', a 'credibility gap' and a 'communications gap' (2014: 1). Why do consultants detect gaps in so many places? This question should be especially interesting to social scientists, who are pretty apt at spotting 'gaps in the literature' themselves, often while in the process of writing funding applications.

The Oxford English Dictionary (OED 2015) defines the term 'gap' as 'an unfilled space or interval; a blank or deficiency; a break in continuity. Also, a disparity, inequality or imbalance; a break in deductive continuity'. On the one hand, this definition makes reference to a gap's essential attributes, which revolve around notions of difference, absence or non-existence. On the other, there are contextual ones, which refer to a presupposed underlying continuity or unity of the objects around it. I would argue that the contextual attributes in the term 'gap' are stronger than in its synonym 'difference' in the sense that differences may exist between things that have nothing in common, while gaps point more forcefully to a potential unity.

This unity also serves as an ideal that has somehow become disturbed or tarnished as gaps tend to be undesirable (OED 2015) yet, mostly not too great to be overcome. As the consultancy documents above make clear, gaps can be 'bridged', 'filled' or 'closed'. Thus, in postulating gaps rather than differences, otherness or apartness, my colleagues and I usually made the assertion that something was not right, but that it could be fixed if only it was acted upon. If this was true, then consultants may

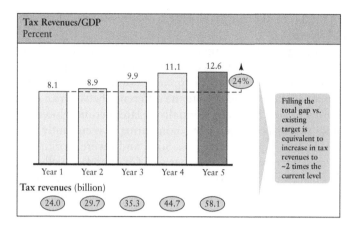

FIGURE 3 *Gaps in a slide.*

have found a lot of gaps because they created a sense of negative abnormality that invited activity. The following lines should outline that gaps did not just exist in PALs but in everyday project work as well.

The gaps that consultants 'uncovered' seemed to exist in highly variegated sectors of the economy and on different analytical scales. Thus they could arise between entire countries, between businesses, business units or between individual employees. While all these gaps were synchronic in nature, diachronic ones were equally important. For example, one of the most relevant slides in our PAL pointed at gaps within a single entity, over time (see figure 3).

In spite of their heterogeneity, the gaps we described had three features in common. First, as in the slide above, we often represented them via the technology of commensuration that is the bar chart. In their simplicity of form, bar charts epitomized abstract labour, in that they could symbolize almost any quantified entity or activity imaginable, perfectly detached from content. When arranged in increasing or decreasing order, they intuitively conveyed to the reader relations of size between the entities in question. While the width of bar charts was mostly meaningless, their perfectly flat tops invited – maybe even imposed – comparison, by allowing the reader to imagine a line stretching out from their tops to above or below the bars nearby. Thus, in the slide above, even temporal differences were thereby made comparable and commensurate in the chart's spatial idiom.

Secondly, gaps always compared an actual entity to its potential self. When a business unit was compared to its planned performance, this was obvious. As long as the premises of the plan were realistic, the gap it depicted would denote the difference between an entity as it was now to how it could potentially be later in time. However, this potential was also invoked when comparing two currently existing entities. For example, when Anne, Sofia and I were working at the health insurance company together (see Chapter 4), a colleague on another team had the task of assessing the insurance company's 'sales performance'. Thus, she got a hold of the sales data and created a bar chart that plotted the amount of new insurance members that each salesperson acquired next to one another, thereby identifying the best- and worst-performing salesperson. Then she tried to find out what lay behind the success of the best of them, hoping to pass her secret on to other sales employees. This in turn would close the performance gaps between sales staff. The top performer thereby served as a role model that her colleagues were expected to emulate, that is, she would be considered a physical manifestation of the potential of her peers. This logic seemed to be at work regardless of the contexts or contents of the gaps in question. Gaps between, for example, two countries, companies, business units or salespeople always pointed at the better-performing entity as a potentially achievable ideal type for the others. Thus, in speaking about gaps, consultants tended to blur the difference between representation and exemplar.

Thirdly, gaps existing on different scales were seen to cause one another. In the example above, the gap between salespeople was part of the reason why the overall sales division was lagging behind others. This in turn was why the company as a whole was not living up to its potential. Our analyses thus tended to point at gaps within gaps within gaps.

Potential worlds

Gaps in the analyses suggest a utopian theme in the PAL, and in our project work more generally, in that our slides tended to aim at ideal states. I will here call these states 'potential worlds' since the term 'potential' nicely captures both a latent possibility and its seemingly high economic prospects, that is, a 'hidden force determined to manifest itself' (Taussig, Hoeyer and Helmreich 2013: S4). At the same time, the term 'world' evokes Leibniz's 'possible worlds', which may be seen as blueprints for what the actual might be like (Look 2013), and which has prophetic and utopian connotations (Guyer 2007). As several of my work mentors taught me, project pitches tended to be structured around two main utopian logics. In the first one, a potential world was desired by the client company and only just out of reach. This logic was known as the *pot of gold*, the *mountain of gold* or the *low hanging fruit*, expressions that emphasize either its high appeal or easy accessibility. The second logic, frequently applied when pitching for cost-reduction projects, was one where the expected future was highly undesirable. It was known among my colleagues as *imminent doom* or the *cliff-hanger*. In these cases hospitals were making losses, company shares were rapidly losing value and government entities did control their budgets. Each of these examples was assumed to end in disaster, that is, in bankruptcy, hostile company takeovers (see Chapter 5) or in the inability of governments to refinance themselves.

The two logics differed somewhat in terms of emphasis. While the *pot of gold* stressed the wonderful potential world, rather than the expected future, the logic of *imminent doom* focused on the horrors that were to be expected if nothing were to be done. However, they had three things in common. They posited stark differences between actual world and expected future as compared to potential worlds; they described potential worlds as preferable over the others; and they held that they could be realized, if action – carried out with the help of consultancy experts – was taken right away. With our support, so the story went, clients would be able to reduce some of the friction between the world that was and the ideals that could be (Tsing 2005). As long as clients were not deemed to live in the 'best of all possible worlds' (Look 2013), more abstract labour might be required to bring it about.

The utopian bent of the PAL was more than a sales strategy. In telephone conferences in which we discussed its 'storyline', the senior consultants responsible repeatedly stated that they were convinced that the country in question could raise much more revenue, if only tax collection practices were improved. No one was sure about the exact size of the potential increase or about the precise steps that the government needed to take, but the belief in a world that would surpass the expected future was held by all colleagues involved. This focus on what could be was held to be an outlook that distinguished management consultants from other people. Senior consultants and trainers often joked about the fact that our profession was full of particularly impatient people since we constantly wanted to improve logistical processes, such as airport queues, traffic jams and bureaucratic procedures. In the light of their utopian analytic techniques and business pitches, the consultants' impatience was not just an indicator of being short on time (Chapter 2), but it showed how preoccupied they were with the tension between the world that was and that which should be. Impatience was their permanent reaction to the current world in which assumedly non-fictional utopias (cf. Moore 1990) had not been realized.

Gaps in the subject

The PAL made a couple of suggestions to the government we hoped to win as client. The government itself had set the condition that in this project it wanted to improve the effectiveness of revenue-raising mechanisms rather than work on legislative change. We thus recommended three main 'levers' through which more revenues could be raised. They were primarily concerned with (1) refining filing and documentation processes, (2) introducing new analytic tools to find out if current revenue sources were sufficiently used and (3) introducing 'performance-tracking measures' for government tax collectors. Each of these suggestions was likely to provide consultants such as ourselves with additional projects over the years to come, again foregrounding the autopoietic nature of our work.

In spelling these suggestions out in detail, our letter was concerned with outlining a series of options that were open to the client in question. In fact, Paul, the partner responsible for our project in Chapter 3, considered the provision of options to be the main function of consultancy work. He argued that, instead of making specific suggestions, consultants should simply outline to their clients what their possibilities were in as clear and realistic a manner as possible. Regardless of whether our PAL actually presented heartfelt suggestions for action or mere options that may be interesting to consider, they pointed to another kind of gap that co-constructed uncertainty in this instance, namely the gap in the subject.

In some strands of contemporary Western thought, for example in the work of John Searle, the idea of a gap is fundamental for description of free human decision-making. In arguing against a deterministic view of human consciousness, Searle holds that humans often experience having several reasons for choosing an action but that they are ultimately in a position to select which particular reason to act on (Searle 2001b: 65). In taking conscious decisions, they have some scope to choose which one of the reasons operating on them will ultimately be effective (ibid.: 66). Searle argues that this and other experiences of human decision-making are indicative of a series of gaps, stating that

> in typical cases of deliberating and acting, there is, in short, a gap, or a series of gaps between the causes of each stage in the processes of deliberating, deciding and acting, and the subsequent stages. If we probe more deeply we can see that the gap can be divided into different sorts of segments. There is a gap between the reasons for the decision and the making of the decision. There is a gap between the decision and the onset of the action, and for any extended action, such as when I am trying to learn German or to swim the English Channel, there is a gap between the onset of the action and its continuation to completion. (2001a: 493–4)

Searle's description of the experience of gaps is linked to discussions of potentiality above, in that he considers them to be 'that feature of our conscious decision-making and acting where we sense alternative future decisions and actions as causally open to us' (2001b: 62).

The view that subjects were capable of 'causally open', conscious decisions was equally implied in the PAL and in public reports of consultancy firms, as they systematically suggested that the readership actually had freedom in deciding how to act on the gaps they faced. Indeed, the PAL's entire structure was devised so as to influence our potential clients in their choice of whether or not to work with us. The same was true for the reports cited at the beginning of this chapter, through which consultancy companies tried to convince potential clients to engage in one kind of activity rather than another.

Consulting slides and official documents greatly overstated the case for client freedom. They presented ideal types of unconstrained decision-making, marked by clear-cut options and hard and fast choices. In fact, management consultants saw their own role as filling all three kinds of gaps identified in Searle's work, in that they wanted to provide clients with the right reasons for making a decision (e.g. by outlining reasonable options); they aimed to translate already taken decisions into corresponding human action (e.g. by organizing workshops aimed at altering staff thought and behaviour); and they tried to ensure the cohesion of extended action (e.g. by increasingly remaining involved in implementing projects over extended periods of time, disciplining and supporting the employees involved). Each of the gaps constitutive of conscious decision-making therefore formed a potential source of consultancy revenue.

The idea of a free client was markedly different from subjects in other anthropological studies that equally deal with uncertainty. In her study of women in Cameroon, for example, Johnson-Hanks (2005) emphasizes that they describe their future 'not as a set of choices and intentional actions but as a sequence of assents: whatever comes along, one may choose to assent to it' (ibid.: 368). Here the subjects' choice is limited to the binary of assent or refusal to what life presents them with. This could hardly be more different from the subjects that consultancy companies addressed, as the latter were constantly expected to will and to change the world into a desirable outcome. If consultants had considered their clients to be mostly predetermined from the outset, there would have been little to no need for advisory services. They therefore had to construct their clients as subjects that may face some constraints but that ultimately had a significant degree of freedom.

In practice, viewing clients as principally defined by their freedom and as suffering from the responsibility assumed to come with it guided only a small part of our daily work. Instead, day-to-day consulting practice was keenly aware of factors that constrained unencumbered decision-making, such as the emotional states of clients, their aesthetic preferences and the power hierarchies that dominated their lives. During all of my projects, whenever partners or senior consultants had not been present at one of my meetings with clients, they asked in subsequent debriefs about the personal reactions of the people I had talked to. They were keen to know which aspects of a discussion had got clients angry, concerned or bored, whom they liked and whom they did not want to work with, if any gossip had come to the fore and so on. Their constant concern with such personal ties and emotions, as well as with slide aesthetics and the narrative arcs of slide shows (Chapter 4), showed that management consultants never fully ascribed to the story of personal freedom and largely unconstrained choice. While they adhered to many of the tenets of rational choice in official discourse, they followed a 'substantive approach' to economics (Ortiz 2005: 63) in most of their daily work practice.

Intriguingly, in the PAL, the balance between freedom and constraints that delimitated the decisions open to clients was tilted differently, depending on the kind of subject in question. When addressing high-ranking government officials who might buy our services, the gaps involved in decision-making received a lot of attention. Yet when speaking about the lower-ranking government officials involved in raising revenues, it stressed the constraints under which they were operating. Tax collectors might not be incentivized to work towards the right goals, they might be using outmoded tools and techniques, or they might not know how to target the right revenue channels. A skilful manipulation of such constraints was assumed to lead them to behave differently, in line with the goals of our plans. Thus, consultancy documents such as the ones mentioned here made a difference between two kinds of subjects. While the managers who hired us were at least on paper considered to suffer from the freedoms involved in decision-making, their subordinates were understood to work primarily according to workplace constraints. In short, freedom had to remain unequally distributed. If all subjects were considered as free as the high-ranking government officials we addressed, the imponderabilities of the social world would be too large to plan ahead. If all subjects were as constrained as low-level employees, there would be little need for expert advice at the top. The last missing piece in this construction of uncertainty was the assumption that subjects could actually have an influence on which potential world would come about.

The presence of experts

The PAL had a couple of reassuring elements to it. One slide was entitled 'revenue gaps are a common problem across many countries', depicting an overview of such gaps in developing and developed countries. It was followed by explanations as to how our extensive experience in raising government revenues and our capacity-building skills would 'ensure local ownership and the ability to implement results'. Moreover, it included shortened CVs of our team, held to combine 'broad and deep experience in government reform with detailed knowledge of the government in question'. Finally, the letter ended on a more personal note, stating that we were 'truly excited' at the prospect of partnering with the client in question and that we were 'committed to ensuring the success of this undertaking'.

These reassuring elements confirmed our belief that the client's problems could in fact be overcome and that all kinds of gaps mentioned or insinuated earlier could indeed be filled. The reaffirmation of client influence may be cast aside as a mere formality, but I would like to suggest that the entire structure of the PAL, as well as those of most consultancy reports, was geared towards a subject that was held to have the power to shape the world. The uncertainty we created would result in profitable activity only when the subjects in question believed that their actions could make a relevant difference to the status quo.

This is not a given. For example, in Sheper-Hughes's seminal study of shantytown dwellers near the city of Bom Jesus in Northeast Brazil, she showed how mothers relate to their children in an environment of high infant mortality. Rather than actively engaging with their newborns' health problems so as to ensure their survival, these mothers developed an ability to face child death with stoicism and equanimity (1993: 275). They distinguished between those infants thought of as survivors and those considered doomed from the start, letting the latter die in acts of 'mortal selective neglect' (ibid.). In these cases, the mothers' response to uncertainty was inertia. I would argue that this risk of resorting to inertia is always present in uncertain environments (cf. Luhrmann 1998). While stark differences between a potential and an actual world may incite activity, they may just as well lead to apathy and despair.

To summarize the argument so far, consultancy companies have been shown to co-construct profitable uncertainty in three movements. They postulated attractive potential worlds, held that subjects were capable of making free decisions (project commissioners more so than their subordinates) and argued that the actions of clients could have a relevant if partial influence on whether or not these worlds would be realized. The following paragraphs will show that within consultancy companies a very similar logic was at work.

Potential worlds II

Consultancy companies were peculiar in that they provided their recruits and employees with an exceptionally clear idea of how their career status was supposed to improve. Thus, the German websites of different consulting companies, for example, presented internal hierarchies in highly similar terms. Their junior consultants mostly did analyses and would eventually be responsible for subsections of a project, *team leaders* ran a project on a day-to-day level, junior partners built client relationships and partners fostered and expanded these relationships and thereby the business (see Figure 4).

Each moment of career advancement was supposed to follow a predefined period of time, equally made known to consultants in official documents and through informal conversations. Consulting companies were in this respect a direct extension of schools and universities, allowing career-minded students to continue constantly 'moving up' after university was over. Differences in pay that corresponded to each career step were referred to in much vaguer terms, as they increasingly relied on mostly unspecified end-of-year bonuses. Nevertheless, every consultant knew that with each step up the ladder salary increases would grow both in absolute terms and relative to one's base salary.

A second, frequently underestimated way in which consultancy companies established desirable potential worlds was by claiming that they could provide employees with any kind of project they might fancy. For example, at a recruiting event for students of the social sciences in Berlin, which I co-organized, the consultant in charge of the event provided me with a series of slides on the basis of which we

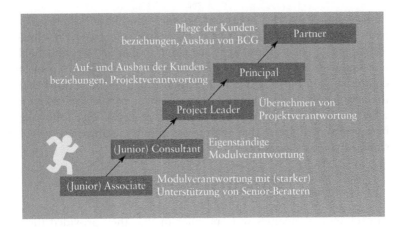

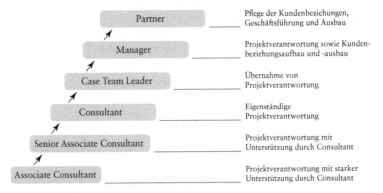

FIGURE 4 *Career descriptions.*[2]

were supposed to present our labour. Right after introducing ourselves, our first slide made reference to the vast variety of organizations we worked for. Entitled 'Our clients include major private sector firms as well as governments and NGOs', the slide allowed us to talk about the exciting public sector projects we had already worked on. The next two slides in the *deck* mentioned a few of our past NGO clients. The students attending the event were visibly interested in macroeconomic and social questions and they responded favourably to the diversity of projects. Several senior consultants had also mentioned in interviews and informal conversations that consulting was the perfect job for anyone who did not know what to do with one's life, since one could really do anything.

The self-presentation of our company as a place of radical project diversity continued throughout our working lives. The *assessment day* during which I had been hired had begun with a presentation that highlighted how varied consulting work was. Trainers, interviewees, career coaches and intranet blogs continued in the same vein presenting with pride that our consultants could work on 'exotic' projects, such as helping a major NGO fight malaria, and that we would at times work in *remote* locations, far from the usual infrastructure of taxis, hotels and major airports. A senior colleague of mine loved recounting the story of how he had worked in a small village in the Mediterranean, where, in the absence of a major hotel, they had decided to rent a bungalow for the whole team. I myself had become a consultant partially for this reason. While my main aim had been to pay off my five-digit student debt, I had also hoped that consulting would allow me to work with governments and large NGOs in developing countries. My contribution to the PAL reflected my own desire to make the promise of an exciting diversity of projects beyond the immediate demands of the behemoths of the German economy possible.

All that said, the focus on potential worlds was not all positive in consulting. First, our jobs were highly precarious and the industry was known for its *up or out* system. In short, *up or out* meant that those consultants considered unable or unwilling to work at the same level as their peers were incited to leave the firm. As mentioned before, internal estimates pointed to a turnover of about 20 per cent of staff per year. Consulting careers were thus highly liquid in nature, similar to other jobs in finance (Ho 2009). While being laid off as a consultant was not usually as tragic as it was among lower-income professions, it was still closely tied up with ideas of personal failure (Chapter 5), and my colleagues visibly dreaded their biannual career assessments in which promotion would be wonderful, while no promotion meant being one step closer to getting fired. Their anxiety was palpable and they could discuss the reasons for why they might or might not get promoted for days on end.

One of our office coaches had told my group of recent recruits on the first day of work that *up or out* should not be seen so much as a threat, but as a possibility for career development. After all, the flip side to the resulting job uncertainty was that the doors for advancing in the company were always open and that with each step up higher salary increases could be guaranteed. *Team leaders* and partners religiously repeated this argument when worries or complaints about precarity were uttered. For them, job uncertainty was the logical extension of upward mobility. Consultants thus lived the values that they themselves tried to advance in public sector projects (Ho 2009). A good example for this is the notorious German labour market reforms under Gerhard Schröder during the early 2000s, in which two major consultancy companies had been involved in rendering the country's job market much more 'flexible' for employers and much more precarious for employees (ibid.; *Der Spiegel* 2004).

Free employees in theory and practice

My willingness to contribute to the PAL on top of doing normal project work was largely an attempt to actualize the potentially infinite variety of consulting projects. However, it also reflected the widespread conviction that employees were free to build their own networks with senior consultants and partners. My own mentor, who made this point, was keen to add that one could work less in our firm, but that 'our employees usually did a little more'. My colleagues and I were to hear this view many times afterwards, when people assured us that we were always happy to 'go the extra mile' or 'to notch up performance'.[3] In the light of the *up or out* system this warning that simply doing project work would not be enough was spread among us from day one, in training camps, private conversations and intranet blog posts. Official rhetoric constantly stressed how *driven* we all were collectively and that we had great *passion* for client work. Keeping consultants 'on the edge'[4] in this way explains why juniors were so keen to organize the Christmas party, got involved with free NGO consulting, supported recruitment activities or helped out with logistical issues of their home offices, all on top of daily project work that easily took up 12 hours a day. Importantly, this rhetoric also stressed that working harder was to be the expression of the consultants' personal choice, rather than a top-down command. Like our clients, we were free to do less, but would have to live up to the consequences of our own decisions.

The freedom of employees to work very long hours differed in some respects from that of clients. The extreme dedication to work which consulting companies demanded from their staff was supposed to be an expression of employee nature (Rose: 1999). As frequent references to our *passion* for client work implied, the consultants' choice to work during most of their waking lives was supposed to arise from their innermost core. Consulting was thus seen as a test of whether one's essence corresponded to that of our employer. As one of my interviewees had put it during my assessment day, they were finding out whether our company and we 'made a good match'. If this match was good, work would be the site at which one's freedom could be expressed. So while managers of client companies were suffering from too much freedom, and their employees were largely seen as predetermined by structural constraints, consultants were in turn considered free in the sense of living up to their assumed positive liberty to work hard and to succeed.

In practice, the impediments to realizing potential careers were numerous. First, far from being the autonomous, bold individuals as whom they liked to present themselves, management consultants were heavily reliant on working with whatever client was in a position to pay them. In order to generate the vast revenues on which their business model of expensive travel, luxurious parties and prime-location offices relied, they needed to place their staff on whichever project was about to start. In Germany, these projects mostly lay with large financial or manufacturing companies. At several companies, consulting staff were thus allocated by enlisting employees in a *staffing pool*, that is, a list showing the date by which each currently occupied consultant would be 'free' to be placed elsewhere. Partners and *team leaders* would either participate in staffing calls or use online databases to announce confirmed projects and negotiate who would be assigned to them. Consultants picked from the *pool* ran the risk of getting placed on an unattractive project, which might involve a lot of stress and sleep deprivation, or may stand in contrast to their personal interests and ethics.

For example, many of my colleagues tried to circumvent working in particularly taxing environments by either avoiding certain partners and *team leaders* who were known for their breakneck work ethic or evading notoriously tough sectors, such as finance, altogether. Avoiding them was difficult as, when they called to place one on their upcoming project, one had to pretend to already have another project confirmed and to be unfortunately unavailable. One colleague had compiled a list on his smartphone of partners and *team leaders* who had a reputation for being 'slave drivers' as he said. While some of my more senior colleagues who saw this list during a day out were not impressed with it, as it indicated a dangerous lack of commitment to the company as a whole, others asked for a copy, hoping it might help them in their quest for a healthier *work–life balance*. A considerable amount of mostly early-career consultants, including myself, also had reservations about working in the arms or tobacco industry, while projects in the public and the development sectors were highly coveted. Dozens if not hundreds of applicants were known to try getting placed on relatively few internationally announced projects that supported governments or large NGOs.

The difficulty of choosing project work was even more complex than its relative scarcity might suggest. One of the junior partners I worked with, for example, had long tried to specialize in the field of development. He told me over a quick coffee in the office that while he generated a series of projects with public sector clients, many of his more senior colleagues thought that a proper consultant should also be working in the private sector, where larger project budgets worth several millions of Euros could be generated. Development work was deemed 'exotic'[5] in the sense of being exciting but also somehow intrinsically irrational and worthless. According to him there was a clear hierarchy of projects in which public sector activity was considered *soft* and less valuable, while work in the private sector was considered to be tougher and closer to the ideal of true consulting. This hierarchy, he argued, was much stronger in Germany than in the UK, where he was equally active. Therefore, he had now changed his official job role, so that an international committee of partners would in the future assess his work performance. Partners in Germany, he thought, would be far less willing to promote him.

Internal hierarchies that limited project variety were in fact everywhere in consulting. Even the most skilful consultants I met did not manage to build a career exclusively in public sector or NGO projects, as manufacturing and finance stood in much greater esteem. Mergers and acquisitions were considered tough and intimidating, as they had a reputation for awful working hours that seamlessly span from weekdays into weekends. These hierarchies were so prevalent that some of my colleagues argued that consultants had essentially two ways of going about their careers. They could either choose to work on interesting topics and get laid off after about two years or focus on prestigious ones so as to try to make it to partner. Whether and how it would be possible to find a middle ground in between these two extremes was an endless source of anxious discussions.

As part of writing the PAL it was my role to update the CVs of the senior consultants on our team. I did this mainly by looking them up on our intranet so as to write favourable summaries of their past projects. On the frequent occasions when the intranet lacked detail or turned out to be plainly inaccurate, I was obliged to contact the partners or their secretaries, asking them countless times to fill in the CV templates that I had sent. However, partners remained almost impossible to reach. Their secretaries assured me that they were incredibly busy, constantly travelling or participating in client meetings but that they would do their best so as to get back to me as quickly as possible. However, it was hard for me to gauge if this was true or if they simply did not care about my requests. Co-authoring the PAL turned out to be a substantial amount of work, yet it was not considered a full-time activity. It was the kind of job that consultants did on the side or in between projects when they had little else to do.

At the same time, I was working on another project in a German health insurance company with *Team Leader* Sofia (Chapter 4). My involvement in the PAL was clearly not in Sofia's interest since she would be evaluated with reference to the success of her own project work, regardless of whether or not I was involved in other issues on the side. Therefore, I tried to secretly send PAL-related emails or browse the intranet in her presence without arousing her suspicion. However, as an experienced *team leader*, Sofia quickly found out that I was helping another team. Some of the PAL telephone conferences actually took place during the day, and Sofia sat opposite me in our *team room* most of the time. So on one of the first occasions after I had casually left our office to take a call, she forthrightly inquired what I was having *calls* for. When I told her about the PAL, she warned me that she would rate my performance at the end of our project only with respect to the work that contributed to our shared activity and that my additional jobs would not be taken into account. While Sofia and I worked as a close and supportive team within the confines of our project, breaking these confines meant that our interests as individualized employees stood in tension with one another. Our assumed freedom to act in accordance with our nature was thus limited by corporate structures in which individuals rather than teams were assessed, paid, promoted or laid off.

The partially influential employee

My second task in writing the PAL was to compile a series of reference cases, that is, descriptions of past projects that would position my team as experts on tax and revenue issues in the clients' eyes. I therefore searched the company intranet for documents, which unfortunately provided mostly superficial information on such cases. Then I asked the people involved in compiling these documents to provide me with more detail, concerning the size of past teams, their overall budgets, project achievements and any merits worth highlighting in the current project pitch. However, nobody in the PAL team really knew which aspects of our past work potential clients would find convincing enough to hire us. Should we focus mostly on past tax and revenue improvement projects or on public sector work with prestigious clients in general? Should we present cases mainly in developing countries or would projects with the governments of rich nations be seen more favourably? Should we present clients with a few selected cases in great detail or with as many cases as possible? All of these questions received a great deal of discussion from my senior colleagues. A surprisingly large part of our job thus consisted in guessing what exactly it was that clients did, what they expected from our projects and whether these expectations could reasonably be met. This was one of the decisive ways in which we could influence whether or not our work would eventually be considered a success.

Our partial influence was not just evident in writing PALs, but it applied to successful consulting practice more generally. Once accepted, a PAL did not specify the exact work activities that needed to follow during the months to come. As a document of just a few pages, it was usually far too short to contain this much detail.

Clients tended to commission our work on the basis of only a rough idea of what we would do. Upon hiring us they did not have exact knowledge of our upcoming day-to-day activities as these would be spelt out during so-called *kick-off* meetings at the beginning of a project. Here, consultants usually presented a Gantt chart, that is, a calendar on a PowerPoint slide, that would state in rough terms when they would engage in which kind of work. Yet, even these charts continued to make relatively generic statements such as 'define business model' or 'derive organizational structure'. Due to the opaque nature of the PAL and the Gantt chart, the precise definition of the work expected from consultants occurred during weekly *steercos* with the client in charge of a project, when the project was already underway. If clients seemed content with the results we presented, this meant that enough work had probably been carried out and that we had contributed to project success. If they were not, work routines needed to change, usually increasing in intensity in order to still make the project successful. Abstract labour was thus marked by a constant definition and redefinition of what it was actually about and guessing at client desires was an essential part thereof. Consultants could thus in part influence project success if they managed to guess what exactly clients desired.

Consider the following interview with a junior consultant describing his least-favourite project, in which this issue turned out to be particularly problematic:

> One project went really poorly and I did not like it at all. The main reason was that the team of clients and us had very different ideas. In a way we never really agreed on what exactly should be our goal and how we could reach it. It was due to coordination problems. We simply did not manage to work together and [as a result, our team] worked into many different directions. However, the client was not satisfied with this and it never led to a kind of answer that they desired. … I also did not really know where my place was in the team, did not really understand what my main task was and where it all should lead. That's when I needed a lot of support from the *team leader*, which was tough.

In its strong self-referentiality our labour thus derived an additional layer of both abstraction and opacity, allowing a host of diverse legitimation techniques to play an even more important role than already described in previous chapters. This is part of the answer to the question posed in the Introduction of this book. Consultants could not easily summarize what their job was about since defining and redefining its purpose was a considerable part of it. According to what would sell a project, consultants could position themselves as personal confidants of management, or sources of outside knowledge, rigorous overseers of staff or motivational speakers, permanent additional manpower or visiting experts. As long as they fended off accusations of incompetence or of being overpriced, they could remain in the business, attempting to tap into the relationships they had with clients, harnessing their uncertainties in their favour. Uncertainty as to the nature of our work thereby kept the autopoietic aspects of it alive.

The interview excerpt above also shows that the position of consultants within the consultancy company mirrored their relationships with clients. Just like they had to routinely guess what client desires may be, they equally had to carefully assess what kind of work partners and *team leaders* and other superiors expected of them. While official company rhetoric stressed hard and fast criteria on the basis of which consultants would be assessed after every project, career advisors and senior colleagues taught us informally that building social relationships with partners and *team leaders* was the best way to be successful.

The rhetoric of building social relationships and of working in teams often meant submitting to authority. As my somewhat explosive and seemingly self-assertive *Team Leader* Michael once put it, after getting yet another spontaneous job request from a partner over the phone: 'You know, when you work as *team leader* you simply need to bend over forward and every partner can have a go.' His angry reference at getting raped by partners highlighted that the uncertainty at work could be used to increase pressures to submit. It was hard to assess how many PowerPoint slides were really needed and how many analyses were enough to make a partner happy. Michael's remark also showed that in consulting, references to submission and domination continued to be expressed in heavily gendered terms (Chapter 3).

Indeed, consultancy companies did their best to use the climate of uncertainty among their staff to heighten work activity. This started with recruiting. It was a standard expression among colleagues that consultancy companies hired *insecure overachievers*, that is, people who worked too much but remained uncertain as to whether their work was quite enough. The term 'overachiever' was meant as a self-compliment, but several interviewees pointed out to me that it also referred to people who were willing to submit to institutional demands. In their opinion, hiring from leading international universities such as Harvard and Oxford did not just ensure that consultancies employed bright staff or people with the required habitus. It also guaranteed that they would employ university graduates trained into working hard towards strictly enforced deadlines. They would deal with uncertainty by working more rather than less.

Consolations of optimistic pragmatism

Here is how *Team Leader* Matthias describes the key competencies in consultancy, with reference to a study in product pricing.

> I believe that most of all you need to have a healthy amount of pragmatism. When you analyse data you typically have way too much of it, with too many complexities and imponderabilities. You also have too little time and you are expected to quickly produce results. Thus it is extremely important to be able to still see the forest in spite of all the trees. You must always tell yourself that you might theoretically do analyses for 30.000 different products, but that in fact the 10 biggest products make up 70% of total volume. Thus we will concentrate on these 10 products. We will also not analyse the whole universe but we will focus on a single market, such as Germany, where we can roll out the price change that we have in mind. This might be because Germany is a large market or because we have client support there. Such simplifications, prioritisations and pragmatic detours are absolutely crucial. Especially if you still want to have a life, rather than working all the time.

In this interview excerpt, Matthias seamlessly links pragmatism as a tool against pervasive epistemic uncertainty to the personal goal of working less. Pragmatism and a constant emphasis on simplification did not just define the consultant as a charismatic other (see Chapter 5). Instead, it was simultaneously an epistemic stance, time management technique and an economically useful response to persisting uncertainty, a belief in meaningful activity in the face of potentially endless doubt. Many other expressions used by colleagues pointed in the same direction. Consultants should have a 'strong drive towards the goal', communicate *top-down*, practise *elevator pitches* and excel in the art of simplification.

A second way to deal with uncertainty was a somewhat relentless and always forceful optimism that did not rely on downplaying daunting challenges but that prided itself in tackling them head-on. Gaps could always be bridged. Moreover, successful consultants were known to wholeheartedly insist on the quality of their past, present and future work and on the amazing impact that they had had for their clients. Anything else would not just have undermined the justifications of high daily consultancy fees, but it would also have pointed to the more foundational problem that the world remained for one reason or another uncontrollable.

As one former consultant who now teaches development and area studies at university told me, she still uses consultancy reports about social issues and public sector problems in her teaching for precisely this reason. They serve as an interesting counterweight to the more pessimistic accounts about private and public sector activity, frequently found in parts of the press and in some academic journals. While in the social sciences, questioning the status quo often includes its condemnation (Ortner 2016), the critical work of consultants immediately foregrounded the pragmatic and monetizable remedies to the problems at hand. Impatience and a drive for market activity had to trump condemnation and further reflection. The profit motive is certainly an important cause for consultants to react to their own critical work in this way. However, I would here like to point out the abstract nature of their labour as another crucial factor. Since abstract labour lends itself to the creation of a myriad of sources of uncertainty, as the paragraphs above have shown, one of the greatest risks that consultants face is equanimity and stasis.

Limits to profitable uncertainty

The peculiar mixture of potential worlds, freedoms and influence in this setting had a series of side effects. On the one hand, consultancy companies could not force their employees to work beyond their immediate tasks on individual client projects. Activities such as recruiting, organizing the Christmas party or training recently hired staff were to some degree optional. On the other hand, *team leaders* could not force their team to work *only* for the project in question. The freedom of employees thereby turned out to be the flip side of the uncertainty of guessing at the desires of their superiors. Even if *team leaders* and junior consultants sat together for most hours of the day, not all emails sent by junior consultants could be double-checked, not all calls could be listened to and not all analyses could be fully understood. Most junior consultants quickly learnt how to make these uncertainties work for themselves. In my case, *Team Leader* Sofia had rapidly grasped that I had no reason to be in *calls* unless I was doing something on the side. However, as a general rule she did not exactly know how long the work that she asked from me should take. The imperfections of her oversight gave me some leeway to write a few more emails every day regarding the letter that I was helping out on.

I quickly found out that all consultants made sure to signal to their superiors and especially to their clients through occasional emails or phone calls that they might be working constantly. The profitable uncertainty that pervaded consulting thereby rendered the performative aspects of work more important than they otherwise would be. I use the term 'performative' here in the twofold sense of working 'as if' one was engaging in labour and as foregrounding the fact that labour is not just product oriented but in part constituted by its own performance. Performing work at 'full capacity'[6] did develop into something like an art form. Consultants had to signal in informal conversations with clients and bosses that their work was a lot, without coming across as lacking motivation for it. Most of my bosses also knew how to keep finished analyses in the back pocket until the right moment came to present them to clients. Sofia was proud of 'front loading' her work, that is, getting it done early in the project and releasing it slowly. When Andreas, the *team leader* introduced in Chapter 3, had finished a slide or an analysis that he did not pass on to partners and clients right away, he commented on it at times by saying that he did not want to 'shoot all our powder in one go'.[7] While presenting our work results too late might have given us a reputation of being either not *driven* or not smart enough, presenting them too early would simply result in additional demands. Other colleagues were known to preschedule their emails so as to have them sent either very late at night or very early in the morning. This would simulate constant work activity and even less sleep. *Upward management* and *downward management*, that is, exerting power over colleagues and clients on all spectrums of corporate hierarchy, was considered to be a crucial *skill* for consultants, and using the ambiguities that arise in environments of uncertainty was a key part thereof.

On an *office Friday* the interplay of these uncertainties became most obvious. Usually, consultants worked from their home towns during that day. Partners and *team leaders* tried to ensure that they would work as hard as possible by providing them with challenging tasks early on. However, the physical distance between them meant that the pace of work was generally more relaxed. In fact, this lack of team control during one day of the week was an institutionalized mechanism, meant to allow consultants to do their own administrative work, such as handing in their expense sheets, catching up with colleagues from their hometowns, maybe seeing a doctor or working from home to be closer to their children. At the same time, all consultants made sure to signal to their superiors and especially to their clients through occasional emails or phone calls that they were working constantly.

The performative aspects of work were heightened by structural features, such as project work and labour in a partnership. Doing project work meant working in different teams and on different issues every few months. Thereby, consultants did not have a superior who got to know them well and then decided about their advancement. Instead, they had many superiors, all of whom gave them grades – from one to five – after intense, yet fairly brief periods of interaction. On the basis of these grades and of verbal reports of former colleagues, an independent panel of partners then decided what the consultant's overall grade should be and whether it was sufficient for advancement in the company. In this structure based on transient social ties, the notion of having 'a job' with a consultancy company was in some respects a euphemism, since consultants needed to apply for a new project every couple of months, sometimes weeks. Employees were here constantly in a process of either proving themselves in their 'new position' or applying to be allowed to prove themselves anew.

Partners graded consultants in spite of having relatively few interactions with them. After all, they were in charge of several project teams at a time, they were usually travelling and they predominantly communicated with their secretaries, *team leaders* and clients. The partners therefore relied on individual *team leaders* and on a handful of personal observations in their assessments. The assessment panel, in turn, had to rely on the collective agreement of all partners who had worked with a consultant over the past year. With this many steps in the grading process, what counted most was the rough 'overall impression'[8] that a consultant had made, since no-one had the time or energy to look into performance specifics. Such impressions depended on content as much as on showmanship, on rational assessment as much as on personal affinity, and consultants were often highly uncertain what the outcome of their assessment would be.

A final aspect that fostered performative pressures on consultants was that, in this environment, understandings of charisma were based on certainty and reassurance (see Chapter 4). In spite of creating uncertainty by means of the mechanisms described above, our PAL for example, consultants were not supposed to foster an outwardly sceptical attitude towards their own judgements and analytic conclusions (Briggs 1991). Instead, they needed to present themselves as providers of certainty who would help clients overcome the assumed challenges ahead. This double role was made evident in the fact that regular company employees saw us as agents of uncertainty – who questioned their jobs, their productivity, the necessity of the products they worked on and so on – while management appreciated us as providers of stability. It was considered one of the primary skills of consultants to perform certainty vis-à-vis management, but it could also lead to moments of profound alienation. Here is how Eva, a former colleague of mine, talked about this tension:

> Communication was hard for me, even during my first project with [*Team Leader*] Hannes. [He did not want to hear about] problems and did not appreciate it when I pointed out errors in the system. It could be a good thing but you had to bring a solution at the same time, as anything else was deemed destructive. You had to say: We do not have a problem but we have a *slight bump on the road*, and in general everything is great, and I will have a think about the following couple of steps,

and eventually all will be *tip top*. For example, Hannes had prohibited me from using the words 'but' or 'problem'. Problems did not exist. Our *obligation to question everything* was pure *hypocrisy*. ... A Senior Partner recently said to a Junior Partner 'I always seem to have to convince you to carry out an analysis.' He was talking to the guy who worked until 4 am every day of the week and who started his days at 8 am. This was not a lazy person. He was a critical person, who knew a lot and who saw problems in an analysis. The Senior Partner does not understand that, because he is not as involved, and [as consultant] you simply are not allowed to say that something is hard. You have to say that things are totally awesome, and that you will suggest an analysis. You have to pretend that things make sense.

Despite performative attempts at dealing with the uncertainties of this kind of work, the risk remained that heightened economic activity would tip over into stasis. Here is Eva again on how she encountered problems at work and one day at the office simply could not move anymore:

It felt like being paralysed. This is how I remember it. It led me to develop strong feelings of uncertainty and to feel like I was paralysed at the end of the project. I think this is what a burnout must feel like. Maybe it was one, I do not know. So I got myself a coach so as to avoid this from happening again, because I was also suffering from panic attacks. ... When I tried to talk to my *Team Leader* about it, because I did not know how this would continue, he asked me whether this was really necessary. The coach helped me understand that I should stop this kind of behaviour. She also gave me a sedative because panic attacks – apart from being extremely bothersome – are also paralysing. They do not allow you to do anything anymore and you begin *catastrophising* as they say in English, that is, you think everything is horrible. She did not want me to take them regularly, but even taking half a pill was helpful. You know that it does not render you totally freaky but it has a kind of a talisman effect, in the sense that I know that I have something that helps me.

Eva responded to the problems associated with an uncertain environment with total paralysis. The performative pressures meant that she had no way of seeking help without completely losing face, and it was only through the support of an outsider and the use of a talisman that she was able to return to economic productivity. Like many of her colleagues she eventually decided to leave the company after only about three years into the job. She did not leave right after her worst project, but decided to change job after a more successful one, as doing the former would have had too much of a negative impact on her self-esteem. Today she works in her own management consulting business, at her own pace. From the perspective of our former employer, however, she eventually chose inertia over further attempts to fulfil what she could have been within company boundaries.

The potential client of ours in the PAL equally chose not to work with us. Writing our letter did get my team a *pitch* invitation, yet the *pitch* was lost for reasons unknown to most people involved in it. My *team leader* argued that the competition in the pitch had simply been cheaper. Rather than wondering further about it, we did not dwell in the uncertainties of this past decision, accepted that this project was not going to actualize itself and focused in a pragmatic and optimistic manner on other tasks at hand.

Conclusion

This chapter has shown that abstract labour lends itself to the construction and use of a profitable uncertainty, a pervasive condition that shapes relationships within consultancy firms and with their clients. In my field site, uncertainty was established for employees and clients by postulating potential worlds and holding that economic subjects were both free and influential with respect to their actualization. Uncertainty turned out to be heterogeneous in nature in that its excess could lead to stasis, rather than further economic activity, and consultants reacted to it with pragmatism, optimism, declarations of expertise work performance and ultimately stasis. The chapter has also foregrounded that the anthropological study of freedom (Laidlaw 2014 a,b) and that of economic activity under capitalism should go hand in hand since different forms and assumed distributions of freedom were here harnessed for monetary gains.

Conclusion:

In the Business of Critique

This book has argued that the work regime of management consultants is best described as 'abstract labour'. As knowledge workers, consultants bought and sold abstractions, that is, representations that constantly referred to entities and activities that lay far beyond the concrete, observable environment. These abstractions both reflected and instantiated corporations, thereby enabling managerial rule and shareholder value. Their work was abstract in a second sense, namely in that it enabled managers to foster their position of power over thousands of corporate employees at a time. While the relations of consultants and managers with corporate subordinates would strongly impact the latter's economic lives, they were marked by an emotional and affective disengagement, facilitated by physical reclusion and an enclosure of one's emotions and affects to within the sphere of management. Apart from these epistemic and social components of abstraction, consulting was considered several steps removed from the origins of corporate value creation, enabling arguments in favour of its overarching importance. Lastly, it was abstract in that it remained ultimately opaque, both for clients and their employees, and frequently for the consultants involved in it.

Economic anthropologists have frequently associated the term 'abstraction' with entities or processes that are inherently negative or to some degree unreal in nature (e.g. Comaroff and Comaroff 1999; Miller 2002, 2003). While this may reflect popular or materialist understandings of the term 'abstract', I would like to convey that this kind of critique did not easily apply to my field site (cf. Harper 2000: 29–30; Holm 2007). My colleagues sometimes doubted whether the degree of abstraction with which they were operating might not be too high, yet they never questioned the act of abstraction itself. Moreover, they seemed to suffer frequently from the fact that work became in many ways hyperreal. It almost fully determined their daily behaviour, from the food they ate to the clothes they wore, and the ways they spoke. It equally seemed to alter their ways of thinking about the world, profoundly affecting their conceptions and perceptions of time (Chapter 2), knowledge (Chapter 4) and personhood (Chapter 5). Abstract labour was equally hyperreal in the sense that it made strong physical, emotional and social demands on the people involved in it, their families and friends, as well as all those corporate employees eventually affected by it.

However, the fact that this kind of work was in many senses removed from its concrete referents meant that it enabled a panoply of ways in which it could be challenged or justified. Assertions that their jobs were meaningless (e.g. Graeber 2013) went hand in hand with (self-) congratulatory celebrations of the tremendous economic impact that consultants had. Rather than ending this book with my personal judgement on this issue, I will leave it up to the reader to decide whether and under which circumstances the act of speeding up other people's working lives and creating spreadsheet and slide show representations of corporate entities constitute useful, meaningful or otherwise desirable activities. What can be said based on the previous chapters is that the kind of consulting work described here, geared at strengthening the power of top management, carried out in seclusion from affected publics and structured around constant performances of social elitism facilitates the short-term creation of social inequality.

In this chapter, I would like to draw attention to the similarities and differences between German business consultants and British social anthropologists. I have studied the latter group over a year, as part of a postdoctoral research project at the University of Cambridge. During this time, I conducted over fifty interviews with anthropologists trained in Britain, most of whom held a PhD in the subject, asking them whether and how they considered their work to have an influence beyond academia. The comparison between them and German business consultants is meant to fulfil two purposes. On the one hand, it should elucidate the nature of abstract labour a little more. On the other, it is meant as an intervention in the current trend of blurring the lines between the work of consultants and that of anthropologists. It argues that both groups carry out fundamentally different kinds of work, and that while they may surely learn from one another, their jobs should not be turned into one and the same.

Anthropology as abstract labour?

In many ways, anthropologists also engage in abstract labour. They tend to describe entities that lie beyond their concrete environment, and they frequently do this from the comfortable physical seclusion of the university campus. Their work is often removed from the assumed origins of capitalist moneymaking (i.e. our books are not geared at broad audiences and usually do not sell very well) and carrying it out may get hyperreal in many ways. Indeed, anthropological work warrants being considered a strongly morally inflected profession, that is, a vocation which people 'live for' rather than living off (Weber 2004). Thus anthropologists consider their work to be important far beyond its economic pay-off and they deem themselves to remain part of their profession even when their official job titles say otherwise (Spencer, Jepson and Mills 2011). This vocational view of the discipline has come through very strongly in the interviews with anthropologists on which this chapter is based. The vast majority of the fiction writers, journalists, NGO workers, state officials and private sector employees I talked to continued to consider themselves anthropologists regardless of whether or not this was written on their business cards. A similarly intense identification with the discipline was evident in academic writing, where anthropological work was frequently depicted as a means by which researchers came to understand more about themselves (Kuper 2010: 141), tried to establish relations of correspondence with the world (Ingold 2013: 7) or engaged in practices of reflective self-formation (Laidlaw 2014: 216). Anthropologists in the UK thus did not mechanically respond to economic incentives, but they partook in a moral economy (Thompson 1971), in that their work activity was structured to a significant extent around non-economic considerations of what constituted a right and a good life in the light of the values, norms and affects they abide by (Fassin 2009, 2012; Herzfeld 2015). This is quite different to the work of management consultants, where vocational understandings are much harder to establish (Chapter 5).

However, two trends blur the currently existing lines between anthropology and consulting. First, consulting is becoming an increasingly interesting job prospect for anthropology graduates. As part of the humanities and social sciences, their mean annual starting salary currently lies around £18k (De Vries 2014: 28–31), and their likelihood of getting a professional job after graduation sits firmly within the lower third of university degrees (ibid.: 33–6). In times when the average UK student leaves university with an astonishing £44k of debt (ibid.), choosing to study anthropology as a subject can thus mean selecting a level of indebtedness of roughly 250 per cent of future annual income, if one manages to obtain a professional job in the first place (Graeber 2014). The situation does not improve markedly for those anthropologists who attempt to build an academic career. Between 2006 and 2012 the number of PhD graduates in the UK expanded by 20 per cent, leading to the creation of a new periphery of academic workers with increasingly insecure job prospects, who labour around the existing core of established elders (Alfonso 2014; Mills 2003: 22). Among my interviewees, the difficulties of this situation seemed to affect women more than men. The prospects of childcare were hard to combine with moving from one temporal research contract to another, pushing several women out of the academic job market after their PhD but before obtaining the security of academic tenure. In this climate of relatively high debt and unsatisfactory job prospects, consultancy constitutes one lucrative job option, not least because the public and private sectors are increasingly looking to use ethnography as part of market research, policy appraisal, workforce assessment and even journalism (*The Atlantic* 2007; Stein 2016).

Secondly, the British government is aggressively increasing its demands on social anthropologists to make their work 'policy relevant'. Thus, the country's regular audit exercise for the measurement of academic productivity, known as the 'Research Excellence Framework' (REF), included in its last instalment an assessment of how much 'impact' anthropologists (and academics more widely) could claim to have on wider society. This audit is taken very seriously by British academics, since whichever institution gets the best grades is likely to receive a larger share of the roughly £2bn that is allocated to higher education institutions per year.[1] While government calls at increasing the discipline's practical relevance are both necessary and have broadly been supported by UK anthropologists for close to a century (see for example Ingold 2016: 383; Malinowski 1929, 1930, 1945), its current audit system incentivizes them to target their advice and support at corporate institutions (Stein forthcoming; Jarman and Bryan 2015). The REF thereby pushes academics to turn themselves into consultants, in the hope of obtaining more research funding.

The business of critique

Similarities and increasing overlaps of anthropology and consulting raise the question whether significant differences exist between the two. I will here point out three of these, namely the purposes of both kinds of labour, the ways in which they create and overcome their abstract nature, and the time frames under which they operate. First, the previous chapters have shown that while the work of German management consultants was frequently based on the utopian and decentring act of building potential worlds (Chapter 5), this was not its main purpose. The worlds they invoked could never be outlandish, merely interesting or clashing with business-internal 'common sense' (Geertz 1983). Instead, the kinds of critique that consultants were allowed to engage in had to remain closely circumscribed by everyday realism and market imperatives so as to be of practical efficacy understood to as fulfilling the prerogatives of management, corporate profit or shareholder value. Critical work was here subsumed to planning, which in turn had to be deemed useful by project-commissioning managers. Thereby, the critique of management consultants was based on an *a priori* normative stance towards the world. It was a denunciatory project grounded in and justified by a desire for social change along the lines of business logics. Critical work in consulting was thus both epistemically and normatively subsumed to business logics, rather than the other way round.

An immediately politically inflected understanding of critique may often be a driving force for anthropological work as well, even if it is mostly geared at social justice rather than business imperatives (Graeber 2014; Nader 1969; Sheper-Hughes 1995). However, the British anthropologists I interviewed predominantly valued their discipline because it had provided them with an altered approach to the world as such (Eriksen and Stein 2017; Stein 2016: 28). In describing anthropology as 'eye-opening', 'mind-blowing', or rendering people 'more understanding and open minded', they stressed that they had learnt to cultivate a sense of wonder and unease towards the most basic categories of social life. It is through this acquired disposition that anthropology continued to be valued by them as a source for empirically grounded, yet largely imaginative thought, rather than as a form of planning for practical purposes. In fact, anthropology has always been a critical activity, one marked by systemic scepticism (Carrithers 2005: 435) that goes so far as to question not just market rationales, but the ontological foundations of social life itself (Heywood 2017; Scott 2016). Thereby, work of anthropology is critical in a more general, epistemic sense of undermining taken-for-granted views and providing its writers, readers, speakers and listeners first and foremost with empirically grounded alternatives as to how human lives can be led. This more profoundly critical nature can be traced back to the European Enlightenment, as part of which anthropology arose not only as a driver of European colonialism, but also as a persistent quest for knowledge that destabilized the established conceptual orders of all peoples involved (Hastrup 2007). The anthropology of audit cultures has shown that this kind of work aims at producing critique, rather than subsuming critical work for business.

At least two defining aspects of anthropology enable this strongly critical function. First, the discipline has historically been driven by a willingness for cross-cultural and cross-temporal comparison. For the anthropologists I interviewed, finding out that family life, political institutions and everyday patterns of production, consumption and exchange could be organized very differently had a lasting effect. The mere act of being confronted with a description of the lives of others already bears the potential of instilling an enduring critical mindset in students and readers of anthropological work, one that may be equally unsettling as it is liberating. As Hannerz has put it: 'Any claim that anthropology can have to unusual critical insight is in fact based on its special relationship to diversity – to the knowledge that other ways of thinking and acting are possible' (2010: 49). Anthropology, as the most radically comparative social science, makes the most out of this knowledge by systematically likening topics and entities that other academic disciplines may deem perfectly incommensurable (Lazar 2012; Strathern 2005: 91).

Secondly, anthropological scholarship, whether conducted in the depth of the Amazon or in the boardrooms of Wall Street investors, tends to look for conceptual paradoxes, inconsistencies and internal inadequacies (Berliner et al. 2016). They may describe how the incompatibility between simultaneously present moral systems push indigenous people of Papua New Guinea into crisis (Robbins 2004) or how US central-bankers make up for the imperfections of their technocratic knowledge through the use of semiotics (Holmes and Marcus 2006). This is not the result of an unfounded desire for complexity and complication but a technique that allows anthropological scholarship to conceive of the world differently from most people whose struggle for survival or whose intense daily job requirements punish rather than encourage such excessively critical attention.

A defining feature of the alternative modes of thought thereby created is that practitioners and readers of anthropology do not have to, nor should they, think along the lines of immediate short-term utility, or prevalent corporate or political lines of allegiance. As a discipline in which argumentative fit triumphs over practical utility, and in which researchers create moments of uncertainty regardless of whether or not the latter may or may not be profitable (Strathern 2006), anthropology will frequently sit uneasily with the desires of corporate elites. In fact, anthropologists working with corporate elites in the public and private sectors have shown that the latter deal often in creating authoritative interpretations (Mosse 2005, 2006). Their frequently tenuous power positions rely to a significant extent on producing and protecting authorized views of social life, the inadequacy of which becomes obvious when directly confronted with alternative interpretations or references to their own inconsistencies and blind spots (ibid.).

A second major difference between consulting and the work of anthropology lies in how they attempt to both create and overcome their abstract nature. The previous chapters have shown that consultants create a mix of rhetoric and episteme so as to speak about a vast amount of social phenomena in an idiom of spreadsheets, slides and workshops that evoke precision and control over empathy. This is done in the service of a clearly predefined audience, that is, the managers who may commission further projects for them. This, as well as a fluctuation between being social insiders and outsiders, allows them to justify their own work as relevant, enabling management to legitimate their position of intra-corporate dominance. Consultants thereby turn themselves into a technology of abstraction, in the sense that management could use them to relate to their products, capital, staff, suppliers and clients without getting to know them on an empathetic level. One way in which this tension between abstraction and intimacy became obvious during my fieldwork was when colleagues joked by expressing highly personal topics in consultancy terms. Colleagues would frequently announce the birth of their children via email to the entire office, jesting about how the birth of their child meant that they would 'embark on a new project'. Another strongly gendered joke sent to me from male and female colleagues was a publicly available slide show. Written by someone who must have been a male American management consultant during the 1990s, it depicted his attempt at analysing his relationship with his girlfriend in consulting terms (see excerpt Figure 5) and ended in his girlfriend breaking up with him because of his lack of 'empathy, companionship, affection [and] love'.

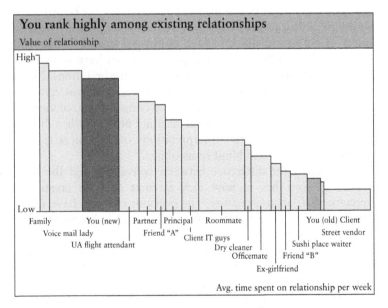

FIGURE 5 *A slide depicting intimate relationships.*[2]

In anthropology, this relationship between knowledge creation and audience is inverted in two ways. First, anthropologists produce research papers and books for a largely unknown audience, and even in teaching they might be presenting ideas to hundreds of students at a time, rather than to a handful of closely known managers. More importantly, anthropological work does not overcome its abstract nature in making itself relevant for current and future clients, but in aiming at an empathetic understanding of its research subjects (Geertz 1973). This engagement may be such that it leads researchers to get politically involved in the lives of the people they study. One illustrative example for this is the research experience of Marcus Colchester, anthropologist and founder of the NGO Forest Peoples Programme that promotes the rights of indigenous people. For his PhD research he spent over two years living in the upper Orinoco river of current-day Venezuela, an experience that he describes thus:

> I became more and more indignant … , in particular when I saw so many people dying of introduced diseases because mining was coming into the area at the time. I was working for the government of Venezuela as a regional coordinator for the national census … , working out that 25% of the population of some villages had died in the past year. These people were obviously deeply traumatised and I had seen them dying and getting ill in the places where I was working as well, which was terribly upsetting. Traumatic almost. So I decided I had to do something about all this institutional neglect and racism rather than just pursuing my own interests. That is when I converted from being an academic to being an activist.

Martina Salvatierra,[3] who got her PhD in anthropology in the late 1990s, describes a similar experience. She is now a senior World Bank official involved in responding to the Syrian Refugee Crisis in parts of the Mediterranean, and explains the lasting effect of anthropology on her work as follows:

> [For my PhD research] I have stayed in a refugee camp for a year and a half. Just to have that experience as a development practitioner is transformative. I will fortunately never know what it is like to be poor or be faced with those constraints and

challenges, but I have gone as far as it is possible to understand what it feels like to live as a poor person day by day. Hopefully everything I do today [at the World Bank] will be designed with that in mind.

Anthropologists thus often develop a heartfelt desire to endow their work with a broader sort of social efficacy that is not restricted to the requirements of corporate managers (see also Simpson 2016: 3). Empathy does not just allow anthropologists to overcome the abstract nature of their work, by creating long and profoundly qualitative accounts of the lives of people under study. It also stands in the service of critique in the sense that anthropological scholarship gives considerable importance to the conceptual apparatus of their research subjects. Reluctant to either take on the concepts of the people they study fully or dismiss them in their entirety, anthropology thrives in the tension between providing a mere account of what people think and denouncing them for being mistaken or otherwise misguided (Fassin 2009b, 2012). In striking a balance between epistemological engagement and detachment that is closer to its research subjects than that of consulting, anthropology manages to confront its readers with radically different conceptions of the world that they can neither fully take on nor easily dismiss. It thereby leaves its readers in a state of epistemic and normative suspension that strengthens the critical rather than the pragmatic potential inherent in comparative work.

Moreover, ethnographic research has a considerable degree of serendipity built into it (Rivoal and Salazar 2013). Consider the following account by one anthropologist interviewee:

[My research trajectory] has been, a slightly unlikely one and I could not have replicated it if I wanted to. I was initially interested in fair trade so I went to Ghana to look at the impact it was having on small scale producers. While I was there, I developed an interest in the issue of child labour in cocoa production. This was over 16 years ago at a time when nobody was talking about this topic and the people I researched were considered very obscure. ... Within less than six months of starting my PhD, a team of investigative journalists from the UK went to West Africa and found children were working in cocoa production. This caused a huge scandal and suddenly everyone wanted to talk about the issue. It was on the front page of the papers, and campaigning groups and [politicians began holding] chocolate companies to account. ... My PhD went in a matter of days from complete obscurity to everyone wanting to know more about it.

The research project described here led to a follow-up study commissioned by a cocoa producer so as to guide a £3.2m investment to reduce child labour. It thereby blurred the lines between anthropological research and consultancy work in various ways. However, both its epistemic and its political effects were largely unforeseeable. Unlike the work of consultants, where key hypotheses of what needs to be done in a company are defined before a project even officially starts, anthropology is decisively serendipitous in nature. This has become so enshrined in the discipline that British anthropology PhD students are actively encouraged in their training to be very open to a potential mismatch between the topic of interest outlined in their research proposals and the issues that their post-fieldwork writing actually deals with. This serendipity does not end with the writing process, but stretches into the afterlife of ethnographic publications (Fassin 2015, 2017). In the critical work of anthropologists, unforeseen research avenues are thus much more openly embraced than in consulting.

Lastly, a third crucial difference worth pointing out is the temporality with which consultants and anthropologists operate. Since critique in consulting is subsumed to business concerns, its time frames are as well. Thus, Chapter 2 has shown that speed is not just a feature of how consultants are meant to work, it is in fact a product of their labour. In the light of this, consultants always need to pretend to be faster than corporate employees, and faster than the potential competition. This drives them to conduct research and analyses in extremely short time frames, leaving little possibility for detailed qualitative engagement with the thousands of entities that they are meant to analyse within months, weeks, at times even just days.

Anthropology on the other hand, is slow. Long-term fieldwork is the key in the production of its critical stance, since its extended time frames allow the researcher to develop a degree of intimacy vis-à-vis the people under study that will prevent her from simply discarding their views as irrelevant. Thus anthropologists are known to spend years, at times even decades, working in the same countries, regions and sometimes even with the same research subjects. These longer time frames enable them to tease out the intra-discursive inconsistencies, as well as the tensions between word and practice, conscious and unconscious knowledge, formal and informal modes of living with which their research subjects operate. Thus, longer time frames are a necessary prerequisite for qualitative research.

While this slowness may stem from and foster the empathy built between anthropologists and the people they study, it equally enables the researcher to develop an eye not just for those aspects of social life that are immediately relevant for her research hypothesis, but also for all those moments of incompleteness and contingency that challenge the conceptual apparatus with which she embarked on a research project in the first place (Candea 2007: 180). As a practice of lasting embodied, social and conceptual displacement, it removes the researcher from the foundations of her own life, forcing her – in a best case scenario – to re-evaluate them in its light (Kapferer 2006). The epistemic and at times normative moments of critique are here more frequently geared towards the self, trying not to force others to correspond one's own utopian vision, but questioning whether one's own vision is the right one. Self-formation, in so far as it is part of anthropology, is less constrained by business concerns and more driven towards conceptual self-doubt. The time frames for critical work, the development of empathy and the radical undermining of one's own conceptual apparatus thus have to be much longer than those of managerial or shareholder performance cycles.

In the light of these differences between consulting and anthropological work, the reader might ask herself what the social efficacy of anthropology may be. Is anthropology just a tool for widely interested academics to satisfy their personal curiosity? That would make for a weak justification for the provision of a publicly funded institutional space such as a university to carry it out. According to the interviews on which this chapter is based, the social efficacy of anthropology is at least twofold. First, for my interviewees, the most important social effect of anthropology is that it presents us with an empirically informed conceptual space that stands apart from the dominant discourses of our states, markets, families as well as ethnic or religious leaders. This space is critical in that it conveys the insight that the world could be otherwise which was to them an end in itself (Carrithers 2005). Anthropology is a kid of empirically grounded form of science fiction, in that it provides the peoples who engage with it the opportunity of thinking about their world in a new way (Eriksen and Stein 2017: 236). One of my interviewees, a full-time fiction writer who had studied anthropology later in life, continues to read academic articles and attends events organized by Britain's Royal Anthropological Institute precisely for this reason. He argues that anthropology persistently provides him with 'a new perspective' that he integrates into his work. It serves as a seemingly endless intellectual resource for his writing. This endows his work with a degree of nuance in understanding social life that is rarely found elsewhere. Thereby, anthropology contributes significantly to the work of journalists, filmmakers and policy researchers who spoke with me.

One recent illustration for this alternative stance is the work by Liberatore (2017) on Somali Muslim women living in London. The author begins her book by tracing public debates around culture and religion in the UK from the 1960s until today, showing how concepts such as cultural identity, integration and cohesion have been mobilized in order to turn Muslims, particularly Muslim women who wear the *hijab* or *niqab*, into objects of concern and scrutiny. Yet, Liberatore makes clear that her study does not pursue the goal of resolving a 'problem' pertaining to Somalis. She explicitly refuses to take on public and popular anxieties of how to 'integrate' these women into the British cultural mainstream. Instead, she questions why these women have come to be understood as a problem in the first place, thereby turning her ethnography into an attempt of '"speaking with" rather than "speaking to" or "for" Somalis' (ibid.). Her anthropological work allows us to engage with topics that currently dominate the British media in a manner that is hard to find in the all too quickly polarizing spheres of journalism and political discourse.

Ultimately, it is likely that the presence of the critical discursive space that anthropology provides (together with other social sciences and the humanities) drives the constant renewal and refinement of dominant discursive paradigms. For example, here is how a senior UK anthropologist and public intellectual put it in an interview:

Anthropology has a great deal of impact. ... In terms of my own research the impacts have been of many different kinds, on the community I study, on students and on the discipline as a whole, which is what you'd expect. ... When I began working on the topic of gender most people really did not know what gender was. I was part of a really extremely large group of people internationally, who were all collaborating in one way or another [so as to] develop the idea of gender. Now, nearly every country in the world has a gender policy. ... The impact of the academy is often very significant.

Conclusion

This chapter has compared the work of German business consultants to that of social anthropologists, foregrounding that both are abstract in a variety of ways. Consultants carried out 'abstract labour' in that they bought and sold abstractions, enabled managers to rule at a distance, remain removed from economic value creation and conducted work that ultimately remained opaque, both for clients and frequently for the consultants involved in it. In many ways, the work of anthropologists is also abstract, in that they describe entities that lie beyond the concrete environment, frequently from a comfortable distance. Needless to say, the links of their work to moneymaking are equally, if not more tenuous.

That said, in the light of the societal pressures that work to turn anthropology into consulting and that claim that consulting and anthropology can be one and the same, I have here pointed out three differences between the two kinds of work. They differ in purpose in that consulting rests subsumed to business logics, while anthropology engages in a more radical and encompassing form of critique. Moreover, they create and overcome the abstract nature of their work in different ways. Consultants evoke precision and control over empathy in the service of a clearly predefined managerial audience. Thereby they work directly on social relationships in that they enable management to relate to a myriad of entities without developing empathy towards them. Anthropologists, on the other hand, cater to a wider and less well-known audience, rather than a handful of managers. While their work is based on the use of concepts that are not necessarily experience-near, it tries to overcome this abstract nature by conveying an empathetic understanding of the people they speak about. The empathy and serendipity that mark anthropological work and enhance its critical value rely on long-term research and the production of engaging descriptions, rather than overnight slide production. Since anthropology works to create a critical discursive space in which thought can be less bound up than in corporate or otherwise pragmatic efficacy, it seems to be a polar opposite of consulting, which subsumes critique to managerial demands. In renewing and changing the basic categories through which we conceive of social life, anthropology also stands in considerable tension to consulting, which holds them stable and applies them in the service of business and busyness.

While this chapter insists on the differences between anthropology and consulting, it does not deny that both kinds of work could operate hand in hand. Anthropologists driven towards making a more directly visible and immediate impact on the world may want to think about how they can engage with the corporate world (including NGOs and state entities) so as to work towards the goals of social justice and cultural respect that have long been part of our discipline's history. Management consulting as I have encountered it in the field might not be the best way to do this, since it was too often part and parcel of creating social inequality. Yet, maybe other forms and audiences of corporate advice given by anthropologists are conceivable. In the same vein, I hope that at least a few management consultants will have found this book interesting. If it has enabled them to think about their work in even a slightly different light, then it has fulfilled its purpose. After all, anthropology does not subsume critique under business, but remains in the business of critique.

NOTES

Introduction

1 See http://ec.europa.eu/eurostat/statistics-explained/index.php/
File:Table_2_Unemployment_rate,_2003-2014_(%25).png (accessed
14 October 2015).

2 All names of companies and individuals in this book have been
anonymized. Numbers, diagrams and some key expressions have
equally been altered.

3 For an introduction to the literature from which this vocabulary was
borrowed, see for example Womack, Jones and Roos 1990, Womack
and Jones 2003, Boltanski and Chiapello 2011: 124–7.

4 In so far as their abstractions render other people's work
homogeneous, consultants could even be said to be an enabling
force for 'abstract labour' in Marx's original sense of the term
(Mohun 1991).

5 Rimowa is a traditional German suitcase brand preferred by business
travellers. It is known for its high quality and its inflated prices.

Chapter 1

1 For a description of autopoiesis in the work of EU officials, see Shore
(2000: 27).

2 For a discussion of the many different kinds of shareholder value, see
Ho 2009b and Froud et al. 2006.

3 See, for example, IBM management consulting: http://www-935.ibm. com/services/us/gbs/consulting/ (accessed 17 October 2015).

4 See, for example, Repucom: http://repucom.net (accessed 17 October 2015).

5 See, for example, Dalberg: http://www.dalberg.com (accessed 17 October 2015).

6 The country's largest matchmaking company is called Parship Elite Group. It operates the country's two major partnership websites, one of which is called Elite-Partner (Handelsblatt 2016).

7 'Hochbegabte'.

8 The number has been altered for confidentiality reasons.

9 'Auszeichnung'.

Chapter 2

1 The Marxist concept 'ursprüngliche Akkumulation' used here is sometimes translated into English as 'primitive accumulation'.

2 'durchgetaktet'.

3 'reinquätschen'.

4 For reasons of confidentiality I will not comment on the location of the mill.

5 All numbers have been altered for confidentiality reasons.

6 Quote slightly altered to ensure anonymity; improvement potential could in theory also be 'identified' if time gains were converted into potential revenue increases, which would in turn drive up profit. However, management was interested in saving costs, not in increasing revenue.

7 'Eingreiftruppe'.

8 'am Anschlag arbeiten'.

9 This progression has been altered slightly for confidentiality reasons.

10 'Mithalten'.

11 'Zeit gespart', 'Zeit gewonnen'.

12 For an example of temporality geared at permanence that is closer to home, see Ringel (2014).

Chapter 3

1 Technically, a senior partner from Norway and another one from France were also part of our team, yet they were absent most of the time.

2 'Affekte'.

3 German: 'abgebaut werden', literally 'get deconstructed'.

4 'etwas no needful machen'.

5 'In der Schublade verschwinden'.

6 An instrument that divides work progress into green (on track), yellow (slightly behind) and red (major issues).

7 'Relationship building machen'.

8 'was sagen'.

9 'Entscheidungsfreude', literally, 'Joy in decision-making'.

Chapter 4

1 Known as 'public statutory health insurance funds'.

2 Split into 8.2 per cent paid by employees and 7.3 per cent paid by employers. The money had to be paid directly by employers, so that the employees never got involved in the payment process. The national employment agency paid both amounts for the unemployed.

3 Figures have been altered for reasons of confidentiality.

4 'komisch', a term meaning both strange and funny.

5 'sich reinbohren'.

6 'sich ins Modell reinfräsen'.

7 'Wunschkonzert'.

8 'mit dem Rasenmäher drüber'.

9 'Zahlen schrubben'.

10 'Führungskräfte', literally 'leading forces'.

11 The latter was an unfortunate term since each of these groups referred to employees of some sort, a fact that would eventually lead to some confusion.

12　The model has been simplified and anonymized. All numbers in this and in all following figures are fictional.

13　The location of staff needs to remain confidential.

14　'versliden'.

15　This slide has been rebuilt with some modifications to ensure confidentiality.

16　'Kästchen rücken'.

17　https://www.joinbain.com/apply-to-bain/interview-preparation/crack-the-case.asp (accessed 23 October 2015).

18　http://www.bcg.com.cn/en/newsandpublications/publications/books/book20090309008.html (accessed 23 October 2015).

Chapter 5

1　'Brückentechnologie'.

2　'Restrisiko'.

3　See for example http://www.opp.com/en/tools/mbti/myers-briggs-history.

4　https://books.google.com/ngrams/graph?content=MBTI%2CMyers-Briggs&year_start=1940&year_end=2008&corpus=15&smoothing=3&share=&direct_url=t1%3B%2CMBTI%3B%2CCc0%3B.t1%3B%2CMyers%20-%20Briggs%3B%2CCc0 (accessed 23 October 2015).

5　http://www.myersbriggs.org/type-use-for-everyday-life/mbti-type-at-work/ (accessed 23 October 2015).

6　See for example Deloitte's company-specific 'Business Chemistry' personality test: http://deloitte.wsj.com/cfo/2015/08/26/the-power-of-business-chemistry-3/.

Chapter 6

1　Quotes from the letter have been slightly altered for confidentiality reasons.

2　Adapted from http://www.bcg.de/karriere/entwicklung/moglichkeiten/default.aspx (accessed 8 July 2014) and Bain Germany career website http://www.joinbain.de/career/#qualification-428 (accessed 8 July 2014).

3 'immer noch eine schippe drauflegen'.
4 'am Anschlag halten'.
5 'exotisch'.
6 'ausgelasted sein', 'keine Kappa haben'.
7 'nicht unser ganzes Pulver auf einmal verschießen'.
8 'Gesamteindruck'.

Conclusion

1 See for example http://www.hefce.ac.uk/pubs/year/2016/CL,232016/ (accessed 13 November 2016).
2 Online at: http://www.slideshare.net/nitinagarwalin/bcg-consultants-love-life.
3 Some names have been changed.

BIBLIOGRAPHY

AAA (American Anthropological Association) (2012). Principles of Professional Responsibility. Online at http://ethics.aaanet.org/ethics-statement-0-preamble/ (accessed 14 October 2015).

Abram, S. (2014). 'The time it takes: Temporalities of planning'. *Journal of the Royal Anthropological Institute* 20(S1): 129–47.

Abrams, P. (2006). 'Notes on the Difficulty of Studying the State'. In *The anthropology of the state: A reader*, A. Sharma and A. Gupta (eds). Oxford, Blackwell: 112–30.

Adam, B. (1994). 'Perceptions of time'. In *Companion Encyclopedia of Anthropology*, T. Ingold (ed.). London and New York, Routledge: 503–27.

Ade, M. (2016). *Toni Erdmann*. Germany and Austria, NFP Marketing & Distribution Enfilade, 2016.

Agamben, G. (2005). *State of Exception*. Chicago and London, The University of Chicago Press.

Alfonso, A. (2014). How Academia Resembles a Drug Gang. Online at https://alexandreafonso.me/2013/11/21/how-academia-resembles-a-drug-gang/ (accessed 11 November 2016).

Amrute, S. (2014). 'Proprietary Freedoms in an IT Office: How Indian IT Workers Negotiate Code and Cultural Branding'. *Social Anthropology* 22(1): 101–17.

Anders, G. (2008). 'The Normativity of Numbers: World Bank and IMF Conditionality'. PoLAR – *Political and Legal Anthropology Review* 31(2): 187–202.

Anderson, B. (1991). *Imagined Communities: Reflections on the Origin and Spread of Nationalism*. London, Verso Books.

Appadurai, A. (ed.) (1996 [1993]). 'Number in the Colonial Imagination'. In *Modernity at Large – Cultural Dimensions of Globalization*. Minneapolis and London, University of Minnesota Press: 114–39.

Aristotle (2007 [350BC]). *On Rhetoric – A Theory of Civic Discourse*. New York and Oxford, Oxford University Press.

Armbrüster, T. and M. Kipping (2002). 'Strategy Consulting at the Crossroads: Technical Change and Shifting Market: Conditions for Top-Level Advice'. *International Studies of Management & Organization* 32(4 Management Consultancy: Issues, Perspectives, and Agendas): 19–42.

Armbrüster, T. and J. Glückler (2007). 'Organizational Change and the Economics of Management Consulting: A Response to Sorge and van Witteloostuijn'. *Organization Studies* 28(12): 1873–85.

Armbrüster, T., J. Banzhaf and L. Dingemann (2010). *Unternehmensberatung im öffentlichen Sektor – Institutionenkonflikt, praktische Herausforderungen, Lösungen [Consulting in the public sector – Insitutional conflict, practical challenges, solutions].* Wiesbaden, Gabler.

Arendt, H. (1958). *The Human Condition.* Chicago and London, University of Chicago Press.

Augé, M. (1995). *Non-Places – Introduction to an Anthropology of Supermodernity.* London, New York, Verso.

Arnold, P. E. (1976). 'The First Hoover Commission and the Managerial Presidency'. *The Journal of Politics* 38(1): 47–70.

Bain & Company (2005). Closing the delivery gap: How to achieve true customer-led growth. Online at http://www.bain.com/publications/articles/closing-the-delivery-gap-newsletter.aspx (accessed 24 October 2015), Bain & Company.

Bain & Company (2011). The Great Eight – Trillion Dollar Growth Trends to 2020. Online at http://www.bain.com/publications/articles/eight-great-trillion-dollar-growth-trends-to-2020.aspx (accessed 19 October 2015).

Bain & Company (2014). Join Bain. Online at https://joinbain.com/apply-to-bain/what-bain-looks-for/ (accessed 20 October 2015).

Bain & Company (2015a). A supportive culture. Online at https://ww.joinbain.com/why-bain/a-supportive-culture/default.asp (accessed 20 October 2015).

Bain & Company (2015b). Branchenkompetenzen. Online at http://bain.de/branchenkompetenzen/index.aspx (accessed 20 October 2015).

Bain & Company (2015c). Managementkompetenzen. Online at http://bain.de/branchenkompetenzen/index.aspx (accessed 20 October 2015).

Berliner, D., M. Lambek, R. Shweder, R. Irvine and A. Piette (2016). 'Anthropology and the Study of Contradictions'. *Hau: Journal of Ethnographic Theory* 6(1): 1–27.

Barchitta, P. D. (2013). *A Salesman Walks into a Classroom – The Art of Sales Meets the Science of Selling.* Bloomington, iUniverse.

Barth, F. (2002). 'An Anthropology of Knowledge'. *Current Anthropology* 43(1): 1–18.

Bauman, R. and C. L. Briggs (2003). *Voices of Modernity: Language Ideologies and the Politics of Inequality*. Cambridge, England; New York, Cambridge University Press.

BCG (Boston Consulting Group) (2013a). The U.S. Skills Gap: Could It Threaten a Manufacturing Renaissance?. Online at https://www.bcgperspectives.com/content/articles/lean_manufacturing_us_skills_gap_could_threaten_manufacturing_renaissance/ (accessed 24 October 2015).

BCG (Boston Consulting Group) (2013b). Bridging the Gap – Meeting the infrastructure Challenge with Public-Private Partnerships. Online at http://www.bcg.com/documents/file128534.pdf (accessed 24 October 2015).

BCG (Boston Consulting Group) (2013c). Mind the Gap: What Scenario Analysis Says About the Future of the U.S. Power Industry. Online at https://www.bcgperspectives.com/content/articles/energy_environment_strategy_mind_the_gap_what_scenario_analysis_says/ (accessed 24 October 2015).

BCG (Boston Consulting Group) (2014a). Branchenexpertise. Online at http://www.bcg.de/expertise_impact/industries/default.aspx (accessed 20 October 2015).

BCG (Boston Consulting Group) (2014b). Funktionale Expertise. Online at http://www.bcg.de/expertise_impact/capabilities/default.aspx (accessed 20 October 2015).

BCG (Boston Consulting Group) (2014c). Training und Entwicklung. Online at http://karriere.bcg.de/karriere/training-entwicklung.aspx (accessed 23 October 2015).

BCG (Boston Consulting Group) (2015a). Mentoring and Feedback [Mentoring und Feedback]. Online at http://www.bcg.de/karriere/entwicklung/mentoring_feedback/default.aspx (accessed 23 October 2015).

BCG (Boston Consulting Group) (2015b). Mobile Internet Contributes More than $700 Billion to Economies of 13 Major Countries. Korea. Online: https://www.bcg.com/d/press/10feb2015-mobile-internet-economies-countries-837 (accessed 10 April 2017).

BDU (Bundesverband Deutscher Unternehmensberater) (2013). Facts & Figures zum Beratermarkt [Facts & Figures on the Consulting Market]. Bonn.

Bear, L. (2013). 'The Antinomies of Audit: Opacity, Instability and Charisma in the Economic Governance of a Hooghly Shipyard'. *Economy and Society* 42(3): 375–97.

Bear, L. (2014a). 'Doubt, conflict, mediation: the anthropology of modern time'. *Journal of the Royal Anthropological Institute* 20: 3–30.

Bear, L. (2015). *Navigating austerity: currents of Debt Along a South Asian River*. Stanford, CA, Standford University Press.

Bear, L., K. Ho, A. L. Tsing and S. J. Yanagisako (2015). 'Gens: A Feminist Manifesto for the Study of Capitalism. Fieldsights – Theorizing the Contemporary. Cultural Anthropology Online'. *Cultural Anthropology Online.*

Bednarowski, T. (2013). *Get Your Lean On – A Simple, Sensible, Yet Scientific Weight Loss Solution.* Bloomington, Balboa Press.

Benson, P. (2008). 'Good Clean Tobacco: Philip Morris, Biocapitalism, and the Social Course of Stigma in North Carolina'. *American Ethnologist* 35(3): 357–79.

Bloch, M. and J. Parry (eds) (1982). 'Introduction: Death and the regeneration of life'. In *Death and the Regeneration of Life.* Cambridge, Cambridge University Press: 1–45.

BMJV (Bundesministerium der Justiz und für Verbraucherschutz) [Federal Ministry of Justice and Consumer Protection] (1998). Gesetz gegen Wettbewerbsbeschränkungen [Law against limiting competition]. Online at http://www.gesetze-im-internet.de/bundesrecht/gwb/gesamt. pdf (accessed 20 October 2015).

Boltanski, L. and È. Chiapello (2011 [1999]). *Le nouvel esprit du capitalisme.* Paris, Gallimard.

Borneman, J. (1992). 'State, Territory, and Identity Formation in the Postwar Berlins, 1945–1989'. *Cultural Anthropology* 7(1): 45–62.

Borneman, J. (1993). 'Time-Space Compression and the Continental Divide in German Subjectivity'. *The Oral History Review* 21(2): 41–58.

Borneman, J. (2000). 'Politics without a Head: Is the "Love Parade" a New Form of Political Identification?' *Cultural Anthropology* 15(2): 294–317.

Bourgoin, A. and F. Muniesa (2012). 'Making a consultancy slideshow "rock solid": A study of pragmatic efficacy'. *CSI Working Papers Series.* Paris, Centre de Sociologie de l'Innovation Mines ParisTech.

Bourgois, P. (2003 [1996]). *In Search of Respect: Selling Crack in El Barrio.* Cambridge, Cambridge University Press.

Bower, J. L. (2008). 'Insider mit dem Blick von Außen [Insiders with an outside view]'. *Harvard Business Manager* 2. Online at: http://www. harvardbusinessmanager.de/heft/artikel/a-623987.html (accessed 01 May 2017).

Boyer, D. C. (2000). 'On the Sedimentation and Accreditation of Social Knowledges of Difference/ Mass Media, Journalism, and the Reproduction of East/West Alterities in Unified Germany'. *Cultural Anthropology* 15(4): 459–91.

Boyle, G. J. (1995). 'Myers-Briggs Type Indicator (MBTI): Some psychometric limitations'. *Australian Psychologist* 30: 71–4.

BPB (Bundeszentrale für Politische Bildung) (2012). 'Ausblick'. Online at https://www.bpb.de/politik/grundfragen/deutsche-verhaeltnisse-eine-sozialkunde/138446/ausblick.

Briggs, J. L. (1991). 'Expecting the Unexpected: Canadian Inuit Training for an Experimental Lifestyle'. *Ethos* 19(3): 259–87.

Camus (1955). *The Myth of Sisyphus, and Other Essays*. New York, Vintage.

Canback, S. (1998). 'The Logic of Management Consulting Part 1'. *Journal of Management Consulting* 10(2): 3–11.

Candea, M. (2007). 'Arbitrary locations: in defence of the bounded field-site'. *Journal of the Royal Anthropological Institute* 13(1): 167–84.

Candea, M., J. Cook, C. Trundle and T. Yarrow (eds) (2015). 'Introduction: Reconsidering Detachment'. In *Detachments: Essays on the Limits of Relational Thinking*. Manchester, Manchester University Press: 1–35.

Carsten, J. (1995). 'The Substance of Kinship and the Heat of the Hearth: Feeding, Personhood, and Relatedness among Malays in Pulau Langkawi'. *American Ethnologist* 22(2): 223–41.

Carrier, J. G. and D. Kalb (2015). *Anthropologies of Class – Power, Practice and Inequality*. Cambridge, Cambridge University Press.

Carrithers, M. (2005). 'Anthropology as a Moral Science of Possibilities'. *Current Anthropology* 46(3): 433–56.

Carrithers, M. (2010 [1996]). 'Person'. In *Encyclopedia of Social and Cultural Anthropology*, A. Barnard and J. Spencer (eds). London and New York, Routledge: 532–5.

Carrithers, M., S. Collins and S. Lukes (1999 [1985]). *The Category of the Person – Anthropology, Philosophy, History*. Cambridge, Cambridge University Press.

CDU CSU and FDP (2009). Wachstum. Bildung. Zusammenhalt. Koalitionsvertrag zwischen CDU, CSU und FDP. [Growth. Education. Solidarity. Coalition Agreement between CDU, CSU and FDP]. Online at http://www.bmi.bund.de/SharedDocs/Downloads/DE/Ministerium/koalitionsvertrag.pdf?__blob=publicationFile (accessed 20 October 2015).

Chandler, A. D. (1998 [1962]). *Strategy and Structure – Chapters in the History of the Industrial Enterprise*. Cambridge, MA, MIT Press.

Chandler, A. D. (2004 [1990]). *Scale and Scope – The Dynamics of Industrial Capitalism*. Cambridge, MA and London, Belknap Press of Harvard University Press.

Chong, K. (2012). *The Work of Financialisation: An Ethnography of a Global Management Consultancy in post-Mao China*. PhD, London School of Economics and Political Science.

Christensen, Clayton M., Dina Wang, and Derek Van Bever. (2013). 'Consulting on the Cusp of Disruption'. *Harvard Business Review* 91.10 (2013): 106–14.

Chute, H. (2008). 'Comics as Literature? Reading Graphic Narrative'. *PMLA* 123(2): 452–65.

Civitas (2013). Healthcare Systems: Germany. Online at http://www. civitas.org.uk/nhs/download/germany.pdf (accessed 19 October 2015)

Clyne, M. G. (1995). *The German Language in a Changing Europe.* Cambridge, Cambridge University Press.

Cohen, G. A. (2000). *If You are an Egalitarian, How Come You're So Rich?* Cambridge, MA and London, Harvard University Press.

Comaroff, J. and J. L. Comaroff (1999). 'Occult Economies and the Violence of Abstraction: Notes from the South African Postcolony'. *American Ethnologist* 26(2): 279–303.

Cook, J., J. Laidlaw and J. Mair (2009). What if There is No Elephant Towards a Conception of an Un-sited Field. In *Multi-Sited Ethnography – Theory, Praxis and Locality in Contemporary Research.* M. A. Falzon (ed.) Farnham, Ashgate: 47–73.

Crewe, E. (2007). 'La Loyauté Dans Une Paire De Collants. Règles, Rites Et Symboles À La Chambre Des Lords'. *Ethnologie Française* 37(2): 243–54.

Crowell, S. (2004). 'Existentialism'. *Stanford Encyclopedia of Philosophy.* E. N. Zalta (ed.). Online at http://plato.stanford.edu/entries/ existentialism/ (access 24 October 2015).

Davenport, T. H. (1998). 'Putting the Enterprise into the Enterprise System'. *Harvard Business Review* 76(4): 121–31.

David, R. J. (2012). 'Institutional Change and the Growth of Strategy Consulting in the United States'. In *The Oxford Handbook of Management Consulting*, M. Kipping and T. Clark (eds). Oxford and New York, Oxford University Press.

Der Spiegel (2011a). Ein Tag mit einer Beraterin – Cash Cows und Fragezeichen [A day with a management consultant – cash cows and question marks]. Online at http://www.spiegel.de/karriere/berufsleben/ ein-tag-mit-einer-beraterin-cash-cows-und-fragezeichen-a-774990-2. html (accessed 20 October 2015).

Der Spiegel (2011b). Verstehen Sie Beratersprech? [Do you understand consultant-speak?]. Online at http://www.spiegel.de/karriere/ berufsleben/kauderwelsch-quiz-verstehen-sie-beratersprech-a-775151. html (accessed 20 October 2015).

Der Spiegel (2011c). Viel Stress, viel Geld [A lot of stress, a lot of money]. Online at http://www.spiegel.de/karriere/berufsleben/berater-gehalt-viel-stress-viel-geld-a-775548.html (20 October 2014).

Der Spiegel (2013a). Spendable Ministerien: Bundesregierung zahlte eine Milliarde an Berater [Generous minsteries: Government paid

1bn to consultants]. Online at http://www.spiegel.de/wirtschaft/
soziales/bundesregierung-beauftragte-berater-fuer-eine-milliarde-
euro-a-921241.html (accessed 19 October 2015).

Der Spiegel (2013b). Klempner, Jetset, Eulenspiegel [Plumber,
Jetset, Trickster]. Online at http://www.spiegel.de/karriere/
berufsleben/a-904270.html (accessed 24 October 2015).

Der Spiegel (2014). Wir wollen die besten Männer und Frauen [We want
the best men and women]. Online at: http://www.spiegel.de/politik/
deutschland/bundeswehr-von-der-leyen-ueber-familienleben-und-
ausruestung-a-972498.html (accessed 10 April 2016).

Der Spiegel (2016). McKinsey erhielt mehr als 20 Millionen Euro
vom Bund [McKinsey received over 20 million Euro of government
money]. Online at: http://www.spiegel.de/wirtschaft/unternehmen/
fluechtlinge-in-deutschland-mckinsey-erhielt-mehr-als-20-millionen-
euro-a-1118698.html (accessed 05 January 2016).

Destatis [German Federal Statistics Office] (2015). 62% des
Bruttoeinkommens stammen aus Erwerbstätigkeit [Salaries make
up 62% of gross income]. Online at https://www.destatis.de/DE/
ZahlenFakten/GesellschaftStaat/EinkommenKonsumLebensbedingungen/
EinkommenEinnahmenAusgaben/Aktuell_Bruttoeinkommen.html
(accessed 14 October 2015).

De Vries, R. Earning by Degrees – Differences in the career outcomes
of UK graduates. Online at http://www.suttontrust.com/wp-content/
uploads/2014/12/Earnings-by-Degrees-REPORT.pdf (accessed 14 July
2016), The Sutton Trust.

Die Zeit (1976). Wenn der Doktor kommen muss [When the doctor needs
to come]. Online at http://www.zeit.de/1976/21/wenn-der-doktor-
kommen-muss/komplettansicht (accessed 20 October 2015).

Die Zeit (2004). Die Berater-Republik [The Consultancy Republic].
Online at http://www.zeit.de/2004/07/Berater (accessed 19 October
2015).

Die Zeit (2006). McKinsey und ich [McKinsey and I]. Online at http://
www.zeit.de/2006/21/McKinsey_21 (accessed 19 October 2013).

Dobler, Gregor (2016). '"Work and rhythm"revisited: rhythm and
experience in northern Namibian peasant work'. *Journal of the Royal
Anthropological Institute* 22(4): 864–83.

Douglas, M. (2001 [1966]). *Purity and Danger – An Analysis of the
Concepts of Pollution and Taboo.* London and New York, Routledge.

Douglas, M. (ed.) (2003 [1970]). 'The two bodies'. In *Natural Symbols
– Explorations in Cosmology.* London and New York, Routledge:
72–92.

DPG – Deutscher Paritätischer Wohlfahrtsverband Gesamtverband
e.V. (2015). Die zerklüftete Republik. Bericht zur regionalen

Armutsentwicklung in Deutschland 2014 [The split republic. Report on Germany's regional poverty developments 2014]. Online at http://www.der-paritaetische.de/armutsbericht/service-download/ (accessed 14 October 2010).

Duden (2014). Betriebsblind. Online at http://www.duden.de/rechtschreibung/betriebsblind (accessed 20 October 2015).

Edersheim, E. H. (2004). *McKinsey's Marvin Bower: Vision, Leadership, and the Creation of Management Consulting.* Hoboken, NJ, Wiley.

Englund, H. (2006). *Prisoners of Freedom – Human Rights and the African Poor.* Berkeley, Los Angeles and London, University of California Press.

Ericson, R., D. Barry and A. Doyle (2000). 'The moral hazards of neoliberalism: lessons from the private insurance industry'. *Economy and Society* 29(4): 532–58.

Eriksen, T. H. (2001). *Tyranny of the Moment – Fast and Slow Time in the Information Age.* London and Sterling, VA, Pluto Press.

Eriksen, T. H. and F. Stein (2017). 'Anthropology as Counter-Culture: An Interview with Thomas Hylland Eriksen'. *The Journal of the Royal Anthropological Institute* 23(1): 233–38.

Ernst, B. and A. Kieser (2002). 'In Search of Explanations for the Consulting Explosion'. In *The Expansion of Management Knowledge – Carriers, Flows and Sources.* K. Sahlin-Andersson and L. Engwall (eds). Stanford, CA, Stanford University Press: 47–73.

Escobar, A. (1991). 'Anthropology and the Development Encounter: The Making and Marketing of Development Anthropology'. *American Ethnologist* 18(4): 658–82.

Escobar, A. (1995). *Encountering Development – The Making and Unmaking of the Third World.* Princeton, Princeton University Press.

EU (European Union) (2012). 'The Situation in the EU: How Is the Gender Pay Gap Measured?'. Online at http://ec.europa.eu/justice/gender-equality/gender-pay-gap/situation-europe/index_en.htm.

Fabian, J. (1983). *Time and the Other – How Anthropology Makes its Object.* New York, Columbia University Press.

Fassin, D. (2009). 'Une Science Sociale Critique Peut-Elle ÊTre Utile?'. *Tracés. Revue des Sciences Humaines* 9: 199–211.

Fassin, D. (2009a). Les économies morales revisitées. *Annales HSS* 6, 1237–66.

Fassin, D. (ed.) (2012). 'Introduction: Toward a Critical Moral Anthropology'. In *A Companion to Moral Anthropology.* Malden, MA, Wiley-Blackwell: 1–19.

Fassin, D. (2015). 'The Public Afterlife of Ethnography'. *American Ethnologist* 42(4): 592–609.

Fassin, D. (ed.) (2017). 'Introduction. When Ethnography Goes Public'. In *If Truth Be Told.* Durham and London, Duke University Press.

Faubion, J. D. (2011). *An Anthropology of Ethics*. Cambridge, Cambridge University Press.

Faust, M. (2000). 'Warum boomt die Managementberatung – und warum nicht zu allen Zeiten und überall? [Why is management consulting booming? And why not everywhere and at all times?' *SOFI-Mitteilungen* 28: 59–90.

Ferguson, J. (1994 [1990]). *The Anti-politics Machine:'Development, 'Depolitization, and Bureaucratic Power in Lesotho*. Minneapolis, University of Minnesota Press.

Fink, D. (2014). *Strategische Unternehmensberatung [Strategy Consulting]*. Munich, Vahlen.

Fisher, M. S. (2012). *Wall Street Women*. Durham, Duke University Press.

Forbes (2010). Avoid the Commoditization Trap. Online at http://www.forbes.com/2010/04/23/commoditization-trap-branding-leadership-managing-marketing.html (accessed 23 October 2015).

Fortune (2013). Have we all been duped by the Myers-Briggs test?. Online at http://fortune.com/2013/05/15/have-we-all-been-duped-by-the-myers-briggs-test/ (accessed 23 October 2015).

Foster, R. (2014). 'Corporations as Partners: "Connected Capitalism" and the Coca-Cola Company'. *PoLAR – Political and Legal Anthropology Review* 37(2): 246–58.

Friedrichs, J. (2009). *Gestatten: Elite: Auf den Spuren der Mächtigen von morgen [May I introduce myself: I am the elite: Investigating tomorrow's people in power]*. Munich, Hoffman und Campe.

Frankfurt, H. G. (2005). *On Bullshit*. Princeton and Oxford, Princeton University Press.

Froud, J., S. Johal, A. Leaver and K. Williams (2006). *Financialization and Strategy: Narrative and Numbers*. London and New York, Routledge.

Furnham, A. (1996). 'The big five versus the big four: the relationship between the Myers-Briggs Type Indicator (MBTI) and NEO-PI five factor model of personality'. *Personality and Individual Differences* 21(2): 303–7.

Gabriel, Y. (2008). 'Against the Tyranny of PowerPoint: Technology-in-Use and Technology Abuse'. *Organization Studies* 29: 255–76.

Geertz, C. (1973). ' "From the Native's Point of View": On the Nature of Anthropological Understanding.' *Bulletin of the American Academy of Arts and Sciences* 28(1): 26–45.

Geertz, C. (1983). Common Sense as a Cultural System. *Local Knowledge – Further Essays in Interpretive Anthropology*, New York, Basic books: 73–93.

Gell, A. (1988). 'Technology and Magic'. *Anthropology Today* 4(2): 6–9.

Gell, A. (1992). *The Anthropology of Time – Cultural Constructions of Temporal Maps and Images*. Oxford, Berg.

Gell, A. (1998). *Art and Agency – An Anthropological Theory*. Oxford, Clarendon Press.

Gershon, I. (2016). 'I'm not a businessman, I'm a business, man: Typing the neoliberal self into a branded existence'. *HAU: Journal of Ethnographic Theory* 6(3): 223–46.

Gingrich, A. (1998). 'Review Essay: Toward an Anthropology of Germany: A Culture of Moralist Self-Education?' *Current Anthropology* 39(4): 567–72.

Gingrich, A., E. Ochs and A. Swedlund (2002). 'Repertoires of Timekeeping in Anthropology'. *Current Anthropology* 43(S4): S3–S4.

Golub, A. R. (2014). *Leviathans at the Gold Mine*. Durham and London: Duke University Press,

Graeber, D. (2012). 'Dead zones of the imagination – On violence, bureaucracy, and interpretive labor'. *Hau: Journal of Ethnographic Theory* 2: 105–28.

Graeber, D. (2013). 'On the Phenomenon of Bullshit Jobs – A Work Rant'. *Strike Magazine* Summer: Online at http://strikemag.org/bullshit-jobs/ (accessed 20 October 2015).

Graeber, D. (2014). 'Anthropology and the Rise of the Professional-Managerial Class'. *Hau: Journal of Ethnographic Theory* 4(3): 73–88.

Graeber, D. (2015). *The Utopia of Rules: On Technology, Stupidity and the Secret Joys of Bureaucracy by David Graeber*. Brooklyn, Melville House.

Grabka, Markus M., and Christian Westermeier. (2014). 'Anhaltend Hohe Vermögensungleichheit in Deutschland' DIW-Wochenbericht 81.9 (2014): 151–164..

Graeber, D. (2001). *Toward an Anthropological Theory of Value: The False Coin of Our Own Dreams*. New York, Palgrave.

Gregory, C. (1982). *Gifts and Commodities*. London, Academic Press.

Gregory, C. (1994). Exchange and Reciprocity. In *Companion Encyclopedia of Anthropology – Humanity, Culture and Social Life*, T. Ingold (ed.). London and New York, Routledge: 911–39.

Gudeman, S. (2016). *Anthropology and Economy*. Cambridge, University Press.

Gudeman, S. and A. Rivera (1990). *Conversations in Colombia – The Domestic Economy in Life and Text*. Cambridge, Cambridge University Press.

Gupta, A. (2012). *Red Tape – Bureaucracy, Structural Violence and Poverty in India*. Durham and London, Duke University Press.

Gupta, A. and J. Ferguson (1997). *Anthropological Locations – Boundaries and Grounds of a Field Science*. Berkeley, Los Angeles, London, University of California Press.

Guyer, J. I. (2007). 'Prophecy and the near future: Thoughts on macroeconomic, evangelical, and punctuated time'. *American Ethnologist* 34(3): 409–21.

Handelsblatt (2016). 'Pro Sieben Parshipt Jetzt [Pro Sieben Is Now on Parship]'. Online at http://www.handelsblatt.com/unternehmen/ dienstleister/kauf-der-parship-elite-group-pro-sieben-parshipt-jetzt/14497720.html (accessed 01 October 2016).

Hann, C. and K. Hart (2011 [1988]). *Economic Anthropology – History, Ethnography, Critique*. Cambridge, polity.

Hannerz, Ulf. (2010). 'Diversity Is Our Business'. In *Anthropology's World: Life in a Twenty-First Century Discipline*, U. Hannerz (ed.). London, Pluto Press: 38–59.

Harvey, D. (1992 [1990]). *The Condition of Postmodernity – An Enquiry into the Origins of Cultural Change*. Cambridge, MA and Oxford UK, Blackwell.

Hardt, M. (1998). 'Affective Labour'. *Boundary* 26(2): 89–100.

Hardt, M. and A. Negri (2000). *Empire*. Cambridge, MAand London, England, Harvard University Press.

Harper, R. (2000). The social organization of the IMF's mission work – An examination of international auditing. *Audit Cultures – Anthropological Studies in Accountability, Ethics and the Academy*. M. Strathern. London, Routledge: 21–55.

Harris, O. (2007). '*What makes people work?'* In *Questions of Anthropology*, R. Astuti, J. Parry and C. Stafford (eds). New York and Oxford, Berg: 137–67.

Hart, K. (2000). *The Memory Bank: Money in an Unequal World*. London, Profile Books Ltd.

Hart, K. (2010). 'Models of Statistical Distribution – A window on Social History'. *Anthropological Theory* 10(1–2): 67–74.

Hart, K. and C. Hann (eds) (2009). 'Introduction: Learning from Polanyi'. In *Market and Society: The Great Transformation Today*. Cambridge, Cambridge University Press: 1–17.

Hartmann, M. (2000). 'Class-Specific Habitus and the Social Reproduction of the Business Elite in Germany and France'. *The Sociological Review* 48(2): 262–82.

Hartmann, M. (2004). 'Eliten in Deutschland: Rekrutierungswege Und Karrierepfade'. *Aus Politik und Zeitgeschichte* B 10: 17–24.

Harvey, R. C. (2005). 'Describing and Discarding "Comics" as an Impotent Act of Philosophical Rigor'. *Comics as Philosophy*. J. McLaughlin (ed.). Jackson, University Press of Mississippi: 14–26.

Harvie, D. (2005). 'All Labour Produces Value for Capital and We All Struggle against Value'. *The Commoner* 10: 1–40.

Hastrup, K. (2007). 'Ultima Thule: Anthropology and the Call of the Unknown'. *The Journal of the Royal Anthropological Institute* 13: 789–804.

Heidegger, M. (2006 [1927]). *Sein und Zeit [Being and Time]*. Tübingen, Max Niemeyer Verlag.

Herf, J. (1997). *Divided Memory – The Nazi Past in the Two Germanys.*
Cambridge, MA and London, Harvard University Press.

Herles, B. (2013). *Kaputte Elite – Ein Schadensbericht aus unseren
Chefetagen [Broken Elite – A damage report from the boardroom].*
Munich, Knaus.

Hermez, S. (2015). 'When the state is (n)ever present: on cynicism
and political mobilization in Lebanon'. *Journal of the Royal
Anthropological Institute* 21(3): 507–23.

Herzfeld, M. (1993 [1992]). *The Social Production of Indifference –
Exploring the Symbolic Roots of Western Bureaucracy.* Chicago and
London, The University of Chicago Press.

Heywood, P. (2015). 'Equivocal Locations: Being "Red" in "Red
Bologna"'. *The Journal of the Royal Anthropological Institute* 21(4):
855–71.

Heywood, P. (2017). 'The ontological turn'. In *The Cambridge
Encyclopedia of Anthropolgy*, F. Stein, H. Diemberger, S. Lazar, J.
Robbins, A. Sanchez and R. Stasch (eds). Online at http:// www.
anthroencyclopedia.com, 1–10.

Hilgendorf, S. K. (2007). 'English in Germany: Contact, spread and
attitudes'. *World Englishes* 26(2): 131–48.

Hill, A. (2013). Roland Berger set to go it alone. Financial Times.
Online at https://www.ft.com/content/53b6fa34-6711-11e3-a5f9-
00144feabdc0 (accessed 01 May 2017).

Ho, K. (2005). 'Situating Global Capitalisms: A View from Wall Street
Investment Banks'. *Cultural Anthropology* 20(1): 68–96.

Ho, K. (2009a). 'Disciplining Investment Bankers, Disciplining the
Economy: Wall Street's Institutional Culture of Crisis and the
Downsizing of "Corporate America"'. *American Anthropologist*
111(2): 177–89.

Ho, K. (2009b). *Liquidated – An Ethnography of Wall Street.* Durham,
Duke University Press.

Hochhuth, R. (2004). McKinsey kommt [McKinsey comes]. Brandenburg
an der Havel, Brandenburger Theater.

Holm, P. (2007). Which Way Is Up on Callon? In *Do Economists Make
Markets? On The Performativity of Economics*, D. MacKenzie,
F. Muniesa and L. Siu (eds). Princeton and Oxford, Princeton
University Press: 225–44.

Holmes, D. R. (2009). 'Economy of Words'. *Cultural Anthropology* 24(3):
381–419.

Holmes, D. R. (2014). *Economy of Words – Communicative Imperatives
in Central Banks.* Chicago and London, The University of Chicago
Press.

Holmes, R. D. and G. E. Marcus (2006). 'Fast Capitalism: Para-Ethnography and the Rise of the Symbolic Analyst'. In *Frontiers of Capital – Ethnographic Reflections on the New Economy*. M. S. Fisher and G. Downey (eds). Durham and London, Duke University Press: 33–58.

Hull, M. S. (2012). *Government of Paper – The Materiality of Bureaucracy in Urban Pakistan*. Berkely, Los Angeles, London, University of California Press.

Ingold, T. (2013). 'Knowing from the inside'. In *Making – Anthropology, Archaeology, Art and Architecture*, T. Ingold (ed.). London and New York, Routledge: 1–17.

Ingold, T. (2016) 'That's Enough About Ethnography!'. *Hau: Journal of Ethnographic Theory* 4(1): 383–95.

Jacob, M.-A. (2007). 'Form-Made Persons: Consent Forms as Consent's Blind Spot'. *Political and Legal Anthropology Review* 30(2): 249–68.

Jaeggi, R. (2014). *Alienation*. New York, Columbia University Press.

James, D. (2015). *Money from Nothing – Indebtedness and Aspiration in South Africa*. Stanford, CA, Stanford University Press.

James, W. (1995 [1907]). 'Pragmatism's Conception of Truth'. In *Pragmatism*, T. Crofts and P. Smith (eds). New York, Dover Thrift Editions: 76–92.

Jarman, N. and D. Bryan (2015). 'Beyond the Academy – Applying Anthropological Research, a Case Study of Demonstrating Impact in the U.K. 2014 Ref'. *Anthropology in Action* 22(2): 36–41.

Johnson-Hanks, J. (2005). 'When the Future Decides: Uncertainty and Intentional Action in Contemporary Cameroon'. *Current Anthropology* 46(3): 363–85.

Jordan, Ann T., and D. Douglas Caulkins (eds) (2013). 'Expanding the Field of Organizational Anthropology for the Twenty-first Century'. In *A Companion to Organizational Anthropology*. New York, Wiley-Blackwell: 1–23.

Jung, C. (2015 [1921]). Psychological Types. Online at http://psychclassics.yorku.ca/Jung/types.htm (accessed 25 October 2015), York University, Ontario.

Juran, J. M. (1994 [1975]). 'The Non-Pareto Principle; Mea Culpa'. *Selected Papers*, Juran Institute. 18: 47–50.

Juran, J. M. (2005 [1960]). 'Pareto, Lorenz, Cournot, Bernoulli, Juran and Others'. In *Joseph M. Juran – Critical Evaluations in Business and Management*, J. C. Wood and M. C. Wood (eds). New York, Routledge: 45.

Juran, J. M. and A. B. Godfrey (1999 [1951]). *Juran's Quality Handbook*. New York, McGraw-Hill.

Kahn Jr, E. J. (1986). *The Problem Solvers: A History of Arthur D Little, Inc.* Boston and Toronto, Little, Brown and Company.

Kaplan, S. (2010). 'Strategy and PowerPoint: An Inquiry into the Epistemic Culture and Machinery of Strategy Making'. *Organization Science* 22(2): 320–46.

Kaplow, L. (2004 [1987]). 'Pareto principle and competing principles'. In *The New Palgrave Dictionary of Economics*, S. N. Durlauf and L. E. Blume (eds). New York, Macmillan 6: 295–300.

Kapferer, B. (2006). 'Anthropology and the Dialectic of Enlightenment: A Discourse on the Definition of Ideals of a Threatened Discipline'. *The Australian Journal of Anthropology* 18(1): 72–94.

Karpferer, B. (2013). 'How anthropologists think: configurations of the exotic'. *Journal of the Royal Anthropological Institute* 19(4): 813–36.

Keane, W. (1997). *Signs of Recognition – Powers and Hazards of Representatino in an Indonesian Society.* Berkeley, Los Angeles and London, University of California Press.

Kelly, T. (2006). 'Documented lives: fear and the uncertainties of law during the second Palestinian intifada'. *Journal of the Royal Anthropological Institute* 12(1): 89–107.

Kendzior, S. (2011). 'Digital distrust: Uzbek cynicism and solidarity in the Internet Age'. *American Ethnologist* 38(3): 559–75.

Kertzer, D. I. (1988). *Ritual, Politics, and Power.* New Haven and London, Yale University Press.

Kipping, M. (1999). 'American Management Consulting Companies in Western Europe, 1920 to 1990: Products, Reputation, and Relationships'. *The Business History Review* 73(2): 190–220.

Kipping, M. and I. Kirkpatrick (2005). 'The Development of the Management Consultancy Business: A Co-evolution Perspective'.

Knorr Cetina, K. and U. Bruegger (2002a). 'Global microstructures: the virtual societies of financial markets'. *American Journal of Sociology* 10(4): 905–50.

Knorr Cetina, K. and U. Bruegger (2002b). ' "Traders" Engagement with Markets – A Postsocial Relationship'. *Theory, Culture & Society* 19(5/6): 161–85.

Knox, H. and P. Harvey (2015). 'Virtuous detachments in engineering practice – on the ethics of (not) making a difference'. In *Detachments: essays on the limits of relational thinking.* M. Candea, J. Cook, C. Trundle and T. Yarrow (eds). Manchester, Manchester University Press: 58–79.

Koch, R. (2013). *The 80 20 Manager: Ten Ways to Become a Great Leader.* London, Hachette Digital.

Krause, P. (2015). 'Einkommensungleichheit in Deutschland'. In *Wirtschaftsdienst*, Peter Krause (ed.). Heidelberg, Springer: 572–4.

Kunze, Rolf-Ulrich (2000). '75 Jahre Studienstiftung Des Deutschen Volkes: Zeit-Und Wissenschaftsgeschichtliche Perspektiven Zu Einem Deutschen Sonderweg Der, "Hochbegabten"- FöRderung [75 Years of the German National Merit Foundation: Historical and Scientific Perspectives on Germany's Exceptional Way of Funding the "Highly Gifted"]'. Bonn, 2000.

Kuper, A. (2010). The original sin of anthropology. *Paideuma: Mitteilungen zur Kulturkunde* 56: 123–44.

Laidlaw, J. (2002). 'For An Anthropology Of Ethics And Freedom'. *Journal of the Royal Anthropological Institute* 8(2): 311–32.

Laidlaw, J. (2014a). 'The "question of freedom" in anthropology. In *The Subject of Virtue – An Anthropology of Ethics and Freedom*. Cambridge, Cambridge University Press: 1–25.

Laidlaw, J. (2014b). *The Subject of Virtue – An Anthropology of Ethics and Freedom*. Cambridge, Cambridge University Press.

Lane, P. R. (2012). 'The European Sovereign Debt Crisis'. *Journal of Economic Perspectives* 26(3): 49–68.

Latour, B. (1993). *We Have Never Been Modern*. Cambridge, MA, Harvard University Press.

Latour, B. and S. Woolgar (1986 [1979]). *Laboratory Life – The Construction of Scientific Facts*. Princeton, Princeton University Press.

Lazar, S. (2008). *El Alto, Rebel City: Self and Citizenship in Andean Bolivia*. Durham, Duke University Press.

Lazar, S. (2012a). 'A Desire to Formalize Work? Comparing Trade Union Strategies in Bolivia and Argentina'. *Anthropology of Work Review* 33(1): 15–24.

Lazar, S. (2012b). 'Disjunctive comparison: citizenship and trade unionism in Bolivia and Argentina'. *Journal of the Royal Anthropological Institute* 18(2): 349–68.

Lazar, S. (2014). 'Historical narrative, mundane political time and revolutionary moments: coexisting temporalities in the lived experience of social movements'. *Journal of the Royal Anthropological Institute* 20 (Suppl. S1): 91–108.

Lazonick, W. (1992). 'Controlling the Market for Corporate Control: The Historical Significance of Managerial Capitalism'.

Lazonick, W. (1993 [1991]). *Business Organization and the Myth of the Market Economy*, Cambridge, Cambridge University Press.

Lazonick, W. and M. O'Sullivan (2000). 'Maximizing Shareholder Value: A New Ideology for Corporate Governance'. *Economy and Soceity* 29: 13–35.

Lazzarato, M. (1996). 'Immaterial Labor'. In *Radical Thought in Italy – A Potential Politics*. P. Virno and M. Hardt (eds). Minneapolis and London, University of Minnesota Press: 133–51.

Leach, E. R. (1971 [1961]). *Two essays concerning the Symbolic Representation of Time. Rethinking Anthropology*. London, The Athlone Press, University of London: 124–36.

Leif, T. (2005). Gelesen, Gelacht, Gelocht – Vom Irrsinn der Beraterrepublik [Read, laughed, shelved – The folly of the consulting-republic]. Online at https://www.youtube.com/watch?v=7cpXcXLQEUk (accessed 14 October 2015), Südwestrundfunk.

Leif, T. (2006). *Beraten und verkauft: McKinsey & Co. – Der große Bluff der Unternehmensberater [Consulted and Sold: McKinsey & Co – The great bluff]*. Munich, Bertelsmann.

Levy, S. (2014 [1984]). A Spreadsheet Way of Knowledge. Online at https://medium.com/backchannel/a-spreadsheet-way-of-knowledge-8de60af7146e (accessed 19 October 2015).

Liberatore, G. (2017). *Somali Muslim British*. Lse Monographs on Social Anthropology London, Bloomsbury.

LiPuma, E. and B. Lee (2004). *Financial Derivatives and the Globalization of Risk*. Durham and London, Duke University Press.

Lloyd, J. B. (2012). (The Myers-Briggs Type Indicator® and mainstream psychology: analysis and evaluation of an unresolved hostility). *Journal of Beliefs & Values* 33(1): 23–34.

Lockwood, B. (2004 [1987]). 'Pareto efficiency'. In *The New Palgrave Dictionary of Economics*. S. N. Durlauf and L. E. Blume (eds). New York, Macmillan 6: 292–5.

Look, B. C. (2013). 'Leibniz's Modal Metaphysics'. *The Stanford Encyclopedia of Philosophy* Spring 2013: Online at http://plato.stanford.edu/entries/leibniz-modal/ (accessed 05 January 2017).

Luhrmann, T. (1998). 'Partial Failure: The Attempt to Deal with Uncertainty in Psychoanalytic Psychotherapy and in Anthropology'. *The Psychoanalytic Quarterly* 67(4): 449–72.

Lukács, G. (1971). *History and Class Consciousness – Studies in Marxist Dialectics*. Cambridge, MA, The MIT Press.

Lupton, T. and C. S. Wilson (1959). 'The Social Background and Connections of "Top Decision Makers"'. *The Manchester School* 27(1): 30–51.

MacClancy, J. (2002). *Exotic No More: Anthropology on the Front Lines*. Chicago and London, University of Chicago Press.

Maguire, M. (2014). 'Counter-terrorism in European Airports'. In *The Anthropology of Security – Perspectives from the Frontline of Policing*, M. Maguire, C. Frois and N. Zurawski (eds). London, Pluto Press: 118–39.

Mahmud, L. (2014). *The Brotherhood of Freemason Sisters: Gender, Secrecy and Fraternity in Italian Masonic Lodges*. Chicago and London, The University of Chicago Press.

Malinowski, B. (1929). 'Practical Anthropology'. *Africa: Journal of the International African Institute* 2(1): 22–38.

Malinowski, B. (1930). 'The Rationalisation of Anthropology and Administration'. *Africa: Journal of the International African Institute* 3(4): 405–30.

Malinowski, B. (1931). 'The Role of Magic and Religion'. In *Encyclopedia of the Social Sciences*, E. R. A. Seligman and A. S. Johnson (eds). New York, Macmillan Publishing Co.: 634–42.

Malinowski, B. (1945). 'The New Tasks of Modern Anthropology'. In *The Dynamics of Culture Change. An Inquiry into Race Relations in Africa*, P. M. Kaberry (ed.). New Haven, Yale University Press: 1–14.

Malinowski, B and R. Redfield. (1948). *Magic, Science and Religion and Other Essays, Vol. 3*. Boston, MA, Beacon Press: 1–71.

Malinowski, B. (2002 [1922]). *Argonauts of the Western Pacific*. London, Routledge.

Manager Magazin (2014). McKinsey gegen den Rest der Welt [McKinsey against the rest of the world]. Online at http://www.manager-magazin. de/magazin/artikel/baur-fuehrt-mckinsey-im-ueberlebenskampf-der-unternehmensberater-a-951828.html (accessed 19 October 2015).

Marcus, G. E. (1995). 'Ethnography in/of the World System: The Emergence of Ethnography'. *Annual Review of Anthropology* 24: 95–117.

Marsh, S. (2009). *The Feminine in Management Consulting: Power, Emotion and Values in Consulting Interactions*. New York, Palgrave Macmillan.

Marshall, A. G. (2011). *Resolve Your Differences – Seven Steps to Dealing with Conflict in Your Relationship*. London, Bloomsbury.

Martin, E. (1994). *Flexible Bodies – Tracking Immunity in American Culture from the Days of Polio to the Age of AIDS*. Boston, Beacon Press.

Marx, K. (1988 [1844]). *Economic and Philosophic Manuscripts of 1844 and the Communist Manifesto*. Amherst and New York, Prometheus Books.

Marx, K. (2005 [1872]). *Das Kapital*. Köln, Parkland Verlag.

Massey, D., P. Quintas and D. Wield (1992). *High Tech Fantasies: Science Parks in Society, Science and Space*. London and New York, Routledge.

Mathur, N. (2014). 'The reign of terror of the big cat: bureaucracy and the mediation of social times in the Indian Himalaya'. *Journal of the Royal Anthropological Institute* 20: 148–65.

Mauss, M. (1938). 'Une catégorie de l'esprit humain: la notion de personne celle de "moi" '. *Journal of the Royal Anthropological Institute* LXVIII: 263–81.

McDonald, M. (2015). 'Some Merits and Difficulties of Detachment'. In *Detachments: Essays on the Limits of Relational Thinking*, M. Candea, J. Cook, C. Trundle and T. Yarrow (eds). Manchester, Manchester University Press: 1–35.

McKenna, C. D. (1995). 'The Origins of Modern Management Consulting'. *Business and Economic History* 24(1): 51–8.

McKenna, C. D. (2006). *The World's Newest Profession – Management Consulting in the 20th Century*. Cambridge, Cambridge University Press.

McKinsey & Company (2009). The Economic Impact of the Achievement Gap in America's Schools – Summary of Findings. Online at http://dropoutprevention.org/wp-content/uploads/2015/07/ACHIEVEMENT_GAP_REPORT_20090512.pdf (accessed 24 October 2015).

McKinsey & Company. (2011a). 'Book Excerpt – Daniel Kahneman: Beware the "inside view"' Retrieved 05 May 2014. Online at http://www.mckinsey.com/insights/strategy/daniel_kahneman_beware_the_inside_view.

McKinsey & Company (2011b). The emerging equity gap: Growth and stability in the new investor landscape. Online at http://www.mckinsey.com/insights/global_capital_markets/emerging_equity_gap (accessed 24 October 2015).

McKinsey & Company (2012). The social economy: Unlocking value and productivity through social technologies. Washington, McKinsey Global institute.

McKinsey & Company (2014). Digital divide: The impact of closing Africa's Internet gap. Online at http://www.mckinseyonmarketingandsales.com/sites/default/files/pdf/06_Digital%20divide.pdf (accessed 24 October 2015).

McKinsey & Company. (2014b). 'Unsere Kompetenzen [Our competencies]'. Online at http://mckinsey.de/unsere-kompetenzen.

Mead, M. (1973). 'Changing Styles of Anthropological Work'. *Annual Review of Anthropology* 2: 1–27.

Merkel, A. (2011). Regierungserklärung von Bundeskanzlerin Angela Merkel zur Energiepolitik 'Der Weg zur Energie der Zukunft' (Mitschrift) ['Government declaration by chancellor Angela Markel regarding energy politics 'The way towards the energy of the future' (transcript)]. Online at http://www.bundesregierung.de/ContentArchiv/DE/Archiv17/Regierungserklaerung/2011/2011-06-09-merkel-energie-zukunft.html (accessed 20 October 2015).

Miller, D. (2002). 'Turning Callon the Right Way Up'. *Economy and Society* 31(2): 218–33.

Miller, D. (2003). 'The Virtual Moment'. *The Journal of the Royal Anthropological Institute* 9(1): 57–75.

Mills, D. (2003). 'Quantifying the discipline: Some anthropology statistics from the UK'. *Anthropology Today* 19(3): 19–22.

Mitchell, T. (1991 [1988]). *Colonizing Egypt*. Berkeley, Los Angeles, London, University of California Press.

Mitchell, T. (1998). 'Fixing the Economy'. *Cultural Studies* 12(1): 82–101.

Miyazaki, H. (2003). 'The Temporalities of the Market'. *American Anthropologist* 105(2): 255–65.

Miyazaki, H. (2006). 'Economy of Dreams: Hope in Global Capitalism and Its Critiques'. *Cultural Anthropology* 21(2): 147–72.

Miyazaki, H. (2013). *Arbitraging Japan – Dreams of Capitalism at the End of Finance*. Berkeley, Los Angeles, London, University of California Press.

Miyazaki, H. and A. Riles (2007). 'Failure as an Endpoint'. In *Global Assemblages – Technology, Politics and Ethics as Anthropological Problems*, A. Ong and S. J. Collier (eds). Malden, US; Oxford, UK; Victoria, Australia, Blackwell: 320–33.

Mohun, S. (1991 [1983]). 'Abstract Labour'. In *A Dictionary of Marxist Thought*, T. Bottomore (ed.). Oxford, UK, Blackwell: 1-2.

Mol, A. (1999). 'Ontological politics. A word and some questions'. *The Sociological Review* 47(S1): 74–89.

Moore, H. (1990). 'Visions of the good life: Anthropology and the study of utopia'. *Cambridge Anthropology*: 13–33

Mosse, D. (2005a). *Cultivating Development : An Ethnography of Aid Policy and Practice*. London, Pluto Press.

Mosse, D. (2005b). 'Global Governance and the Ethnography of International Aid'. In *The Aid Effect – Giving and Governing in International Development*. D. Mosse and D. Lewis (eds). London and Ann Arbor, Pluto Press: 1–37.

Mosse, D. (2011). 'Politics and Ethics: Ethnographies of Expert Knowledge and Professional Identities'. In *Policy Worlds – Anthropology and the Analysis of Contemporary Power*, C. Shore, S. Wright and D. Però (eds). New York and Oxford, Berghan: 50–67.

Muehlebach, A. (2011). 'On affective Labor in post-Fordist Italy'. *Cultural Anthropology* 26(1): 59–82.

Muehlebach, A. (2012). *The Moral Neoliberal – Welfare and Citizenship in Italy*. Chicago and London, The University of Chicago Press.

Munn, N. D. (1992). 'The Cultural Anthropology of Time: A Critical Essay'. *Annual Review of Anthropology* 21: 93–123.

Naber, J. (2013). Zeit der Kannibalen [Age of Cannibals]. Berlin.

Nader, L. (1969). 'Up the Anthropologist – Perspectives gained from studying up'. In *Reinventing Anthropology*, D. Hymes (ed.). New York, Vintage: 248–311.

Navaro-Yashin, Y. (2002). 'Fantasies for the State: Hype, Cynicism and the Everyday Life of Statecraft'. *Faces of the State – Secularism and*

Public Life in Turkey. Princeton and Oxford, Princeton University Press: 155–87.

Nietzsche, F. (1996). *On the Genealogy of Morals*. Oxford and New York, World's Classic.

Niewiem, S. and A. Richter (2004). 'The changing balance of power in the consulting market'. *Business Strategy Review* 15(1): 8–13.

O'Sullivan, M. (2002). 'Corporate Governance in Germany: Productive and Financial Challenges'. In *Corporate Governance and Sustainable Prosperity*, W. Lazonick and M O'Sullivan (eds). New York, Palgrave Macmilan UK: 255–300.

OED Oxford English Dictionary (2015). Gap. Online at http://libsta28. lib.cam.ac.uk:2318/view/Entry/76658?rskey=8ca0ZU&result=1#eid (accessed 23 October 2015).

Ong, A. (1987). *Spirits of Resistance and Capitalist Discipline: Factory Women in Malaysia*. Albany, State University of New York Press.

Ong, A. (2006). Corporate Players, New Cosmopolitans, and Guanxi in Shanghai. In *Frontiers of Capital – Ethnographic Reflections on the New Economy*. M. S. Fisher and G. Downey (eds). Durham and London, Duke University Press: 163–91.

Ortiz, S (2005). Decisions and choices: the rationality of economic actors. In *Handbook of Economic Anthropology*, J. Carrier (ed.). Cheltenham, Edward Elgar: 59–78.

Ortner, S. B. (2016). 'Dark Anthropology and Its Others: Theory since the Eighties'. *Hau: Journal of Ethnographic Theory* 6(1): 47–73.

Pande, A. (2014). *Wombs in Labor: Transnational Commercial Surrogacy in India*. New York, Columbia University Press.

Parkes, S. (1997). *Understanding Contemporary Germany*. London and New York, Routledge.

Parmenter, D. (2007). *Pareto's 80/20 Rule for Corporate Accountants*. New York, John Wiley & Sons, Inc.

Persky, J. (1992). 'Retrospectives: Pareto's Law'. *The Journal of Economic Perspectives* 6(2): 181–92.

Pickles, A. (2017). 'To Excel at Bridewealth, or Ceremonies of Office'. *Anthropology Today* 33(1): 20–3.

Pine, J. (2016). 'Last Chance Incorporated'. *Cultural Anthropology* 31(2): 297–318.

Pittenger, D. J. (1993a). 'The Utility of the Myers-Briggs Type indicator'. *Review of Educational Research* 63(4): 467–88.

Pittenger, D. J. (1993b). 'Measuring the MBTI and coming up short'. *Journal of Career Planning and Employment* 54: 48–52.

Planet Money (2015). Spreadsheets. Online at http://www.npr.org/ sections/money/2015/02/25/389027988/episode-606-spreadsheets (accessed 19 October 2015).

Polanyi, K. (2001 [1944]). *The Great Transformation*. Boston, Beacon Press.

Porter, M. (1996). 'What Is Strategy?' *Harvard Business Review*. Online at https://hbr.org/1996/11/what-is-strategy (accessed 23 October 2015).

Postone (2003 [1993]). *Time, Labour and Social Domination*. Cambridge, Cambridge University Press.

Power, M. (1999). *The Audit Society – Rituals of Verification*. Oxford, Oxford University Press.

Pringle, R. (2005). 'Sexuality at work'. In *Critical Management Studies*, C. Grey and H. Willmott (eds). Oxford, Oxford University Press: 284–303

Quattrone, P. (2015). 'Governing Social Orders, Unfolding Rationality, and Jesuit Accounting Practices: A Procedural Approach to Institutional Logics'. *Administrative Science Quarterly*: 1–35.

Quelch, J. (2007). 'How to Avoid the Commodity Trap'. Online at https://hbr.org/2007/12/how-to-avoid-the-commodity-tra (accessed 23 October 2015).

Rapp, C. (2010 [2002]). *Aristotle's Rhetoric*. Online at http://plato.stanford.edu/entries/aristotle-rhetoric/ (accessed 20 October 2015), University of Stanford.

Rasiel, E. M. (1999). *The McKinsey Way – Using the Techniques of the World's Top Strategic Consultants to Help Yout and Your Business*. New York, McGraw-Hill.

Rasiel, E. M. and P. N. Friga (2002). *The McKinsey Mind – Understanding and Implementing the Problem-Solving Tools and Managment Techniques of the World's Top Strategic Consulting Firm*. New York, McGraw-Hill.

Reed, A. (2006). 'Documents Unfolding'. In *Documents – Artifacts of Modern Knowledge*, A. Riles (ed.). Ann Arbor, The University of Michigan Press: 158–81.

Reid, E. (2015). 'Why Some Men Pretend to Work 80-Hour Weeks'. *Harvard Business Review*. Online at https://hbr.org/2015/2004/why-some-men-pretend-to-work-2080-hour-weeks (accessed 20 October 2015).

Reith, G. (2004). 'Uncertain Times – The notion of "risk" and the development of modernity'. *Time & Society* 13(2/3): 383–402.

Richard, A. and D. Rudnyckyj (2009). 'Economies of Affect'. *The Journal of the Royal Anthropological Institute* 15(1): 57–77.

Riles, A. (1998). 'Infinity within the Brackets'. *American Ethnologist* 25(3): 378–98.

Riles, A. (2001 [2000]). *The Network Inside Out*. Ann Arbor, The University of Michigan Press.

Riles, A. (ed.) (2006). 'Introduction: In Response'. In *Documents – Artifacts of Modern Knowledge*. Ann Arbor, The University of Michigan Press: 1–41.

Riles, A. (2010). 'Collateral Expertise – Legal Knowledge in the Global Financial Markets'. *Current Anthropology* 51(6): 795–818.

Riles, A. (2011). *Collateral Knowledge – Legal Reasoning in the Global Financial Markets.* Chicago and London, The University of Chicago Press.

Ringel, F. (2014). '2 post-Industrial Times and the Unexpected: Endurance and Sustainability in Germany's Fastest-Shrinking City'. *Journal of the Royal Anthropological Institute* 20: 52–70.

Rivoal, I. and N. B Salazar (2013). 'Contemporary Ethnographic Practice and the Value of Serendipity'. *Social Anthropology* 21(2): 178–85.

Robbins, J. (2004). *Becoming Sinners – Christianity and Moral Torment in a Papua New Guinea Society.* Berkeley, CA, University of California Press.

Robbins, J. (2015). 'Ritual, Value, and Example: On the Perfection of Cultural Representations'. *The Journal of the Royal Anthropological Institute* 21(S1): 18-29.

Roland Berger (2011). Purchasing Excellence Study – Purchasing trends and benchmarks 2011 – Production and non-prod.-related materials/ services. Online at http://www.rolandberger.co.uk/media/pdf/Roland_ Berger_Purchasing_Excellence_E_20111201.pdf (accessed 24 October 2015).

Roland Berger (2014a). Expertise. Online at http://www.rolandberger.de/ expertise/ (accessed 20 October 2015).

Roland Berger (2014b). Escaping the commodity trap – How to regain a competitive edge in commodity markets. Online at http://www. rolandberger.com/media/publications/2014-04-22-rbsc-pub-Escaping_ the_commodity_trap.html (accessed 20 October 2015).

Roland Berger. (2014c). 'Logistic im Umbruch: Online handel, intraregionale Warenflüsse und der Trend zu Nischenangebot treiben das globale Wachstum [Logistics in turmoil: online trade, interregaional flow of goods and a trend to niche offers drive global growth]'.

Roland Berger (2014d). Top Management Issues Radar – Aerospace and Defence Industry. Online at http://www.rolandberger.co.uk/media/pdf/ Roland_Berger_TopManagementIssuesRadar_20131210.pdf (accessed 23 October 2015).

Roland Berger (2015a). Join our team. Online at http://www.rolandberger. com/careers/ (accessed 20 October 2015).

Roland Berger (2015b). The Digital Transformation could add EUR 1.25 trillion to Europe's Industrial Value Creation by 2025 – or Diminish it by EUR 605 billion. Munich.

Rosa, H. (2013). *Social Acceleration – A new theory of modernity.* New York, Columbia University Press.

Rose, N. (1999 [1989]). *Governing the Soul – The Shaping of the Private Self*. London and New York, Free Association Books.

Rush Kruger, E. (2011). *Top Market Strategy – Applying the 80/20 Rule*. USA, Business Expert Press.

Russel, B. (2004 [1946]). *History of Western Philosophy*. London, George Allen & Unwind Ltd.

Sahlins, M. (1972). *Stone Age Economics*. Chicago and New York, Aldine Atherton.

Said, E. (2003 [1978]). *Orientalism*. New York, Vintage Books.

Sandel, M. (1984). 'The Procedural Republic and the Unencumbered Self'. *Political Theory* 12(1): 81–96.

Sartre, J. P. (1970). *L'existentialisme est un humanisme*. Paris, Nagel.

Sassen, S. (2001 [1991]). *The Global City*. Princeton and Oxford, Princeton University Press.

Sassen, S. (2011). 'Analytic Borderlands: Economy and Culture in the Global City'. In *The New Blackwell Companion to the City*, G. Bridge and S. Watson (eds). Oxford, Blackwell Publishing: 468–89.

Sauer, K. and M. Sahnau (2002). *FRA-MUC-FRA. Einmal Beratung und zurück [FRA-MUC-FRA. A return trip to consulting]*. Norderstedt, Books on Demand.

Scharff, R. C. (2002 [1995]). *Compte After Positivism*. Cambridge, Cambridge University Press.

Schmitt, C. (2005 [1922]). *Political Theology – Four Chapters on the Concept of Sovereignty*. Chicago, University of Chicago Press.

Schrage, M. (2007). 'The Myth of Commoditization'. *MIT Sloan Management Review* Winter 2007: Online at http://sloanreview. mit.edu/article/the-myth-of-commoditization/ (accessed 20 October 2015).

Scott, J. (1998). *Seeing Like a State : How Certain Schemes to Improve the Human Condition Have Failed*. New Haven and London, Yale University Press.

Scott, Michael W. (2016). 'To Be Makiran Is to See Like Mr Parrot: The Anthropology of Wonder in Solomon Islands'. *The Journal of the Royal Anthropological Institute* 22(3): 474–95.

Searle, J. R. (2001a). 'Free Will as a Problem in Neurobiology'. *Philosophy* 76(4): 491–514.

Searle, J. R. (ed.) (2001b). 'Rationality in Action'. In *Rationality in Action*. Cambridge, MA and London, MIT Press.

Sennett, R. (2006). *The Culture of the New Capitalism*. New Haven and London, Yale University Press.

Sheper-Hughes, N. (1993 [1992]). *Death Without Weeping – The Violence of Everyday Life in Brazil*. Berkeley, Los Angeles and London, University of California Press.

Sheper-Hughes, N. (1995). 'The Primacy of the Ethical: Propositions for a Militant Anthropology'. *Current Anthropology* 36(3): 409–40.

Shore, C. (2000). *Building Europe – The Cultural Politics of European Integration.* London and New York, Routledge.

Shore, C. and S. Nugent (2002). *Elite Cultures – Anthropological Perspectives.* London and New York, Routledge.

Shore, C. and S. Wright (1999). 'Audit Culture and Anthropology: Neo-Liberalism in British Higher Education'. *The Journal of the Royal Anthropological Institute* 54(4): 557–75.

Silver, L. J. (2010). 'Spaces of Encounter: Public Bureaucracy and the Making of Client Identities'. *Ethos* 38(3): 275–96.

Simmel, G. (1908). *Exkurs über den Fremden [Essay on the Stranger].* Berlin, Duncker & Humblot.

Sloterdijk, P. (2013 [1983]). *Kritik der Zynischen Vernunft [Critique of Cynical Reason].* Frankfurt am Main, Suhrkamp.

Smith, A. (1981 [1976]). *An Inquiry into the Nature and Causes of the Wealth of Nations.* Indianapolis, Liberty Classics.

Smith, M. F. (1982). 'Bloody Time and Bloody Scarcity: Capitalism, Authority and the Transformation of Temporal Experience in a Papua New Guinea Village'. *American Ethnologist* 9(3): 318–503.

Spencer, J., A. Jepson and D. Mills (2011). *Where Do All the Anthropologists Go? Research Training and 'Careers' in Social Anthropology.* Online at https://www.researchgate.net/profile/David_Mills21/publication/265007846_Where_do_all_the_Anthropologists_go_Research_training_and_'Careers'_in_Social_Anthropology/links/55f68f5108ae1d9803976fb1.pdf (accessed 11 November 2016).

Spittler, G. (2016). *Anthropologie Der Arbeit: Ein Ethnographisher Verlgeich [the Anthropology of Work: An Ethnographic Comparison].* Wiesbaden, Springer.

Stafford, C. (2007). 'What is going to happen next?' In *Questions of Anthropology,* R. Astuti, J. Parry and C. Stafford (eds). New York and Oxford, Berg: 55–77.

Stasch, R. (2009). *Society of Others: Kinship and Mourning in a West Papuan Place.* Berkeley, Los Angeles and London, University of California Press.

Stein, F. (2015). 'Review: Money from Nothing – Indebtedness and Aspiration in South Africa'. *Social Anthropology.* Forthcoming.

Stein, F. (2016). ' "Anthropology Needs to Go Mainstream" – an Interview with Gillian Tett'. *Anthropology Today* 32(6): 27–9.

Stein, F. (forthcoming). 'Anthropology's "Impact" – a Comment on Audit and the Unmeasurable Nature of Critique '. *The Journal of the Royal Anthropological Institute.*

Stewart, M. (1997). *The Time of the Gypsies.* Boulder, CO and Oxford, Westview Press.

Strathern, M. (2000). *Audit Cultures*. London and New York, Routledge.

Strathern, M. (2005). 'Robust Knowledge and Fragile Futures'. In *Global assemblages: Technology, politics and ethics as anthropological problems*, A. Ong and S. J. Collier (eds). Oxford, Blackwell: 464–82.

Strathern, M. (2006). 'A Community of Critics? Thoughts on New Knowledge*'. *Journal of the Royal Anthropological Institute* 12(1): 191–209.

Strathern, M. (2011). 'An Experiment in Interdisciplinarity: Proposals and Promises'. In *Social Knowledge in the Making*, C. Camic, N. Gross and M. Lamont (eds). Chicago and London, University of Chicago Press: 257–82.

Stricker, L. J. and J. Ross (1962). 'A Description and Evaluation of the Myers-Briggs Type Indicator'. *Educational Testing Service*. Princeton NJ.

Sturdy, A. (2011). 'Consultancy's Consequences? A Critical Assessment of Management Consultancy's Impact on Management'. *British Journal of Management* 22: 517–30.

Sturdy, A., K. Handley, T. Clark and R. Fincham (2009). *Management Consultancy – Boundaries and Knowledge in Action*. Oxford and New York, Oxford University Press.

Sturdy, A., M. Schwarz and A. Spicer (2006). 'Guess Who's Coming to Dinner? Structures and Uses of Liminality in Strategic Management Consultancy'. *Human Relations* 59(7): 929–60.

Süddeutsche Zeitung (2012). Diese Kassen zahlen ihren Versicherten Geld zurück [These insurances pay back money to their members]. Online at http://www.sueddeutsche.de/geld/milliarden-ueberschuss-bei-krankenversicherungen-diese-kassen-zahlen-ihren-versicherten-geld-zurueck-1.1483419 (accessed 19 October 2015), Süddeutsche Zeitung.

Süddeutsche Zeitung (2014). Wie 'echte' Geschäftsleute: Studenten als Unternehmensberater [Just like 'real' businessmen: Students as business consultants]. Online at http://www.sueddeutsche.de/news/bildung/hochschulen-wie-echte-geschaeftsleute-studenten-als-unternehmensberater-dpa.urn-newsml-dpa-com-20090101-140311-99-05237 (accessed 20 October 2015).

Süddeutsche Zeitung (2015). Die Alleskönner. Online at http://www.sueddeutsche.de/karriere/branchenreport-die-alleskoenner-1.2468873 (accessed 10 October 2015).

Taussig, K.-S., K. Hoeyer and S. Helmreich (2013). 'The Anthropology of Potentiality in Biomedicine: An Introduction to Supplement 7'. *Current Anthropology* 54(S7): S3–S14.

Taylor, F. W. (1998 [1911]). *The Principles of Scientific Management*. New York, Dover Publications.

The Atlantic (2007). 'Anthropology Inc'. Online at https://www.theatlantic.com/magazine/archive/2013/03/anthropology-inc/309218/

The Financial Times. (2010). How to bridge the IT alignment gap. Financial Times. Online at http://www.ft.com/cms/s/0/60089a24-e5f3-11df-af15-00144feabdc0.html#axzz3pTD7I6NU (accessed 24 October 2010).

The Financial Times (2013). The strategy consultants in search of a strategy. Online at http://www.ft.com/cms/s/0/f15acee6-0f2d-11e3-8e58-00144feabdc0.html#axzz3oXVOdBov (accessed 14 October 2015).

The Guardian (2010). NHS spending on consultancy: how does your area compare?. Online at http://www.theguardian.com/news/datablog/2010/sep/07/nhs-consultancy-spending-lansley (accessed 17 October 2015).

The Guardian (2013). Nothing personal: The questionable Myers-Briggs test. Online at http://www.theguardian.com/science/brain-flapping/2013/mar/19/myers-briggs-test-unscientific (accessed October 2015).

The Washington Post (2011). Occupy Wall Street protests go global. Online at https://www.washingtonpost.com/world/europe/occupy-wall-street-protests-go-global/2011/10/15/gIQAp7kimL_story.html (accessed 14 October 2015).

Thompson, E. P. (1967). 'Time, Work-Discipline, and Industrial Capitalism'. *Past and Present* 38: 56–97.

Thompson, E. P. (1971). 'The Moral Economy of the English Crowd in the Eighteenth Century'. *Past and Present* 50: 76–136.

Thrift, N. (1997). 'The Rise of Soft Capitalism'. *Cultural Values* 1(1): 29–57.

Thrift, N. (1998). 'The Rise of Soft Capitalism'. In *An Unruly World? Globalization, Governance and Geography*, A. Herod, G. Ó Tuathail and S. M. Roberts (eds). London and New York, Routledge: 25–71.

Thrift, N. (2002). 'Think and act like revolutionaries: episodes from the global triumph of management discourse'. *Critical Inquiry* 44(3): 19–26.

Thrift, N. (2005). *Knowing Capitalism*. London, Thousand Oaks and New Delhi, Sage.

Tomenendal, M. and C. Boyoglu (2014). 'Gender Imbalance in Management Consulting Firms – A Story about the Construction and Effects of Organizational Identity'. *Management and Organizational Studies* 1(2): 30–43.

Töpper, V. (2015). Aufwärts immer, abwärts nimmer [Always up, never down]. *Der Spiegel*. Online at http://www.spiegel.de/karriere/berufsleben/unternehmensberater-das-karriere-prinzip-up-or-out-a-1020499.html (accessed 8 January 2015).

Transparency International UK (2012). Fixing the Revolving Door between Government and Business. C. Krishnan. London.

Tsing, A. L. (2005). *Friction*. Princeton and Oxford, Princeton University Press.

Tufte, E. R. (2003). *The Cognitive Style of PowerPoint*. Cheshire, Graphics Press LLC.

Turner, V. W. (1991 [1969]). 'Liminality and Communitas'. In *The Ritual Process – Structure and Anti-Structure*, V. W. Turner (ed.). Ithaca, New York, Cornell University Press: 94–131.

Verdery, K. (1996). 'The "Etatization" of Time in Ceauşescu's Romania'. In *What was Socialism and What Comes Next?* S. B. Ortner, N. B. Dirks and G. Eley (eds). Princeton, Princeton University Press: 39–59.

Vogl, J. (2010). *Das Gespenst des Kapitals [The Ghost of Capital]*. Zürich, Diaphanes.

von Bieberstein, A. (2016). 'Not a German Past to Be Reckoned With: Negotiating Migrant Subjectivities between Vergangenheitsbewältigung and the Nationalization of History'. *Journal of the Royal Anthropological Institute* 22(4): 902–19.

von Braun, C. (2011). *Der Preis des Geldes – Eine Kulturgeschichte [The price of money – A cultural history]*. Berlin, Aufbau.

Weber, M. (1920). *Die Protestantische Ethik Und Der Geist Des Kapitalismus [the Protestant Ethic and the Spirit of Capitalism]*. Online: Zeno.org.

Weber, M. (2004). 'Politics as Vocation'. *The Vocation Lectures: 'Science as a Vocation' 'Politics as a Vocation.'* Indianapolis and Cambridge, Hackett Publishing Company: 32–94.

Weiden, E. F. (2011). *Folienkrieg und Bullshitbingo: Handbuch für Unternehmensberater, Opfer und Angehörige [Slidewar and Bullshitbingo: A handbook for consultants, victims and relatives]*. Munich and Zurich, Piper.

Weiss, H. (2015). 'Financialization and Its Discontents: Israelis Negotiating Pensions'. *American Anthropologist* 117(3): 506–18.

Welker, M. A. (2009). ' "Corporate Security Begins in the Community": Mining, the Corporate Social Responsibility Industry, and Environmental Advocacy in Indonesia'. *Cultural Anthropology* 24(1): 142–79.

Welker, M. A., D. J. Partridge and R. Hardin (2011). 'Corporate Lives: New Perspectives on the Social Life of the Corporate Form: An Introduction to Supplement 3'. *Current Anthropology* 52: S3–S16.

Westrup, C. and F. Knight (2000). Consultants and Enterprise Resource Planning (ERP) systems. *ECIS 2000 Proceedings*.

Willerslev, R., D. Refslund Christensen and L. Meinert (2013). *Introduction. Taming Time, Timing Death – Social Technologies and Ritual*. Burlington, USA, Ashgate Publishing Limited.

Williams, R. (ed.) (1983 [1976]). 'Elite'. In *Keywords – a Vocabulary of Culture and Society*. New York, Oxford University Press: 112–15.

Wolf-Meyer, M. (2011). 'Natural Hegemonies: Sleep and the Rhythms of American Capitalism'. *Current Anthropology* 52(6): 876–95.

Womack, J. P. and D. T. Jones (2003 [1996]). *Lean Thinking – Banish Waste and Create Wealth in your Corporation*. New York, London, Toronto and Sydney, Free Press.

Womack, J. P., D. T. Jones and D. Roos (1990). *The Machine that Changed the World*. New York, Oxford, Singapore and Sydney, Maxwell Macmillan International.

Wright, S. (ed.) (1994). ' "Culture" in Anthropology and Organizational Studies'. In *Anthropology of Organizations*. London and New York, Routledge: 1–31.

Yates, J. (1984). *Graphs as a Managerial Tool: A Case Study of Du Pont's Use of Graphs, 1904-1949*, Cambridge, MA, Massachusetts Institute of Technology.

Zaloom, C. (2003). 'Ambiguous numbers: trading technologies and interpretation in financial markets'. *American Ethnologist* 30(2): 258–72.

Zaloom, C. (2006a). 'Markets and Machines: Work in the Technological Sensoryscapes of Finance'. *American Quarterly* 58(3): 815–24.

Zaloom, C. (2006b). *Out of the Pits: Traders and Technology from Chicago to London*. Chicago and London, University of Chicago Press.

Zaloom, C. (2012). 'How to read the Future: The Yield Curve, Affect and Financial Prediction'. *Public Culture* 21(2): 245–68.

Zeitlyn, D. (2012). 'Divinatory Logics: Diagnoses and Predictions Mediating Outcomes'. *Current Anthropology* 53(5): 525–46.

Zigon, J. (2007). 'Moral breakdown and the ethical demand – A theoretical framework for an anthropology of moralities'. *Anthropological Theory* 7(2): 131–50.

INDEX

abstract labour 112, 119–20, 135–6, 167
anthropology as 179–90
artistic representation of 37–40
and autopoiesis 112
definition of 5–12, 16–23, 177–8
history of 25–34, 39–40
knowledge and 93–4, 117–18
power and 65–6, 82, 91
and the self 145–6
technologies of 99, 103
temporality of 61
and uncertainty 147–53, 170, 175
absurd 18, 22, 37, 64, 82, 108, 115–18
aesthetics 11, 14, 16–20, 88, 94, 99, 108–10, 113, 156–7
affect 6, 22, 65–6, 91, 108, 117, 137, 177, 179, 184
agency 36, 101, 108
alienation 21, 37, 43, 44, 59–60, 116, 146, 173
audit 29, 180–2
autopoieisis 21, 25, 31, 33, 39–40, 112, 115, 118, 154, 168

bar charts 108, 151–2

capitalism 3, 29–31, 35, 101, 126, 175, 179
American 27, 30, 140
and labour 7–8, 94, 118, 130–1
soft capitalism 31
temporality 21, 41–4, 49, 61
charisma 19, 66, 82–7, 115, 169, 173
comic strips 110–11
commensurability 16, 135–6, 151–2, 182
commodity 22, 43, 120, 129–36, 140, 145–6
commodification 143, 145
commoditization 134–6
commodity fetish 131
common sense 64, 89, 181
corporations 15–19, 25–9, 39, 73, 129, 133, 137, 140, 144–6, 148, 166, 172
boundaries 66, 90
European 30–2
German 14
theory of 5–12, 21–23, 41–7, 49–50, 65–6, 79, 93–4, 118, 120, 177

crisis   35, 183, 185
  dot-com crisis   34
  European sovereign debt
    crisis   123
  Global financial crisis of
    2008   144
critique   23, 34–5, 38–9, 69–70,
  73, 140, 143, 170, 174, 177,
  181–91
cynicism   37, 120, 144–6

detachment   6, 22, 66, 75, 91,
  151, 186

eighty-twenty rule   56–7
elites   1, 22, 34–6, 39, 76, 117–18,
  183, 194
empathy   96, 183–8, 190
enchantment   101, 107
ethics, *see* morality
Excel, *see* spreadsheets
Exception (state of)   47–50, 58, 61
exemplars   42, 44, 51–4, 61, 65,
  98, 152
exoticism   116, 161, 164

fashion   17–19, 83, 86 105
feedback   84–5 120, 132, 136,
  140–6
field site   5–6, 12–21, 42–4, 117,
  140, 145, 147, 175, 177, 191
  aesthetics   16–18
  boundaries   19–21
fieldwork   1–5, 116, 184, 187
financialisation   11, 21, 25, 28–9,
  31, 39
flexibility   10, 33, 35, 124, 123,
  162
freedom   23, 147, 154–7, 159,
  162–3, 166, 170–1, 175
  interpretive freedom   111, 118
friction   34, 153
Fukushima-Daiichi nuclear
  catastrophe   129

functionalism   5, 108
  and anthropology   182
  and consulting   15–18, 32, 35,
    42, 47, 50, 65, 70, 76, 81, 89,
    131–6, 145, 154
  of labour   8
  of technologies   2, 53, 101, 143

Gantt charts   41, 48, 167
gaps   148–58, 170
gender   39, 42, 76–80, 83–5, 98,
  168, 184, 189–90
Glass-Stegall Act   29
Great Depression   28

habitus   11, 38, 60 122, 126, 169
healthcare   30, 95–6, 98, 152, 165
hierarchy
  within consultancies   14–16,
    49–50, 52, 54, 115, 135–6,
    159, 164–5, 172
  corporate   10–12, 18, 27, 65,
    99, 142, 156

ignorance   2, 63–5, 82, 103, 135
imagined communities   5, 112,
  118
income pyramid, *see* hierarchy
indifference   73, 111
individualism   17, 58–9, 71, 87,
  104, 117, 125, 128, 132,
  136–42, 151, 163, 166
inequality   2, 7, 11, 57, 117–18,
  178, 191
  in Germany   39
insurance   28, 32, 63–90, 95–118,
  125, 147, 152, 165

knowledge   122
  and consultants   5, 21–2, 29,
    35, 56, 64–85, 89–94, 97, 158,
    168, 177–8
  corporate   31, 169–70, 178,
    183

embodied 103, 114
ethnographic 20, 182, 185, 188
managerial 9–10, 104, 106–10, 135, 167
and the self 50, 125–7, 139

labour, *see also* abstract labour
immaterial 7
and work 7–9
lean management 129
learning curve 125–7
legitimacy 9, 11, 22, 63–92, 113, 120, 167, 184
liminality 22, 50, 66, 80–1, 90

magic 53, 99–103
modernity 13, 32, 43–4, 95
money 4–5, 12, 46, 48, 50, 93, 95, 121–2, 133–4, 144, 147, 179, 190
and the field 18–21
morality 77, 117, 98, 129, 133, 145–6, 163, 179, 183
moral economy 178–9
moralistic technologies 22, 120, 136–46
multidivisional model 30–1
Myers-Briggs Type Indicator 136–40, 143, 145

narrative 15, 94, 99, 109–11, 157
numbers 3, 67, 88, 94, 98–106, 113–15, 142

optimism 170, 175

performativity 7, 11, 54, 57, 65, 80, 101, 124, 127, 143, 152, 165, 171–5, 178
personhood 8, 22, 36, 119–20, 130–1, 136, 142, 145–6, 178
potential 45–6, 67–8, 100, 155, 163, 166

potential worlds 23, 147, 152–4, 157–9, 161, 170, 175, 181
PowerPoint, *see* presentations
pragmatism 7, 88–9,137, 169–70, 175, 186, 191
presentations 16, 22, 38, 52, 63, 68, 83, 97, 88, 128, 149, 167, 191
aesthetics of 4, 13, 88, 109–10
as craft 2–3, 131, 168
epistemic affordances of 72–3, 93, 106–14, 118, 184
profit 4, 8–9, 22–3, 28, 31, 45–6, 95, 119, 127, 133, 147–75, 181, 183

reification 75, 111–12
relationships 13, 20–1, 57, 59, 118, 131, 184, 190
client-consultant 15, 42–3, 75, 80–5, 94, 103, 115, 118, 159, 177
consultant 143
corporate 5–7, 9–11, 65–6, 90–1, 168, 172–3, 175, 190
intimate 79, 122, 124, 126, 184
rhetoric 22, 28, 46, 64, 84–9, 94, 106, 118, 133, 142, 162, 168, 183
ritual 8, 10–11, 103–6
Royal Anthropological Institute 189

science fiction 188
scientific management 27
self-improvement, *see* morality
serendipity 186–7, 190
shareholder 33, 188
revolution 32–3
value 5, 8–9, 33, 37, 128, 177, 181, 187, 193
shares 37, 153

speed, *see* time
spreadsheets   2, 4, 15, 22, 41–2,
    63, 131, 178, 183
  epistemic affordances of   73,
    93–4, 98–103, 106–7, 112–13,
    118
state of exception   47–51

taxes   32, 95, 151, 153–4, 157, 166
Taylor, F.W.   26
temporality   10
  Intense   21, 42–4, 47–54,
    59–61, 187
  time   23, 40–61, 79, 87–9,
    99,115, 121, 127, 141–3, 152,
    159, 178, 181, 187–8
  full time equivalents   100

time management   54–9, 139,
    169–73
  tragedy of time
    management   58
truth   75, 86, 88, 102, 114, 144

uncertainty   2, 7, 22–3, 31, 67–8,
    88, 104, 147–75, 183
  profitable uncertainty   22–3,
    147–8, 158, 168–71, 175
university   38, 40, 49, 69, 72, 97,
    122, 128, 149 159, 169–70,
    179–80, 188
utility   7, 183
utopia   152–4, 181, 188

vocation   119, 145, 179

For Product Safety Concerns and Information please contact our EU
representative GPSR@taylorandfrancis.com Taylor & Francis Verlag GmbH,
Kaufingerstraße 24, 80331 München, Germany

Printed and bound by CPI Group (UK) Ltd, Croydon, CR0 4YY
08/05/2025
01864406-0002